Beneath the Eagle's Wings

When navies are forgotten
And fleets are useless things,
When the dove shall warm her bosom
Beneath the eagle's wings—

from "The New Age" by
Frederic Lawrence Knowles

Beneath the Eagle's Wings

Americans in Occupied Japan

JOHN CURTIS PERRY

ILLUSTRATED WITH PHOTOGRAPHS

DODD, MEAD & COMPANY, NEW YORK

1 2 3 4 5 6 7 8 9 10

Library of Congress Cataloging in Publication Data

Perry, John Curtis.

Beneath the eagle's wings.
Bibliography: p.
Includes index.
1. Japan—History—Allied occupation, 1945–1952.
2. Americans in Japan. I. Title.
DS889.15.P47   952.04'4   80-15331
ISBN 0-396-07876-1

Grateful acknowledgement is made to the Trustees of Columbia University in the City of
New York for their permission to quote from interviews conducted with Joseph Ballantine,
Hugh Borton, Eugene B. Dooman, Charles L. Kades, and Sir George B. Sansom for the
Columbia University Oral History Collection.

All photographs in this book not otherwise credited are courtesy of the Public Affairs
Department of the U.S. Army.

To the family

Acknowledgments

I WOULD like to thank the following individuals for assistance, encouragement, or specific advice in the preparation of this book: Peter A. Adams; Edward J. Boone, Jr.; Miriam A. Bunker; John Cage; Theodore R. Conant; John W. Dower; Peter K. Frost; David R. Godine; Robert Hale; Richard E. Miller; Ray A. Moore; John M. O'Connell; Arthur Oldman; Susan Pharr; Janet Rigney; Lieutenant General Frank J. Sackton, USA (Ret.); Howard Schonberger; Eiichi Shindo; Jack Sutters; Brigadier General W. M. Thames, USA (Ret.); Hiroshi Wagatsuma; and Blair Watson.

To Bob Russell I owe particular thanks, for he first inspired me to think about writing the book. Capable custodian of the Carleton College Library, Bob kept its tile floors gleaming. In between stripping and waxing, he would sometimes drop by my office to talk. Knowing of my interest in Japan, Bob would reminisce about his experience as a GI there, the major event of his life, he said. From Faribault, Minnesota, to Yokohama, Japan, was a big leap for a Midwestern farm boy who had never been farther from home than neighboring North Dakota.

Terry Basquin typed the manuscript with the cheerful and relentless passion for accuracy she brings to everything she does. And my thanks to Peter R. Weed, editor, whose skillful pencilings helped shape the manuscript.

To all those who were generous enough to comment on and criticize earlier drafts of the book I am particularly grateful. Portions were read by Makoto Iokibe, Richard H. Minear, and Peter

ACKNOWLEDGMENTS

W. Stanley. The entire text was read by Ann Brace Barnes, Albert M. Craig, Dallas and Richard Finn, George R. Packard III, Elizabeth Perry, Edwin O. Reischauer, Frank Joseph Shulman, and Chitoshi Yanaga. I have benefited enormously from their corrections and suggestions. None of them is responsible, of course, for any errors remaining.

J.C.P.

Contents

Foreword

WITH the fighting over in 1945, America's goals were to preserve peace and to sustain prosperity. Depression and war had been the two great challenges to the national well-being. Defeating the Japanese and the Germans had not been easy. But having done so, Americans set out with an aplomb, breathtaking in its audacity, to reform their former enemies, to destroy not only their means but also their will to make war.

Moving into Japan, the Americans sought to take in hand an ancient, distinctive, and highly sophisticated society; to cut, shape, and refit that society to a new pattern, befitting the decorous and modest role Americans wanted for Japan in the international order. In the numbers of people participating, in the scale of what they tried to do, the venture was without precedent.

America's Japan endeavor was one of few instances in which one modern industrial state has entirely occupied another modern industrial state for an extended period—eighty months in this case—trying to change it in some rather basic ways. Military occupations have occurred frequently; the U.S. has participated in many. None was more ambitious than the Occupation of Japan, and none was less punitive.

A punitive Occupation would, in the long run, certainly have failed. After the anger of war subsided, most Americans had the good sense to recognize this, especially given the precedent of post–World War I Germany and the rise of Nazism. Americans strongly desired not to fail in Japan. Building a good society for the

Japanese might somehow justify the enormous outpouring of blood and treasure that had gone into waging the Pacific War.

The later tragedy of America in Vietnam stemmed in part from an exaggerated notion of American creative powers, a self-assurance buoyed by earlier success in Japan, and a belief that the techniques so usefully employed in one Asian country were readily transferable to another. But we must not read the catastrophe of Vietnam into an earlier past. Other American encounters in Asia were happier, the Occupation of Japan, despite all expectations to the contrary, especially so.

How can we reconcile the successes of the occupiers—and these were great—with the many reasons the Americans ought to have failed: their ethnocentrism, their racism, and their ignorance of Japan? Fortunately some of the occupiers were both well informed and free of prejudice. Even more important, many Japanese eagerly subscribed to the noble aims of the Occupation, contributing mightily to all its accomplishments.

Japan, with fifteen hundred years of civilization in the East Asian world, had never before been defeated in war and occupied by enemy soldiers.* For the Japanese people, occupation by the Americans meant subjection to massive involuntary cultural borrowing. Japan had borrowed heavily before from other cultures, and on an equally large scale, but always on Japanese terms. This time, impetus to learn whatever exercise was set by the instructors was sharpened by the knowledge that until the pupils gave satisfaction the lessons would continue, and the masters would not leave. But what the occupiers sought to create was not necessarily out of joint with what the Japanese already had or wanted to have.

Since the mid-nineteenth century Japan had made rapid advances in building a modern industrial society. The disaster of the Pacific War merely brought a brief lull to that great surge forward. Yet Americans in the Occupation saw only the rice paddies and the

---

*Okinawa was not part of Japan until modern times, and is excluded from this book because the Occupation there had its own special character.

poverty, not the strong social, economic, and political institutions that had girded and propelled Japan's earlier accomplishments and would carry the nation on to the economic miracle of the 1950s and after.

Occupying Japan was a climax for Americans to this country's belief in mission, which during the nineteenth century first developed great strength and tenacity in American life. Taking up "the White Man's burden," in Kipling's phrase—"which circled the earth in a day and became hackneyed within a week"—had been a leading theme in the story of Western overseas expansion in the nineteenth century and before. In 1945, "a sense of superior Christian virtue, a sense of global mission, a sense of responsibility and capability for bringing enlightenment to a dark and superstitious world, for overthrowing ancient and new tyrannies, and for making backward infidels into Christian men of enterprise," neatly sums up the awesome responsibilities Americans felt to be theirs when setting out to evangelize the American way of life to the Japanese.

For hundreds of thousands of American soldiers, to serve in Japan meant life in a totally unknown, non-Christian, racially different culture. That experience, in addition to stretching mental horizons and redirecting some later careers, could provide exhilarating freedom from the social restraints of home, yet offer the simple comforts of dependency. If he wished, the foreigner, especially the male foreigner, could be a child again: pampered, indulged, cosseted. But every visitor would experience the helpfulness of the Japanese. For instance, asking a passer-by directions to get to a camera store might lead the foreign visitor to be escorted the entire lengthy route to that shop. Some liked such attention, but for the independent soul it could be almost suffocating. "I felt the Japanese were manipulating us in a very nice way, that there was a kind of innate feeling of superiority in the way they made the Americans feel superior," one American recalls.

What is extraordinary in the Occupation and its aftermath was the insignificance of the unpleasant. For the Japanese, the nobility of American ideals and the essential benignity of the American presence assuaged much of the bitterness and anguish of defeat. For the Americans, the joys of promoting peace and democracy triumphed over the attendant frustrations and grievances. Consequently, the Occupation served to lay down a substantial capital of goodwill on which both America and Japan would draw in the years ahead.

Introduction

THIS book is about that great American enterprise to change Japan. It is short, and it is primarily about Americans in Japan during the first two years or so after the August 1945 landing. I have not even mentioned the San Francisco Peace Treaty of April 1952, which marked the formal end of the Occupation. One could argue that the spirit of the Occupation lingered much longer, until the Tokyo Olympics in 1964. Or one might say that American eyes shifted away from Japan with the outbreak of the Korean War in June 1950. Certainly the most important acts of the Americans in Japan took place during the early months they were there, and the largest number of Americans to come to Japan did so then.

A comprehensive history of the Occupation, which could easily compass thousands of pages, still needs to be written. The subject is richly complex and the materials plentiful. Voluminous documentary sources, although not always well arranged or easy to get at, are increasingly open to those wanting to read them. Their bulk in fact inhibits the user, but this is a universal embarrassment in the study of contemporary history, making writers of it sometimes wish they were medievalists instead.

Scholars may find this book superficial. It is not intended for them. The subject is a success story that I hope will appeal to the general reader. With all in recent times that the United States seems to have done badly in the world, here is something Americans did right.

The time in question is not so remote that many of the participants and those who know them are not still alive; the events remain of intrinsic interest. Japan has subsequently emerged as a global power. And the American tie with Japan steadily grows in importance, with the Occupation experience a persistingly influential part of that relationship.

The pages following are a work of synthesis, pulling together some of the more recent research in what is becoming a rapidly developing field of study. My focus is less on what the occupiers did to the Japanese than on what the experience meant to those individual Americans most intimately involved with it—and to this nation.

Beneath the Eagle's Wings

Watching the Americans arrive at Atsugi.

Young Japanese naval trainees, ranging in age from twelve to eighteen, enlarge the Atsugi airstrip in preparation for the Americans.

I

The Arrival

ON THE pitted strip of Atsugi Naval Air Base, August 28, 1945, starting at about eight-thirty in the morning, sixteen American planes landed. Appropriately enough, Mt. Fuji, the one image that almost all Americans had of Japan, loomed impassively in the purple distance. Clouds of fighter aircraft hovered protectively above the rapidly descending C-54 "Skymaster" transports. One hundred and fifty Signal Corps men—engineers, radio specialists, interpreters—were in that initial party. Within forty-five minutes of touchdown, the men established radio communication with Okinawa. They set up landing lights and, with the help of Japanese labor, began lengthening the runway and repairing the barracks. They had only one night to prepare a mile-long landing strip.

To watching Japanese it seemed that each American knew "exactly what he had to do, and the efficiency with which the unit went about its work" was impressive. At dawn the next day, Colonel Charles Tench, the commanding officer, radioed that he was ready for the arrival of the main airborne force.

Atsugi Air Base, strategically located about twenty miles west of Tokyo, just on the edge of the great Kanto plain, was near enough to the coast to be within range of naval gunfire, obviously an important reason for its choice by the Americans. Offshore was assembled the mightiest armada in history: four hundred warships, carrying enough planes to darken the sky. This armada was led by twelve American battleships and seventeen aircraft carriers, swelled

1

by an accompanying British fleet of eighteen warships, led by two battleships.

Japanese officers clustered nervously about the landing strip, in full dress uniform with swords. The Americans were in work clothes. The field was surrounded by battered hangars and wrecked aircraft. Someone counted 120 Japanese planes, none of which could fly; they had been damaged in action or had had their propellers removed in accordance with American orders.

The relatively few men carried in by the big American planes were highly outnumbered by the Japanese and highly vulnerable. This was scarcely more than a toehold. That first night the Americans knew they were the only occupying force in a nation where three to four million men were still under arms.

It would be some days, perhaps even weeks, before the number of American troops would be large enough for them to feel at all secure. Only a limited number could be brought in by air, and American bases were several days' steaming distance. Okinawa was nine hundred miles from Atsugi, Saipan fifteen hundred, Manila eighteen hundred. If the Japanese had not surrendered and an invasion had been necessary, the logistics would have been much more formidable than for Normandy in June 1944. That enterprise

The Americans bring their own gasoline.

had not been easy even with England, the ideal staging ground, just across the Channel to supply every man put on the beach with the required five tons of equipment. In the case of Japan, the materiel and the men would have had to come all the way from American shores, over what would have been the longest supply line in history.

The Atsugi force was practically self-sustaining, bringing along food, gasoline, and other necessities. But the first arrivals were dependent upon the Japanese for ground transportation. There were a few American-made automobiles—1938 and 1939 models, with right-hand drive—and some trucks. GIs had to wrestle with the smelly complexities of charcoal-powered engines, wartime Japan's gas-savers.

A bus was the only available transportation to Yokohama for a group that arrived August 30, including Major General William Crist, chief military government officer for Japan. The bus broke down after only two miles. Colonel Charles Kades, the junior member of the party (later to have an important role in the Occupation government), set out on foot in search of alternate transportation. Using sign language and relying on the fact that he was in uniform and was armed, he commandeered a fire engine. In such style General Crist was chauffeured to the door of the undamaged New Grand Hotel in Yokohama, where Allied Headquarters was first established. In a few days the Japanese army would be out of Tokyo and the perimeter of American power would be rapidly but cautiously extended.

August 30 was a day for arrivals at Atsugi. The "Skymasters" started coming in about 6 A.M. Weather was ideal, fortunately, because each plane had only three minutes to land, unload, and take off again. This precise timing excited the admiration of those who watched; it was the biggest airborne operation of the Pacific War. All day the great planes arrived and departed. Some smaller aircraft came and stayed. One observer remembered the Grumman Navy fighters, like giant cicadas with their wings folded, parked at the edge of the strip.

3

Atsugi Operations Tower.

Among those people coming in were 112 press correspondents, ready to handle a big story. They awaited General Douglas MacArthur. For them and for other arriving foreigners at Atsugi, "those Japs certainly had everything organized just like a lawn party," with pavilion tents sheltering tables spread with white linen. The Japanese hosts prepared a superb meal of Hokkaido salmon and roast beef, immaculately served on fine china. "Who ever thought we would come in like this?" an Australian correspondent asked. What a contrast to the immense devastation! How different from the fanatical resistance the Allies had originally expected!

At 2 P.M. the *Bataan* landed. "The Second Coming couldn't have caused more commotion. . . . The General descended from his plane with all the pomp and ceremony of a conquering hero. First, he paused at the head of the automatic ascent ladder, swept the horizon slowly, puffed on his four-inch-tall corncob pipe, then came down. . . . He looked as if he were not unaware of the place in history his setting foot on the sacred soil of Japan would occupy."

4

The Missouri *just prior to the surrender ceremonies.* Lower right, *Commodore Perry's flag, hoisted by him on his first visit to Japan, July 14, 1853.*

Japan surrendered in August before one enemy soldier had arrived in the home islands. For the first time in history an entire nation, a major power, had surrendered without conditions—at least as the victors chose to interpret it—before an invading force had even appeared. Victory came with unanticipated speed; American experts had thought the war might be a prolonged and bloody one. Major George Fielding Eliot, military correspondent for the New York *Herald Tribune,* wrote in July 1944 of the real possibility that "Japan [would] defend her soil to the point where the whole of her cities lie in smoking ruin, and where final military success . . . [could be] attained only when the last Japanese male capable of bearing arms . . . [was] hunted down and destroyed in some mountain fastness."

If Americans had been forced to invade Japan proper, fighting as they had on Okinawa, casualties would have been perhaps more than 700,000, perhaps even a million. If Japan resisted only to the extent Germany had, the Allies would have been "faced with the formidable task of fighting for every inch of Japanese territory over rough terrain, made even worse by the flooded rice fields."

Okinawa showed that the Japanese were fighting harder and better than ever before. Presumably on the home islands this would be intensified. Waiting for the Americans was a huge, fully armed, undefeated Japanese army, backed by an armaments industry that despite bombing and materiel shortages was still, overall, producing at 66 percent capacity. Yet starvation loomed, and supplies of virtually all raw materials needed for military use were exhausted. The Japanese could not protect themselves from enemy air attack. In addition, the vast bulk of that huge, fully armed, undefeated Japanese army was raw, untrained youth. Further resistance would have been suicidal. The war had proceeded "not necessarily to Japan's advantage," the Emperor informed his people in a dramatic radio broadcast, his first, made at noon on August 15. The decision was to surrender. Negotiations began.

Despite this decision for peace, on August 18 two American reconnaissance planes were attacked over Tokyo by fourteen Zero fighters. Furthermore, the Japanese seemed to procrastinate about both the American demand to send envoys to Manila and laying down their arms. Were those in charge sincere? Did they really want all fighting to stop? Admiral William F. "Bull" Halsey, following the news of the surrender, sent a message to his fliers: "It looks like the war is over, but if any enemy planes appear, shoot them down in friendly fashion."

The Japanese via Tokyo radio warned of hotheads who might create "unfortunate incidents." Surrender, they said, would be resented by a considerable portion of Japan's soldiers, of whom many had not personally experienced defeat. Some might well choose now to disobey imperial orders and attempt to continue the struggle.

Those people responsible for guarding the American landing party at Atsugi anxiously watched the skies for a possible appearance by some of the "Special Attack Corps" (suicide pilots) who had recently fled the base with their planes. But nothing happened. All remained quiet.

A great typhoon had earlier swept up from Okinawa, delaying but not destroying the approaching Allies. Lieutenant General Arisue Seizō, commander of the Japanese forces awaiting the Americans at Atsugi, was vastly relieved by the delay. Two more days helped soothe the mood and cool the heads of the Japanese preparing to receive their conquerors. In retrospect at least, the General had been more alarmed by his own fanatics than apprehensive of the foreign enemy. He remembered the *kamikaze* storm that had scattered the threatening Mongol fleet of Kublai Khan seven centuries before. "Truly," he exulted, "we [are] once more saved by the Divine Wind."

The Americans landed not knowing what to expect of the Japanese. Even if most troops followed the imperial command and laid down their arms, guerrilla activity seemed likely, led by fanatic young officers like those who had made Japanese politics so turbulent in the 1930s. Over in Manchuria, for instance, crack troops (as the Americans believed) of the Kwantung army, with an independent industrial base and their own supply of weapons, had a long tradition of flouting orders from Tokyo. At best the Americans anticipated sullen noncooperation or widespread bitterness, possibly erupting in periodic riots. Both before and during the war the Japanese often behaved in ways Americans judged unconventional and irrational. Ritual disembowelment *(hara-kiri),* suicide attacks, and frequent assassinations of politically prominent individuals were parts of what Americans viewed as Japan's bizarre tradition of violence—acts both passive and active, individual and collective.

The first American Navy liberty parties went ashore with "C rations, a canteen, and a carbine" close at hand. Sidearms were standard equipment for everyone during the first anxious weeks. "It's too damn quiet here," one GI said, a sentiment echoed by many.

In early September, as the great fleet of American and British warships stood off Yokohama harbor, a bluejacket pointed out to his buddies a sign painted by Japanese hands on a factory roof: "Three Cheers for the U.S. Navy and Army." This astonishing and seemingly paradoxical Japanese cordiality was not reciprocated by most Americans, at least not right away.

The Americans and their Allies were too outraged over Japan's treatment of prisoners of war to feel friendly toward their former foe. One of the first American objectives was to get the approximately thirty thousand prisoners out and home. As early as mid-August the Americans had assembled, packed, and stored on Guam medical supplies for 31,000 people. Quartermaster stores for 50,000 were prepared on Saipan. All were made ready for air-dropping by B-29s flying low and slowly over the prison camps.

Within a few hours after the American arrival at Atsugi, the first prisoners were freed. Three weeks later virtually all were on their way home. All of the prisoners, the Americans soon learned, were suffering from malnutrition; many were ill and in want of medical attention. Some had been severely mistreated by beating, whipping, or clubbing. Emaciated General Jonathan Wainwright, sym-

8

bol of American defeat in the Philippines, was the highest ranking and best known American prisoner of the Japanese. His nickname, "Skinny," became cruelly appropriate.

Food shortages in Japan may have been a legitimate reason for the diet in the prison camps, but there was no excuse for the brutality. The guards, often Koreans, may have exploited this opportunity to vent their own rage at being oppressed by the Japanese. Japan had clearly violated all conventional international standards for official behavior. Fliers, the direct agents of the torrent of destruction falling on the heads of the Japanese, were singled out for particularly harsh treatment. An even darker side of the POW experience was the discovery that some had been used as subjects for cruel and unusual medical experimentation, such as surgery without anaesthesia. American newspapers began comparing these ghastly episodes to what the Nazis had done.

The evils were quickly exposed. When the prisoners came out, in a few days, the worst was revealed. Many of the victims had suffered horribly and would bear at least psychic scars for the rest of their lives. But the public soon forgot. Anger flared up and then faded away. To most Americans, what was done to Nagasaki and Hiroshima, even to Tokyo, seemed bigger news than what had happened to the relatively few Allied POWs; the horrors of aerial warfare and nuclear bombs had universal implications. Nothing in the literature that came out of the POW experience would compare to the popular impact of John Hersey's book *Hiroshima* (1946), which focused on the agony of the Japanese.

Americans were coming to appreciate in full measure General William Tecumseh Sherman's old truism that "war is hell." In the total warfare of the twentieth century, civilians became an intimate part of the conflict. For Japan during the Pacific War this meant that more civilians were killed than soldiers. Coming into Japan, Americans wondered how they would be approached by the recent enemy.

Hanson W. Baldwin, writer on military affairs for the *New York Times,* warned Americans that their bombing had made "American" synonymous with "destruction." How should Americans behave on meeting Japanese? Since Americans could not conceive of themselves as being friendly to a Japanese conqueror, how could the Japanese be friendly to them? The Japanese simultaneously puzzled over correct behavior toward the Americans. How should a conquered people behave? They had never before been a conquered people.

Anthropologist John Embree had predicted that the Japanese would be cooperative. From his study of Japanese society, he concluded that the Japanese are a pragmatic people and that Americans should respond by being magnanimous, not vengeful. Looking at Japanese history, Embree cited evidence for his point of view: When the province of Satsuma rebelled in 1877 and was crushed by the central government, there were no mass suicides.

More recently, and perhaps more to the point, in Okinawa when the struggle had finished and the Japanese had lost, soldiers may have taken their own lives but civilians surrendered. Embree argued that the Japanese now would want peaceful stability. "General MacArthur's headquarters is as likely to be besieged by pleas for help as by fanatical samurai." He was right, but few people were ready to believe him.

American jeeps circling through rural communities attracted no hostility, merely curiosity. The ice was broken by children—runny-nosed and obviously undernourished, solemn but quick to smile, uninhibited. A Marine lieutenant in the first boat to land at Sasebo, site of one of Japan's largest naval bases, remembers his men fingering their weapons apprehensively, talking as they went in. "All I want is to kill a goddam Jap." Ten minutes after arriving on shore, the Marines were giving chocolate bars to children.

Soon both sides learned they had little to fear from each other. The Japanese had expected that they would be obliged to feed the occupying forces from their own sparse supplies. That the Americans brought their own food made an immediate and powerful impression on Japanese opinion. It set a tone of benevolence, particularly important in those first anxious days.

10

The anger of the Japanese over defeat and deprivation, Americans found, was directed against Japan's own wartime leadership rather than against Americans. Japanese armed forces accepted both the defeat and the anger with remarkably good grace—"oriental stoicism" General Walter Krueger called it—although Japanese anger was not always easily recognized by the much less restrained Americans. Lieutenant General Robert Eichelberger confided to his diary in November 1945: "I am beginning to think . . . [the Japanese] like the American military better than their own."

For most people hatred is hard to sustain. Almost all of the troops who had fought, American or Japanese, soon found they bore no rancor against their former foe. No significant number of people on either side were eager for violence. Everyone simply was glad the war was over. "The big story," wrote Theodore White, a reporter on the scene, "was what did not happen."

Before any Americans touched foot on Japanese soil, certain extremely important matters had already been settled in Washington. The pattern of the Occupation was laid out. Americans had decided that Japan was to be primarily an American affair. Americans judged they had taken the leading part in defeating Japan and were therefore entitled to take the leading role in the peace settlement. Anyhow, the U.S. was the only nation with the troops and the transportation to occupy Japan right away. Allied participation in the Occupation would be only nominal, although the Joint Chiefs of Staff thought it desirable that there be "oriental" troops in the Occupation forces.

As late as May 1946 General MacArthur anticipated the arrival of Chinese troops to take up garrison duty for the Nagoya area. As it worked out, Chinese and Philippine participation did not materialize. Both nations were preoccupied with civil wars and had no men to spare.

Despite an American invitation, the Russians did not send any troops to Japan, presumably because they would have been under American command and permitted to exercise no policy-making

11

powers. The Russians were keen to have their own zone of administration as they did in Germany and Austria; the northern island of Hokkaido would have suited them nicely. But the Americans were determined that Japan not be split into zones, and it was not.

The British Commonwealth was the only other victor directly participating in the Occupation. Beginning in February 1946, forty thousand Commonwealth troops—army, navy, and air, representing the United Kingdom, Australia, New Zealand, and India—arrived in Japan to take up the responsibility of garrisoning all of Shikoku and the western part of Honshu. This was the first time in peace that a Commonwealth force had been called into being, and it was the first time ever that men from these four nations were formed into composite units, "temporarily exchanging their individual national identities for a single British Commonwealth identity."

Because of their earlier experience with the Japanese, the British and Australians were inclined to be much more skeptical, if not downright hostile, than the Americans. Feelings sometimes ran strong. "Nasty little brutes," is how one choleric Englishman characterized the Japanese. Rivalry over commerce, humiliation at Hong Kong and Singapore, the bombing of Darwin and the threat of Japan's invasion of Australia, the suffering of the prison camps —these bitter memories were not wiped out or even assuaged by victory, nor were they offset by the guilt of Hiroshima or Nagasaki and chalked up to the hell of war.

The Australians had the executive authority for the Commonwealth force, which in numbers was surely more than token representation. But Americans retained all military government responsibilities. Beyond the British Commonwealth zone and outside the Tokyo area, "British uniforms were as rare as Japanese generals in Piccadilly."

The London *Economist* rather wistfully remarked that ". . . the immense predominance of Americans in the forces of occupation tends to make the Japanese forget that the British Commonwealth played a considerable part in their defeat, and still exercises great

12

Skirling the pipes outside the Imperial Palace, Tokyo, in celebration of Empire Day, May 24, 1946.

influence in world politics and commerce." The British in Japan were inclined to think of themselves as poor relations, "sitting below the salt," as indeed they were. But they put up a good show, lending pomp and color to the otherwise drab uniformity of the Occupation troops. The changing of the honor guard at the Imperial Palace and the trooping of the colors by the Royal Welsh Fusiliers provided spectacles enjoyed by Japanese and Americans alike.

The Americans were resolved to exclude their Allies from the exercise of ultimate authority over the Japanese, and had reached other decisions as well before arriving in Japan. The Americans had determined to occupy the whole country, not simply certain selected strategic areas. There would be one supreme commander, Douglas MacArthur. And American rule would be indirect.

Invasion had destroyed the institutions of the German state; the victors had no choice but to rule directly there. But hundreds of thousands of Americans already spoke German, a language far

13

easier for Americans to learn than Japanese. Whether there were enough Americans with adequate knowledge of Japan for them to undertake governing it, except in a supervisory manner, is questionable. Since the Japanese Government was still intact, the Americans sought to use it.

World peace depended upon successfully occupying and reshaping the defeated nations. Destroying the enemy meant not simply doing away with his weapons but also eliminating his desire to make war. Americans said it was not their responsibility to "impose upon Japan any form of government not supported by the freely expressed will of the people." But they somehow had to breathe into the Japanese the will to eschew war and to achieve democracy. Only when this was accomplished could they depart at ease.

2

The Baggage

AMERICANS embarked upon the Occupation of Japan with firm purpose and with a body of assumptions, a set of emotional and intellectual baggage. Americans went out to the Western Pacific and to Japan as destroyers, to crush Japanese militarism, determined that Japan should no longer menace American security. But they went also as builders. They wanted to encourage the emergence of a new peace-loving Japan. For this purpose they were convinced that their own culture and values were a suitable model for the Japanese. In fact, Americans saw these as a universally applicable ideal: What's good for us is certainly good for the Japs if they're smart enough to learn it.

Universality is part of an American myth. Of course, other nations have myths they believe foreigners should accept. The Japanese myth, for instance, held that the people of East Asia would cheerfully acquiesce to Japanese rule in what the Japanese were pleased to call the Greater East Asia Co-Prosperity Sphere. Conflict between this myth and the American one contributed to the Pacific War. The Russian Communist myth purported the imminence of world revolution, led by a vanguard of the proletariat. Conflict between this myth, at least as perceived by Americans, and the American myth would provide much of the tension of the postwar period.

Americans are scarcely unique in the high opinion of their own culture. Within the Western tradition the Greeks are remembered for their haughtiness toward the outsider, the barbarian, who

15

Occupation soldier in Japan.

refused to accept the manifestly superior values of Hellenic culture. Beyond the West, the Chinese were an outstanding example of ethnocentricity. Their culture traditionally permitted access by the foreigner, but only if he accepted Chinese ways over his own. Serenely self-confident, the Chinese had a thoroughly offhand attitude toward the outsider and did not care whether he chose to enlighten himself or not. The Chinese were not cultural proselytizers; Americans were, and still are.

The American missionary urge is vigorous and of long standing. It began even before the birth of the Republic and has since been periodically rekindled. Initially many people came to America's shores persuaded of the uniqueness of America as a community they could help to prosper and encourage to spread. The Declara-

16

tion of Independence explicitly articulated a universalist interpretation of America's own cultural values. The American Christian heritage buttressed the idea of universalism. Americans have wanted to mold and shape other cultures to their pattern—and have believed it a divinely sanctioned duty to do so—even though they might know little about these other cultures and not want to know more. Americans have chosen to interpret their world role as essentially altruistic, denying any selfishness in their purpose, assuming a stance of moral earnestness infuriating to other expansive nations.

"The most perfect society now existing in the world," the Frenchman Crèvecoeur said of the new American republic in 1782. Other Europeans agreed; Americans did not dispute the judgment. In the geographical succession of civilizations, as Crèvecoeur and others then saw it, civilization had begun in the East but had reached its peak in the West. It was America's role to "finish the great circle," to carry its fresh young culture, the embodiment of the best that mankind had created, to the far shores of the Pacific, to reinvigorate the decadent, stagnant cultures of Asia. Timothy Dwight, that great man of Yale, put it in verse:

> All hail thou Western world! By heaven designed
> Th' example bright to renovate mankind
> Soon shall thy sons across the mainland roam;
> And claim, on far Pacific shores, their home.

Possibly Dwight had California or Oregon in mind instead of China or Japan. But Thomas Hart Benton was specific when he told his fellow United States senators in 1824: "American pioneers would bring science, liberal principles in government, and the true religion to the peoples of Asia." A contemporary of his, A. A. Bennet, with an eye on St. Matthew's Gospel, promised: "We may look forward to the period when the spark kindled in America shall spread and spread, till the whole earth be illumined by its light."

The great nineteenth-century Protestant missionary impulse, embracing much of American society in its effort to convert the hea-

17

then, both fed on and gave nourishment to these feelings. The sentiments persisted. Douglas MacArthur would be entirely comfortable with them.

Early in the twentieth century, at a time of growing concern for America's responsibility in international affairs and when the needs of the economy had begun to assume greater importance in American life, Woodrow Wilson urged an audience of Detroit businessmen "to carry liberty and justice and the principles of humanity wherever you go, go out and sell goods that will make the world more comfortable and more happy, and convert [these people] to the principles of America."

The ideal of universalism thus fused with practical economic considerations (the drive for exports, the desire for access to raw materials, outlets for capital) to form the larger concerns of those Americans who thought at all about such things as they fought, subdued, and prepared to occupy Japan.

By 1945, Americans assumed a reformist vision of international politics, suggesting that even the nation-state might be obsolescent in a world moving toward political unity. Spheres of influence were a traditional way in which great powers had divided their responsibilities and kept the peace. But such divisions were totally unacceptable to Americans who now wanted an "open-door world" for goods and for ideas.

Americans ended the war immensely satisfied with the effort that had brought them victory. They were full of their own vitality and energy. The goals of the war had been simple to state and easy to accept. The war was popular; virtually all Americans believed they had no choice but to resist Japanese aggression.

Among American advantages, as the aged Secretary of War Henry L. Stimson assessed them in the summer of 1945, was moral superiority. Americans had this, he asserted, because they had been victims of a "sneak attack": Pearl Harbor. Japanese ignorance of America had led them to that monumental blunder that furnished Americans with a powerful sense of righteousness in the pursuit of their war against Japan. Overnight the American nation united behind the war effort.

Despite the strategic priority of defeating Hitler first, many in America saw Japan as the chief enemy. Even during 1942 and 1943, the U.S. sent as many men off to fight the Japanese as to do battle against the Germans and Italians. "Praise the Lord and pass the ammunition," went the popular song, summing up America's spirit during the war years. Americans never doubted victory.

At war's end American power was at its peak and the world looked to the U.S. The other powers were either crushed by defeat or exhausted by victory. The U.S.S.R. was the only potential competitor. But Russian military power was not global; it was regional and confined, limited by weakness at sea and in the air. By contrast, on land America was weak, but its fleet and air forces possessed awesome and unrivaled might. America emerged from the war with a new ability, at least in theory, to exercise its military power anywhere in the world.

During those early months of peace newspapers carried frequent accounts of record-breaking flights by American planes. American technology, its seemingly unrivaled skill at inventing and using machines, was causing the world to shrink. The war against the Japanese led Americans to bridge the vast spaces of the Pacific, and the production of American factories and shipyards, stimulated by military demand, seemed limitless. The uncertainties of the Depression were left behind. American resources had never appeared so substantial.

In world affairs America was ready, at least with the financial and military resources, to take Great Britain's place as paymaster of the Allies, global policeman, and workshop of the world. The mantle and instruments of power were America's as well. America was not only mistress of the seas but also of the skies. Nuclear monopoly supplemented military muscle of the traditional kind, now condescendingly labeled "conventional."

Yet wealth and power did not bring a total sense of ease and

Members of the Far Eastern Advisory Commission listen to Colonel John R. Hall describe effects the atomic bomb had on Hiroshima.

security. Americans worried about the uncertain implications of nuclear warfare. Their stockpile of weapons was limited. Rapid dismantling of wartime armed forces, bitter squabbling over whether the Army, Navy, and Air Force ought to be pulled together into one body, and the often painful inflationary readjustment of the economy from war to peace made the early postwar years anything but serene.

During the war a good bit of ambiguity characterized American attitudes toward the Soviet Union. Americans exaggerated both the strength of the U.S.S.R. and the international appeal of its ideology. Americans assumed on the part of the Russians a masterful coherence of policy, worldwide, of the sort they wanted for themselves but which in retrospect appears highly implausible for any nation to achieve. The American response to this perception was to resist the Soviet Union everywhere.

The cocky insecurity of President Harry S Truman exemplified the tone of timorous bellicosity running through American approaches to postwar foreign relations. Like the President, the nation lacked experience in managing world affairs. Yet many decisions with worldwide ramifications had to be made. Impatience characterized both Mr. Truman's attitude and that of the public. Whether or not the President knew what he was doing, he was quick and decisive in his actions. People liked that; it seemed strong leadership, and Mr. Truman said he never lost sleep over decisions.

The era compelled creativity in American foreign policy. Resolute and energetic personalities—Acheson, Forrestal, Harriman, Lovett, Marshall, McCloy, among others—were there to initiate, shape, and execute it. But of all these able leaders, none knew much about Japan, and none especially cared to learn. Professional diplomat Joseph C. Grew, American Ambassador to Tokyo for ten years before the war and the number-two man in the State Department during the last years of the war, was the only top-ranking American official to have a special interest in Japan. (Stimson had visited Japan before the war and had some appreciation of Japanese culture; it was he who removed Kyoto from the A-bomb target list.)

Grew was not professionally mobile like so many top officials who dart in and out of Government, with highly successful careers in both public and private life. He left office at the end of August 1945, when he reached retirement age. Out of office, Grew was out of power and without any real influence. There was no one with particular sensitivity to American-Japanese relations to replace him at the highest level of Government.

For Americans, Japan was marginal, not a major issue in a postwar world full of problems. Europe came first. Europe was where most Americans had ethnic ties, was the civilization Americans admired and studied, was the most important center next to America of world economic activity. And Europe appeared to be the crucial battleground of the Cold War, at least until after the end of the Berlin airlift in 1949.

Even in Asia, Japan was secondary to the American chief interest, China. Before the war Americans had exhibited no particular interest in Japan's domestic affairs, only in Japanese foreign policy regarding what the Japanese were doing in China and the implications for the U.S. of Japan's rising military power. But Japan for its own

21

sake was remarkably unimportant to Americans. Considering the economic ties, past and potential, between the two nations, this pattern of behavior is odd. Americans had traded with the Japanese more than with the Chinese; Americans had invested more in Japan than they had in China. And Japan was one of America's best customers anywhere in the world. Yet out in the East, China held center stage in American eyes.

China was the focus of the American missionary effort in Asia, and the long political convulsion accompanying the collapse of the Chinese imperial order in 1911 had involved Americans and other Westerners much more intimately in Chinese political life than was the case of Japan. The Japanese were able to preserve scrupulously their political integrity, even at times of greatest weakness, such as at mid-nineteenth century after Commodore Perry's arrival. In 1945, Americans still hoped China would emerge from civil war as a friendly great power, maintaining the stability of Eastern Asia. Instead, Americans were to watch with increasing dismay and anger the climax of the Chinese revolution and the collapse of Chiang Kai-shek's Nationalist republic.

In America there was no Japan lobby as there was a China lobby. Among Japan missionaries and their offspring there was no Pearl Buck, Walter Judd, or Henry R. Luce: all prominent, sympathetic, and persuasive speakers on behalf of a nation they knew firsthand and well. Americans have a romantic notion that deep down the Chinese people cherish Americans; they have never felt that way about the Japanese. Japan was never "ours" in the sense that Americans believed China was. Historically, at least in the twentieth century, it has seemed impossible for America to be friendly for very long to both powers simultaneously. Friendship for one has invariably led to coolness toward the other. Late in the 1940s this worked to the benefit of the Japanese because they were America's helpless dependents. The lights went up on Japan, center stage in East Asia, while American hopes for China dimmed. In the American mind, as the Occupation progressed, Japan came to assume the role of China as loyal Asian ally and at least potential outpost of modern Western Christian civilization.

Why did most Americans know so little about Japan before 1945? The prevailing ignorance, of course, had exceptions. Soon after the war erupted, knowledgeable Americans in Washington were planning the creation of a peaceful democratic postwar Japan based on the British parliamentary model, already well known to the Japanese.

But Japan was both geographically and culturally remote from the Western world, with a tongue that is the most intricate written language mankind has evolved, which has not encouraged many foreigners to tackle it. Japan was too far away to attract any but the most affluent American tourists. And Americans did not learn much about Japanese civilization from immigrants. Japanese influence in gardening, art, and architecture had some mark on American life—shaping the work of Frank Lloyd Wright, for example—but by and large Japanese culture remained strange to Americans.

Some Japanese did emigrate, but discriminatory American immigration laws limited their numbers. And instead of scattering across the nation, they clustered in the Hawaiian islands and along the Pacific coast. In these places their tendency to group together (not unusual for immigrants) was encouraged by the intolerance of their white neighbors. The Japanese newcomers were typically hard working but poor, embodying all the economic virtues of the Protestant ethic. They were farmers for the most part and not conspicuous in the community. The Japanese-American did not become upwardly mobile and truly enter the mainstream of American life until after 1945.

"Inscrutable" was a word Americans commonly used to describe the Japanese, and some admitted the reason they fell back on the word was that they failed to try to understand these people. American perceptions did not penetrate much more deeply than the images of cherry blossoms, *geisha, hara-kiri* (usually mispronounced "harry carry"), and Mt. Fuji. School textbooks neglected Japan, along with the rest of Asia. To educate the troops for possible military government duties in Asian countries, the armed forces found they had to start at the most elementary level. And only in the spring of 1941 did the Government frantically try to remedy the lack of people who could read and speak Japanese by beginning crash programs in language training for members of the armed forces.

Until 1941 the study of Japan in the U.S. had been regarded as highly exotic. In the academic world there were scarcely a dozen people who knew enough of Japanese culture and language to be labeled experts. One of them was Hugh Borton, professor at Columbia University, who recalls that in the early 1930s he was obliged to go to Europe in order to get graduate training in Japanese history. There were no such programs in the United States; there was no person qualified to teach. And on the undergraduate level there were few courses available on Japan or any other part of Asia. American education at all levels was still Eurocentric. The world outside western and central Europe scarcely existed intellectually for Americans, except as places of activity for Western traders, men and women of God, and empire builders. Most Americans were interested in the non-Western world solely for what it had meant to the West.

Americans wanting to read something informative about Japan had little to choose from. The scholarly literature was scanty. Three books were probably the most influential: Sir George Sansom's *Japan: A Short Cultural History* (1931), E. Herbert Norman's *Japan's Emergence as a Modern State* (1940), and the most popular, Ruth Benedict's *The Chrysanthemum and the Sword,* not formally published until 1946.

Sansom was the last of the great amateurs in the field of Western studies of Japan, a scholar-diplomat whose career was largely in the British diplomatic service and who was knighted not for his scholarly achievements but for his work in negotiating a commercial treaty. He was a learned man who read Japanese easily, even ancient and recondite documents, and he knew the country well. His *History,* impressionistic as it is, remains highly readable even today; at the time it was without peer.

Somewhat harder going is Norman's "pioneer work" (in his own words) analyzing the great transition occurring in Japan during the mid and late nineteenth century. Norman, a Canadian, was also a professional diplomat, and a Harvard Ph.D. as well. His career ended tragically in 1957 when, while serving as Canadian Ambassador to Egypt, he jumped to his death from a Cairo rooftop. He then was under severe attack for allegedly having been a Communist. Norman's interpretation of Japanese history is Marxist, but this was not commented on by reviewers when his book was published. More to the point, at least at that time, was the freshness of what he had to say to a Western audience. He drew from a large variety of Japanese language sources, inaccessible to all but a very few Western scholars, for his interpretation of the Meiji Restoration movement of the 1860s, which swept Japan into the modern world. Owen Lattimore, pundit for Americans on Asian affairs, admiringly spoke of Norman as "the most authoritative contemporary analyst of Japan's economy, society, and government." Norman is still read, although subsequent historians have confuted many of his ideas.

Ruth Benedict, a distinguished scholar at Columbia University, was commissioned by the U.S. Government in June 1944 to prepare a study of the Japanese people. "I was asked to use all the techniques I could as a cultural anthropologist to spell out what the Japanese were like." Although her book was not published until after the war, it earlier was circulated rather widely in mimeographed form. The reception was not uncritical, but the book had a large impact. Harold Strauss's review in the *New York Times* said: "Because it pictures a Japan that exists more in tradition than in reality, Miss Benedict's book must be considered primarily of historical interest." But most readers accepted it as an explanation of why the Japanese behaved as they did after the war.

Benedict never visited Japan. Nor did she read Japanese. Instead, she relied on materials published in English and on interviews with Americans of Japanese descent and with Westerners who had lived in Japan. She was therefore handicapped by a narrow range of sources. Moreover, the techniques anthropologists had so skillfully developed for probing and analyzing tiny primitive cultures such as those in the South Pacific were not entirely adequate or suitable when applied to a people as numerous, diverse, sophisticated, and rapidly changing as the Japanese.

Nor was Benedict exempt from the vulnerability of scholarship to the prejudices of wartime. She asserted that the Japanese were the most alien enemy the U.S. had ever fought in an all-out struggle, which is true enough. But while she complained that the Japanese did not accept American conventions of war, she ignored the enormous change in the nature of war, namely massive attack against civilians, a tactic used first elsewhere by others but adopted and vigorously employed by America in the Pacific.

The Chrysanthemum and the Sword was an extraordinary achievement, written well enough to attract a large readership. The imagery of the title alone was arresting, encapsulating the American tendency to think of Japan in terms of violent contrast, the beautiful with the bloody. Although Benedict was guilty of easy generalization, she certainly attempted a more objective view than that of her fellow anthropologist, the Englishman, Geoffrey Gorer.

Gorer has a simple explanation for the less attractive aspects of Japanese behavior. He argues that strict toilet training caused the Japanese to be neurotically aggressive, provoking one critic to remark in 1953 that "the modern psychological approach to the study of Japanese personality [that taken by Gorer] is as far askew as were the approaches of the missionary and the 'old Japan hand.' " Both viewpoints, the critic suggests, take as an implicit starting point that the Japanese are in some way peculiar and abnormal. The Gorer theory was discouraging to those who wanted to reform Japanese behavior. Was it reasonable to suppose that General MacArthur and his associates could modify Japanese toilet training practices?

Not everyone subscribed to the Gorer thesis. Lawrence K. Rosinger, a frequent writer on Far Eastern problems, agreed with Gorer that the Japanese were regimented and chauvinistic, but argued that these traits were not psychologically induced and were not racial. Instead, he said, they came from political, economic, and social conditions—conditions susceptible to change. Therefore the Japanese could be reformed. This line of argument was reassuring to the Occupation forces embarking upon their great endeavor.

Fortune magazine published a special issue devoted to Japan in December 1943. Publisher Henry R. Luce wrote to MacArthur, boasting that the issue was "regarded as by far the most exhaustive semi-popular treatment of the subject." *Fortune* deplored the American ignorance of Japan, attempting to explain it by pointing out the lack of cultural cognates to help Americans understand Japanese motivations and actions, whereas "Europe is a continent we can understand because most of us came from there." *Fortune* stated that ignorance had handicapped American efforts in the war, American ability to make sensible judgments. "Sometimes we describe the Japanese as weaklings, sometimes as supermen, sometimes we insist we can knock off Japan as soon as we get rid of Hitler, sometimes we fear that victory will take decades."

Americans were prone in their naïveté to accept extraordinarily sweeping statements about the Japanese. For example, author Sydney Greenbie in *Asia Unbound* (1943) said the Japanese people may be literate, but "they simply do not know how to think. They are foggy. They are sentimental. They are hysterical and mystical." And James Young, a press correspondent in Japan for thirteen years —long enough to have known better—could write: "The Japanese has no self-consciousness or individual expression."

Eliot Janeway, the well-known writer on economic matters, assured his readers that "Japan is not our intellectual equal. Japan's dominant mentality is either too primitive to accept civilization or too highly developed to be trusted in it." A War Department training film, *Know Your Enemy Japan,* put it quite simply: "We will never know the tough little mind of the Japanese completely." This

27

judgment at least relieved Americans of the need to try.

Joseph C. Grew and others who knew prewar Japan, and dominated planning for peace during the war years, urged separating "the sins of the leaders from the actions of the masses." The real criminals, he believed, were the military clique, not the Emperor. Grew saw the Emperor as a potential instrument of liberal and moderate groups, not the exclusive possession of the military. He warned that harsh treatment of the Emperor by Americans might backfire, making the task of the Occupation much more difficult. Grew worried that the prejudice against Japan, which reminded him of the virulent anti-German feelings in World War I, might lead to a similarly vindictive and unsuccessful peace.

But most Americans seemed ready to think the worst of people of whom they knew so little. Wartime propaganda had to make the Japanese appear utterly vile. This was the best, most easily understood reason for fighting them. Many Americans were quite happy to accept that interpretation. These opinions surfaced in discussing what ought to be done with the Japanese after the war.

George Fielding Eliot, the military analyst, writing in the New York *Herald Tribune,* urged the complete "destruction of Japanese industry so that not one brick of any Japanese factory shall be left upon another, so that there shall not be in Japan one electric motor or one steam or gasoline engine, not a chemical laboratory, nor so much as a book which tells how these things are made."

Professor Ernest Hooton, Harvard anthropologist, recommended that the United States "exile, imprison, and sterilize all members of the Japanese Royal family and all of their blood relations." A November 1944 Gallup poll found that 13 percent of Americans asked would favor killing all the people of Japan left alive when the war ended.

Over the past century or so, American public opinion toward Japan has gone through dramatic shifts, and so has the Japanese view of the U.S. and the West. Before the visits of Commodore Perry in 1853 and 1854, the Japanese were apprehensive about

28

Western incursions and hostile toward most Westerners. The nation had virtually been closed to the outside world since the middle of the seventeenth century. The Dutch were the only Westerners tolerated, because they did not preach Christianity to the Japanese. The sole interest of the Hollanders in coming to Japan was making money from trade. The Japanese did not object to that, for they could profit also. To the Japanese, Americans were much more troublesome.

Americans were frustrated by their inability to trade with Japan or even to stop off there en route to China. Occasionally a whaler, working the rich North Pacific waters, would have the misfortune to be wrecked on the Japanese coast. American castaways sometimes behaved rudely, but in many instances the Japanese treated them abominably. Largely for this reason the American Government began attempts to negotiate with the Japanese. But the American vision was far broader than trade. Writing in 1849, one of the early U.S. envoys was confident that Americans could "convert [the] selfish government [of Japan] into a liberal republic in a short time."

Perry's expedition was viewed by Americans as liberating Japan from feudal barbarism as well as opening the nation to the sunlight of international commerce and intercourse. Perry and his followers did begin an era of amicability in American-Japanese relations. American teachers and technicians, businessmen and beachcombers flocked to Japan. Some Japanese came to America to study.

Japan changed rapidly. The West and modern life were in vogue, and American influence was widespread, particularly at the grassroots level. The Japanese used American readers in their elementary schools, sang with gusto the songs of Stephen Foster with lyrics translated into Japanese, and took up baseball enthusiastically. American attitudes toward the Japanese were friendly—loftily patronizing but basically well disposed.

Friendliness between Japan and America diminished at the turn of the century due to tensions and expansionist competition over the Philippines and Hawaii. The U.S. acquired both, but after the

29

Japanese triumph over Russia in the war of 1904–1905, Americans saw Japan increasingly as competitor, even adversary. In that conflict they judged the Japanese a bit too successful for comfort. Soon both the American and Japanese navies began using each other as the potential enemy in war games.

American fear was intermixed with scorn. Americans tended to dismiss Japanese modernizing as merely the work of clever imitators; Japanese skill at adaptation was consistently put down. Americans conveniently forgot that all cultures borrow, and that their own was conspicuous in that respect. The myth flourished that Japanese culture was simply a derivative one, and it was inflated by the vast American ignorance of both the richness of Japanese folk arts and the extraordinary achievements of the higher culture. One writer went so far as to suggest that Japanese civilization was but a thin veneer, a Potemkin structure erected solely to deceive the West and draw attention away from the miserable state of the common folk, living barely above the subsistence level, ill housed and half starved.

Most Americans had never even seen a Japanese. Only through the five-and-ten-cent store was Japan widely known firsthand, and Americans tended to think of all Japanese culture on those standards. They were reluctant to accept the idea that Japanese technology could rise above the level of shoddy, cheap consumer goods. Outrageous stories were believed, such as the one foreigners liked to tell of the warship built in Japan with stolen foreign plans. Alerted to the possibility of theft, the shipyard had planted a set of drawings with some vital information lacking; the thieves made off with these bogus plans. Because the Japanese did not yet have an adequate grasp of the intricacies of naval architecture, they were chagrined to see the ship they built capsize immediately after it was completed.

Foreigners living in Japan were not necessarily better informed about their hosts or more sympathetic toward them. With the notable exception of missionaries, few felt they needed to learn the language or develop close Japanese friends. Both they and the

Japanese felt comfortable living apart; the foreigners in their Western-style houses, eating Western-style food, dressing in Western-style clothing, and enjoying the society of other Westerners. Japanese labor was cheap, and a foreigner's income went a long way. The life was agreeable, if narrow, not unlike that of European colonial elites elsewhere in Asia. Most foreigners liked it that way. So did the Japanese.

But there were discomforting stirrings of change, particularly after the Russo-Japanese War. Foreigners found growing Japanese pride irritating. When Albert Einstein visited Japan, according to Sir George Sansom, it was said in the foreign community that Japanese newspapers covering the event praised Einstein and his theory of relativity but cautioned that the theory did not necessarily apply to Japan.

As Japan industrialized, Americans felt a growing sense of grievance about Japanese goods flowing to the U.S. and Japanese economic competition. Yet historian William Neumann, commenting much later on the prewar economic animosity, finds "much, if not all . . . unjustified. . . . A United States Tariff Commission report in 1934 found only 8 percent of the total imports from Japan to be substantially competitive." And many of these had come to the American market because of American initiative.

Japanese goods were conspicuous. American textile manufacturers, for example, were vocally unhappy. In 1932 the trade balance shifted in America's favor, as American sales to Japan increased steadily. But this was not in the popular consciousness. A feeling lingered that the Japanese were unfair, ruthless, and highly successful economic rivals, at least within certain fields.

Americans had grown sensitive to Japanese aggression in the 1930s with the bombing of Shanghai, the rape of Nanking, and the sinking of the American gunboat *Panay.* Americans viewed Pearl Harbor as outrageous. To launch an attack while diplomats were still talking seemed treacherous and unprincipled—as if all modern wars were not started with surprise attack, and as if it were not the duty of the military to stay alert and prevent such dastardly surprises. Americans would not speak, even grudgingly, of the brilliance of the Japanese tactical achievement. Instead they dwelt upon the "immorality" of the action. Japanese bombs in Hawaii were aimed only at military targets, not at civilians. But that was not mentioned either.

The Japanese string of sensational victories during the first six months of the war—Hong Kong, the Philippines, Singapore, the Dutch East Indies—changed American attitudes toward Japan. The *samurai* image of Theodore Roosevelt's time, when the plucky "Jap" was seen as killing the Russian "giant," was given a twist away from heroism toward the sinister, even the bestial. The Japanese were now regarded as fanatic militarists, a race apart, like no one else in their willingness to die for the cause. Ironically, America became more persuaded of the inherent implacable quality of Japanese militarism than the Japanese, despite the best effort of their army masters.

Streaking across the arid, desolate Wyoming plain in 1946, the train passed a cluster of abandoned buildings huddled on the bleak landscape, fenced in with barbed wire sprouting out of the sagebrush. "What's that?" the boy asked. "Oh," a woman replied, "that's just an old Jap trap."

"Relocation Centers" was the official euphemism for these prison camps, monuments to white American prejudice and to the wartime suffering of the Japanese-American.

The war simply intensified racial antagonism, it did not create it. In the meeting between East and West, the Japanese had responded with greater initial vigor, more initiative, more curiosity than any other Asian culture, and they made the strongest effort to accommodate their way of life to the modern industrial society of the West. But however they chose to smooth over or eliminate cultural differences, race remained an obvious and irreconcilable distinction, which neither the Japanese nor the foreigner would overlook.

Racism was, of course, not peculiar to Americans or to Japanese. In the pre-World War II era it was practically universal, embedded firmly among scholars and scientists as well as in popular opinion, found both within high culture and folk culture. Herbert Spencer could solemnly talk about the superiority of the "Great White Race." Social Darwinism cast a cloak of respectability over the racial struggle. The ethnic joke lay at the core of popular humor. Race was an extremely convenient means of explaining away complicated differences between cultures.

Racism was one of the ultimate causes of the war. Reading the Hearst press was not necessary to gain awareness of the prejudice, subtle and otherwise, experienced by Japanese immigrants to this country. And the Japanese people were quite familiar with the prescriptive American immigration regulations against Asians, reaching a climax in 1924 with the Exclusion Agreement. Thereafter no Japanese could enter the U.S. and become an American citizen. The American "Open Door" opened only in one direction.

On March 2, 1942, the U.S. Army issued an order approved by Attorney General Francis Biddle and President Franklin Roosevelt that all people of Japanese descent, whether American citizens or not, were to be removed from Washington, western Oregon, most of California, and southern Arizona. One hundred and ten thousand men, women, and children were uprooted from their homes and their belongings and were sent to ten remote camps in what was the greatest single forced migration in American history, accomplished with brutal speed and ruthless disregard for civil liberties.* Military security was the official reason for the policy, to which remarkably few Americans objected at the time.

American authorities did nothing about the Japanese living in Hawaii. Was it simply that there were too many of these people for the Government to subject them to the same treatment as those living on the West Coast? In 1941 more than one third of the people in Hawaii were of Japanese descent. No uprising accompanied the Pearl Harbor attack, not even any significant acts of

---

*That same spring the Canadian Government relocated seventeen thousand of their West Coast citizens of Japanese descent, depriving them of their civil rights.

sabotage. Throughout the war security in Hawaii was uncompromised by the presence of these Japanese-Americans; subversion was no problem. Those on the mainland were allowed no such opportunity to prove their loyalty.

General J. L. Dewitt, military commander for the West Coast, testified before a House Naval Affairs Subcommittee in 1943: "A Jap's a Jap. They are a dangerous element, *whether loyal or not* [italics added]. There is no way to determine their loyalty. . . . The Japanese race is an enemy race. . . ."

In America before the war, Fascism and Nazism enjoyed some support among the Italian and German ethnic groups, but the support was more symbolic than substantive. Of the Japanese-Americans and their sympathy for the aggressive policies of the mother country, one could say the same. Surely it was no greater a problem for the authorities, and probably was less. Certainly no Japanese-American individual or group burst into notoriety like Fritz Kuhn with his German-American Bund. But German-Americans, and Italian-Americans also, held power and political prominence in American life; Dwight D. Eisenhower and Fiorello H. La Guardia were two. No Japanese-Americans then enjoyed such fame; none held high political office.

American wartime propaganda carried a large dose of racism. Other than avenging Pearl Harbor, it was easier to think of respectable reasons for fighting in Europe than in the Pacific. Americans could differentiate between Nazis and Germans; the evils of Nazism were apparent. In the case of the Japanese, most Americans made no separation between government and people.

David MacIsaac in his study of the U.S. Strategic Bombing Survey confides: "One of the highest ranking air commanders of the war has privately confirmed that there existed 'a basic distinction in our thinking' between the Japanese and the German." George Schuyler, columnist for the Pittsburgh *Courier,* a prominent black weekly, explained: "There is greater American satisfaction in humiliating the Japanese than the Germans, just as there was greater enthusiasm for the Japanese war than there was for the German-

Italian one. We all know the reason. It is racial and nothing but racial.''

The images emerging from wartime propaganda emphasized the physical differences between Japanese and Americans. The diminutive was constantly used in a pejorative way. The Japanese were "bandy-legged," "squat," "subhuman," "apelike," "faceless," speaking with "harsh guttural sounds." Cartoons were all buck teeth and glasses.

It is scarcely surprising that black Americans looked on the Japanese with far less hatred than did white Americans. And Japanese wartime propaganda emphasized American racism with telling effect. One Japanese broadcaster, referring to Jim Crow laws, remarked: "If . . . limited rights exist in America, how can Mr. Roosevelt promise them sincerely in the whole world? How can America be fighting for them?''

Whereas Major General Charles Willoughby, MacArthur's chief of Intelligence, could refer to the Japanese treatment of Allied prisoners of war as "the forerunner of Oriental brutality that was still to reach satanic depths in the Korean and Chinese war," the Pittsburgh *Courier*'s view was: "Imagine people who would loose an atomic bomb on two large cities (practically wiping them out with a large part of their populations) wailing about the mistreatment and killing of a few thousand prisoners!" At a time when the American press had little good to say about the Japanese, the *Courier* praised Japanese efficiency, cleanliness, and courtesy.

Most Americans coming to Japan with the occupying forces carried the burden of the propaganda image. Their opinion of the Japanese was low. Not only were these Asians vicious enemies, but they were also inferior to Westerners. Fortunately for some Americans this image was shallowly implanted, and amenable to change. For others, prejudice lingered.

Americans invented the bulldozer. Incorporating raw power with exquisite refinement, its crude strength could be controlled by the most delicate touch. It could be used to destroy and it could be used to build. Scratching out their airstrips and highways with pick and shovel, the Japanese fought the war without benefit of this highly useful machine. Americans introduced it to Japan during the Occupation. Open-mouthed in wonder and admiration, the Japanese watched the speed and ease with which the machine was able to accomplish large tasks.

The bulldozer is both metaphor and totem for the Occupation, as Americans interpreted it. Metaphorically the U.S. undertook to bulldoze Japanese institutions on a massive scale, tearing down and building up, demilitarizing and democratizing. The bulldozer was a totem for the American appreciation—perhaps inordinate—both of what machines can do and the American ability to build and work them.

Wealth and skill buoyed American optimism and inflated American confidence in their power to change the Japanese; what might be called a *pecunia vincit omnia* attitude. American money would overcome all obstacles. The New Dealers, who comprised a fair number of the Americans streaming to Tokyo, were inspired by the idea that social change could be subjected to rationality, that reform could be engineered and legislated. And the occupiers were gloriously uninhibited by the enormity and complexity of what they proposed to do with their former foe.

Douglas MacArthur and his associates in this great enterprise saw themselves as leaders for change, forcing, or better encouraging, the Japanese to join in. As historian Frederick Jackson Turner put it some years earlier, "We ... believed as a nation that other peoples had only to will our democratic institutions in order to repeat our own career." So Americans were now offering the Japanese this glittering opportunity. How would they react?

3

The Itinerary

AFTER the U.S. entered World War II, "Dr. New Deal" became "Dr. Win-the-War," President Roosevelt said, emphasizing where he thought American national energies ought to be focused. Domestic concerns receded before foreign affairs; understandably the country was concentrating on the immediate rather than the distant future. When fighting a war, people are usually too busy to think much about the peace to follow.

In foreign policy, European questions seemed to preoccupy high officials. With so much of the shape of the postwar world undetermined and demanding intense attention and hard analysis, the specific problems of America's relations with Japan were not compelling. Americans felt little sense of urgency. They were certain they would defeat the Japanese—first the Germans, then the Japanese. It might take some time, with bloody assault preceding surrender. Prior to Potsdam Americans expected and planned for the direct military government of Japan. The Italian and German cases seemed to indicate the pattern the U.S. could expect: invasion, fighting, then gradual establishment of Allied military rule.

In a memorandum written for President Truman just before war's end, Secretary of War Henry Stimson advised the new President:

> I would hope that our occupation of the Japanese islands would not involve the government of the country as a whole in any such manner as we are committed in Germany. I am afraid we would make a hash

of it if we tried. . . . Our occupation should be limited to that necessary to (a) impress the Japanese, and the orient as a whole, with the fact of Japanese defeat, (b) demilitarize the country, and (c) punish war criminals, including those responsible for the perfidy of Pearl Harbor.

These were relatively modest and simple objectives in contrast to what was being expansively suggested at lower levels of American Government, and to what ultimately Americans would seek to do. The Japanese would be helped to rebuild a state, an economy, and a society in as remarkable and sweeping a peacetime foreign exercise as any nation has ever undertaken.

Since the fall of 1942, three or four Japan experts in the Division of Special Research in the State Department, gathered from universities as well as from the Foreign Service, had been thinking, writing, and talking about what America ought to do with Japan after victory. From them came the core of American postwar political policies.

The War Department also began planning. Both the Army and the Navy wanted to govern Japan, if only for the recognition of having been the major instrument for victory. Both services prepared. The Army assumed that the job would be theirs, since presumably military government would be erected over the charred ruins of a Japan resisting the Allied invaders to the last person able to wield a sharpened bamboo spear. But the Army was not formally assigned the responsibility of running the Occupation until the war was ending.

Someone digging through War Department files in the early 1940s found the draft of a report on military government prepared many years before by a Colonel J. L. Hunt. He had been in charge of civil affairs in the Rhineland zone Americans occupied after World War I. The American Army had undertaken military government after virtually every war, and the experience had never been a happy one. The men were untrained, uninterested, and wanted only to be back home, a sentiment heartily seconded by those whose land they were occupying. What Hunt said convinced General George C. Marshall and others that this time the U.S. needed to train men for military government.

In the case of Japan America needed people who would know not only the principles and the practices of military government, but also the Japanese language and something about the people, their history and their culture. The need was the impetus for founding three training programs: military government, intensive language instruction, and foreign area studies.

The armed forces (the Navy was also involved, although on a smaller scale) turned to the universities to provide teachers, books, classrooms, and dormitories. Very early in the war the Army at Ann Arbor, Michigan, and the Navy at Boulder, Colorado, began Japanese language and area training. These two programs may have provided more trained Japanese linguists than any others during the war. Certainly their quality was high. Many graduates served in the Occupation; some eventually emerged as leading authorities on Japan. The University of Michigan remains one of the nation's primary centers for Japanese study.

Through Army initiative, "CATS" (Civil Affairs Training Schools) sprang into life. Universities had to scramble to organize these courses. As one University of Washington, Seattle, faculty member recalls: "Two days before the official start of the program we learned that we were not to teach a European but an entirely Far Eastern program, with training in Japanese, Mandarin Chinese, and Korean languages and areas."

For the Army officer assigned to anticipated duty in Japan, the usual pattern was six weeks training in the principles of military government at the University of Virginia, Charlottesville, then six months at one of the six CATS (Chicago, Harvard, Michigan, Northwestern, Stanford, and Yale). At CATS he would spend about half his time in language study, the rest on area studies and military government emphasizing problems peculiar to Japan.

Intensive language study was the inspiration of Mortimer Graves

39

of the American Council of Learned Societies, consultant to the newly established Military Government Division for the Office of the Provost Marshall in Washington. The "Army method," as it came to be called, stressed study of the colloquial spoken language, taught in small classes with the use of native speakers as drill masters. Results were often good; the method seemed a much better and faster way to learn to get along in a language than the old way of working with grammar book and reader. Students were carefully selected and highly motivated. Who, after all, wanted to fail that weekly quiz when it could mean leaving the school and immediate demotion to the ranks? That prospect proved a powerful incentive to concentrated study and to the utmost exercise of brute memory. "When I finished that course, I felt that there was nothing in the world I couldn't do!" recounted one of the students, later a Counterintelligence officer in the Occupation.

Japanese is an exceptionally difficult language. Very few students found the crash courses providing true fluency, unless there was opportunity to continue study. Critics coined the phrase "sunburn effect" to describe the result of this kind of intensive language study; what you learned did not last long. Nevertheless, knowledge of the rudiments often gave the student a sense of confidence. Even if he had to use an interpreter, he was not entirely at sea; psychologically this was important.

The area studies course, for Japan and for other hitherto exotic cultures, was devised to teach prospective military government officers something about the people for whom they were to be responsible. For many professors the course was a novel and, for some, ultimately significant experience in team teaching and interdisciplinary work. The schools had to extend their reach beyond conventional academic circles to find teachers who knew Japan. Businessmen, government officials, missionaries—anyone who had spent some time there before the war was a potential source of information.

Unfortunately not every knowledgeable person can teach. Lectures were sometimes poor, and the courses had a cobbled quality.

Sometimes information was outdated and the ideas so broad as to be quite superficial. Speakers had little time to prepare, students little time to digest. "All you could do," one lecturer remembers, "was give them a feel for the sort of situation they were going to get into."

Meanwhile papers flowed in a steady stream back and forth across the Potomac between the Pentagon and the State Department. In December 1944 the latter formed with the armed forces a policy committee known as SWNCC, the State-War-Navy Coordinating Committee, headed initially by James Dunn (State), John J. McCloy (Army), and Artemus Gates (Navy). The following month a sub-committee was spun off to consider the Far East, chaired by Eugene Dooman, career foreign service Japan specialist; caustic, domineering, and knowledgeable. "Swink," as it was called, pulled together the ideas, discussions, and drafts that would lead ultimately to policy, to those orders that would be sent out to the Supreme Commander in the field.

A few of the many questions these men in Washington pondered were: how much of Japan should be occupied, in what manner and for how long?* How should Americans treat the Japanese—be punitive, forgiving, or simply concerned with maintaining order adequate to extract reparations? What should be done with the existing Japanese Government, the Emperor, and state-supported religion, national and local authority, political parties, codes of law? And what might be salvaged from the old order as timber for constructing a new democratic state and society?

Opinions differed widely. Dooman, for example, questioned whether a victor nation had the right to "reorder the social structure of the vanquished." He worried about preserving Japan's "cul-

---

*One suggestion was that the Japanese army be made to evacuate Hokkaido only and to surrender in Honshu, with ranking Japanese being sent off as hostages to Australia. The Joint War Plans Committee contemplated a Japan divided into zones. Hokkaido and northern Honshu were to go to the U.S.S.R., and China was to have Shikoku. But the idea of zonal government was abandoned long before Germany became an unhappy example of it.

tural integrity." Dr. George Blakeslee, on professorial leave from Clark University, active and quietly influential and, in his early seventies, the senior among planners for Japan in the State Department, believed Japan should share in the benefits of the Atlantic Charter of August 12, 1941, which promised enjoyment of trade, access to raw materials, and a better living standard for all nations.

Secretary of State Cordell Hull overruled Blakeslee, saying that until the Japanese repented and reformed, they deserved little consideration. Hull, a man of "primitive righteousness," consistently took a hard line toward Japan; the former Senator from Tennessee, although scrupulously polite and gentlemanly, had never troubled to conceal his dislike for the Japanese. Even Blakeslee and the Japan specialists who worked with him could scarcely be accused of being swayed by feelings of affection for the Japanese. The sobriquet " 'poor dear Japan' Blakeslee" was unfair; his view and that of his colleagues was simply more optimistic than Hull's. It all depended on how one interpreted Japan's recent history.

Experts in the State Department, although the viewpoint was not confined to those working there, saw the political excesses of the 1930s as an aberration in modern Japanese history. Militarism may have taken over, but the norm was quite different. These men viewed Japan as an essentially benign though increasingly modern and democratic state, which had successfully adopted and adapted much that was good in Western civilization. This analysis was labeled by one critic as "slightly saturated with a Sunday School flavor." Yet these men knew Japan; they had personal experience going back into the period of "Taishō democracy" in the 1920s and even before, and they profoundly appreciated Japan's cultural history and arts.

Old Japan hands wanted reform to grow within a stable political organism; they did not anticipate revolutionary or radical change. To them such a prospect was distasteful, and they judged it unnecessary. The Emperor, after all, had not been invariably, nor was he inevitably, a tool of militarists. Why could he not be transformed into a constitutional monarch, symbol for a democratic state? Here was a comfortable basis for the belief that ruling Japan indirectly was both feasible and desirable. Asia needed Japan. That nation had to resume a place within the international community. And its people must enjoy a decent standard of living, for an impoverished, suffering Japan would be highly susceptible either to revival of virulent nationalism or to the appeal of Communism. Above all, argued the Japan hands, America must not do violence to the feelings of the Japanese; without "cooperation, you never could expect to have a successful occupation."

The Japan hands had to fend off others in the State Department who favored much harsher treatment: Dean Acheson for one, the China specialists, as well as a group of strong-minded and outspoken economists who had been contemplating Japan's future since early in the war. Not that the State Department had a monopoly on dissenting views about Japan. The War Department also had its differing opinions, but they were not as sharp or acerbic.

The economists, recruited from universities, the Office of Strategic Services (OSS), and those federal agencies that had sprouted so vigorously during the New Deal era, were highly competent professionals, for the most part innocent of any knowledge or experience of Japan. Lacking sensitivity to historical or cultural nuance, they tended to lump Japan with Germany. They interpreted both as militaristic enemy states in which big business played a conspicuous role, smothering economic democracy and fueling a drive toward war. The sharpest point of difference between the economists and the Japan experts was what to do about big business. The economists were keen to crush the combines, the *zaibatsu.* Their enthusiasm for trust-busting had deep and respectable roots in the American past, in populism and progressivism as well as more recently in the New Deal.

Those arguing for a severe settlement with the Japanese, a point of view with which an overwhelming majority of the American public agreed, saw Japan as "machine age feudalism," a society by tradition militaristic, seething with irrational and fanatical passions erupting in the 1930s through the thin and fragile crust of respect-

43

able modernity and democracy. Grubbing out these evils would be necessary before reform could be instilled. But first the Japanese had to be forced to lick the dust.

"Unconditional surrender" was the phrase articulated by Franklin D. Roosevelt during a press conference held at the Casablanca summit conference, January 24, 1943, to define the American war aim. His words came out of the Council on Foreign Relations through its president, Norman H. Davis, who had used them earlier in conversation with the President. At the Council the idea of unconditional surrender was provoked by what Americans interpreted as the lessons of World War I and by American resolve not to be cheated of the fruits of victory. This time the enemy would not subsequently be able to claim that he had not actually been defeated.

Unconditional surrender. The phrase was blunt, bellicose, and clean, a simple definition of how the U.S. was going to win. The words captured the public ear, implying both that the loser accepted total defeat and that the victor had won the right to govern and reform the defeated country. The slogan encouraged defiance from the enemy, which Americans did not want; it discouraged the diplomatic initiative, which Americans did want. Once uttered, it was hard to retract without embarrassment. The doctrine had all the power of wartime hatreds behind it, all the missionary zeal of those eager to seize the opportunity to extirpate all evil in Japan, all the sweep and certitude of ignorance.

A number of events caused the American Government to soften the particulars of how they wanted to settle matters with the Japanese, once the latter were subdued: Yalta in February 1945, with growing American suspicions of the U.S.S.R.; President Roosevelt's death that April, followed by the political demise of Henry Morgenthau, Jr., who wanted to turn Germany into a goat pasture and whose harsh ideas for establishing a permanent peace extended to Japan; and finally the fading of the American vision of a friendly China as a great power.

As the war rushed to its end, power accrued in the hands of the Japan experts because they were best equipped to furnish detailed knowledge to American planning and because of the high office of Joseph C. Grew, by sympathy, at least, an ardent member of their company. Grew, Ambassador to Japan for ten years before the war, became Under Secretary of State in November 1944, his authority as the Department's second ranking officer enhanced by the change at the top. The elderly, ailing Hull had given way to Edward Stettinius, the strikingly handsome, prematurely white-haired former chairman of U.S. Steel. Of Stettinius it was said, "There's a lot less than meets the eye." He had had only meager experience in foreign affairs and he deferred to Grew, especially in matters relating to Japan.

In the sultry heat of a Washington August, under stringent time pressure as the war came to an unexpectedly rapid conclusion, "Swink" hammered out a compromise between the flexible spirit of the Atlantic Charter and the rigidity of unconditional surrender. On August 10 the Japanese accepted the Potsdam ultimatum with the reservation that the prerogatives of the Emperor be retained. America modified that stipulation by the ambiguous phrase that the emperor and the Japanese Government would be subject to the Supreme Commander. The Japanese accepted this, hoping desperately that *kokutai,* their national essence, would survive. America thus embarked upon the Occupation feeling quite unfettered and uninhibited.

At the moment of victory the authority of the Japan specialists, who were outnumbered and outmaneuvered by their opponents, began to fade. Grew did not get along with the new Secretary, James F. Byrnes, and he resigned, replaced by Dean Acheson; Dooman retired. The China specialists had the considerable satisfaction of seeing one of their men, George Atcheson, Jr., named senior political advisor in Tokyo to General MacArthur. Grew had vainly tried to get that job for Dooman; but Acheson did not want a Japan hand there.

A second China man, John Carter Vincent, was appointed head

of the Office of Far Eastern Affairs in the State Department. And a third, Owen Lattimore, recently of the Office of War Information although he had never played more than a modest official role, came to be regarded as the nation's leading expert on the Far East, both for China and Japan; no Japan specialist in the mid-1940s spoke with the popular authority of Lattimore.

Grew never became Secretary of State, and after he left the Department his advice was infrequently sought. Dooman's bitterness and frustration festered in retirement; in 1952 he lashed out viciously at his former critics, accusing them of nefariously attempting to weaken Japanese capitalism by insisting on radical economic reform. Yet, in the long run did the loss of these offices to Japan specialists matter? Did their policies fade with their careers?

The breakup of the combines, embodying the underlying notion of a need for thoroughgoing economic change, was included in orders to General MacArthur issued by President Truman on September 6, 1945. As we shall see, the more avid among the reformers would ultimately believe American goals for economic change in Japan to be seriously compromised. And, by and large, what happened in the Occupation would not be displeasing to those Americans who knew Japan best.

By August 1945 more than two thousand Army and Navy officers had been trained for military government duty in Japan. More than half of them were in Monterey, California, awaiting overseas assignment while their newly acquired knowledge and somewhat fragile language skills risked atrophy.

Many were unhappy; it was not so much a matter of "bringing the boys back home" as the boys not wanting to leave in the first place. By V-J Day many of these officers had amassed enough points to be eligible for release from service. In order to retain them, the War Department put them in a special "scarce category," making them ineligible for discharge. Although a public relations officer at Monterey declared, "I cannot see how anyone could have failed to anticipate duty for which their experience and training could not become effective until after cessation of hostilities," many officers did not see it that way. The situation was not helped by a story in the San Francisco *Chronicle,* September 30, that MacArthur was using civil affairs officers in regular staff work, not in the military government duties for which they had been especially trained.

The decision to rule Japan by using the Japanese Government made military government by Americans largely superfluous. Many of the men trained for Japanese duty found themselves sent to Korea instead because the sudden removal of the Japanese imperial authority there created a serious political vacuum. A higher bureaucracy of Koreans did not exist; their Japanese masters had seen to this. So the paradox emerged that Korea, a friendly nation, was to be governed (at least initially) by Americans directly, whereas Japan, an erstwhile enemy, would be ruled indirectly. The *Saturday Evening Post* declared in disgust that Americans were "going to give Japan back to the Japanese."

In the end, Washington simply laid down the broad lines of policy for the Occupation. When Colonel Charles Kades went to Japan among those first arrivals he was not entirely clear as to what his duties would be. Stowed carefully in his office safe, Kades had what he called his bible, a collection of Joint Chiefs of Staff policy statements. But in fact there was no detailed policy waiting to be executed; he and others were to create it. And Supreme Commander Douglas MacArthur enjoyed considerable latitude, indeed relished the opportunity, to do fairly much as he chose.

4

The Machinery

GENERAL Jonathan Wainwright believed America would be obliged to occupy Japan for fifty years. But in Tokyo General MacArthur declared: "The shorter the better. If we're here a year or two, the Occupation will be an outstanding success; if we're here two to three years, it will still be a success; but if we stay too long, it won't be successful." Whether MacArthur thought eighty months "too long" is an unanswered question. Clearly the uncertainty as to the length of time Americans were going to stay caused some difficulty; there could be no long-range planning.

Nor did anyone know how large a garrison might be required. In September 1945 one of the officers there, buoyed by the cooperative spirit of the Japanese, expressed doubt that the occupying Army "need be more than 500,000 men." MacArthur announced in the middle of the same month that he expected to slash his forces in Japan to 200,000 within six months. The number of troops peaked at around 450,000, then fell to MacArthur's goal by February 1946. Characteristically, the General had spoken without consulting Washington; President Truman said he had heard nothing of the matter, but he hoped it would speed up getting the men out of uniform.

By his pronouncement MacArthur provoked a storm of criticism. Did he mean "to toss away the fruits of victory"? From the beginning many were unhappy about what they interpreted as undue compromise with the old order in Japan, manifested by America using the emperor and the existing Japanese structure of govern-

48

ment. These people were still thirsting for a peace of vengeance.

It soon became apparent that questions regarding the character of the Occupation and how long it should last would depend not simply on what was happening in Japan, but upon such wider concerns as the American relationship with Russia and with China. For America in Japan, military priorities were increasingly shaped by the unnerving demands of the Cold War, not the docile behavior of the Japanese. The U.S. had stretched its power all the way across the Pacific, filling at least part of the vacuum left by the collapse of the Japanese imperium, establishing air and naval bases in Japan and on its periphery. Much of Okinawa was now surfaced with concrete to accommodate runways for long-range bombers. The bases on that island, wrested from the Japanese at such heavy cost in the late spring of 1945, as well as Sasebo, Yokosuka, Tachikawa, and others, had growing weight in American strategic planning for possible war against the Soviet Union.

For the American Army, chiefly responsible for occupying Japan, the immediate postwar period was a particularly anxious time. Worrying about both its strategic and tactical roles in the nuclear era, the Army was fighting off what it saw as encroachment by the other services, in the continuing argument over whether or not the armed forces should be unified. While the nation was demobilizing and disarming on a massive scale, and converting industry from war to peace, the Army was struggling to achieve an appropriate equilibrium between the demands of the American public to get the boys back home and the requirements thrust upon it by the responsibilities of America's new leadership in the world. General George C. Marshall and others, attempting during the war to lay out postwar plans, vividly remembered the chaos they had experienced in the Army immediately after World War I. And on a personal level much was at stake. The *Christian Century* dryly reminded its readers that there were sixteen hundred American generals facing demotion (in some cases down to the rank of major or even captain) if the country did not maintain a large standing Army.

In Japan an increasing number of civilians were assuming jobs with the occupying forces and the number of troops was sharply shrinking. Nevertheless, in the Occupation world the Army remained king. Uniformed officers retained top authority. Military command and military law was supreme; civilians, commonly referred to as "DACs" (Department of the Army civilians), were essentially second-class citizens. To be a "DAC dependent" was the bottom, although being a civilian in a high post could be advantageous. Rank was not obvious among civilians. But civilians were obliged to live and work within an atmosphere created and perpetuated by the Army and its ways, which is not to imply that the Army was itself homogeneous or monolithic.

The American Army had become a richly diverse organism as a result of the war. A tiny force of professionals, the old "Regular Army," swelled with millions of transient, civilian, amateur warriors, many of whom were now clamoring for instant release. While in Japan some of these new soldiers shed their uniforms, continuing as civilians in the same jobs. Since many, if not most, of the Occupation Army jobs were not military, the change was of little consequence in terms of the work to be done. Great numbers of people flowed in and out, but both the organization and the atmosphere remained firmly "Army."

Once the occupying forces were in Japan, who was to decide what they were to do? Potentially there were three sources of authority: the Allies, Washington, and MacArthur. The Allies were effectively eliminated before the Occupation even began. In theory the enterprise remained a combined effort of all the nations that had defeated Japan; officially it was always an "Allied" and not an "American" endeavor. In reality, America both formed and executed the program and was never successfully challenged. America's allies were greatly handicapped, either by not being physically present in Japan (the Russians and the Chinese) or, if they were there, by having nothing but garrison duties (the British Commonwealth). The Americans, working directly with the Japanese in Tokyo or indirectly in the provinces, made the real policy. Being there was important, for often the spoken suggestion rather than the written order prevailed; it was not the letter of the directive so much as the nuance to which the Japanese responded.

The Allies clearly hoped to make their wishes felt. The Moscow Conference of Foreign Ministers in December 1945 created the Far Eastern Commission, a body of eleven (eventually thirteen) member nations charged with preparing an agenda for reshaping Japan. America, together with the United Kingdom, China, and the U.S.S.R., had veto power in the Far Eastern Commission, a great power privilege similar to that provided in the United Nations Security Council. The U.S. enjoyed the right to prevent any policy it did not like; in fact, by requesting the Commission to defer any proposed action, America or any of the other great powers could forestall the need to use its veto.

All this was somewhat academic. By the time the Commission began its work, in February 1946, the outline of the Occupation had already hardened. Housed in the handsome former Japanese embassy in Washington, with a budget provided by the American Government, the Far Eastern Commission could review policy as much as it wished. But the Commission would have found it extremely difficult to undo what had already been done. Though powerless, MacArthur nonetheless resented it.

Finally the Commission got together and sent to Tokyo its own version of the Initial Post-Surrender Directive on June 26, 1947, nearly two years after the Occupation had begun! Sir George Sansom, for a time one of its members, neatly summed up the work of the group: "We were supposed to tell MacArthur what to do and of course couldn't."

The second combined body, the Allied Council for Japan, from the start was specified as purely advisory. The eyes and ears of the Far Eastern Commission, it met in Tokyo under the chairmanship of its American delegate, MacArthur's senior civilian political advisor, the State Department's man in Japan. The British Commonwealth, China, and the Soviet Union were the other members of the Council: those Allied states most intimately and most powerfully

W. Macmahon Ball, British Commonwealth Representative from Australia to the Allied Council for Japan.

concerned with Japanese affairs. In practice, the Council had no more power than the Far Eastern Commission; it had little opportunity even to offer advice. MacArthur wanted to hear as little as possible from it.

W. Macmahon Ball of Australia, representing the British Commonwealth and one of the Council's most able, articulate, and aggressive members, justifiably complained that in the meetings "there were no problems of Japan: every problem of Japan came to be considered for its effects on Russian-American relations." The Council became a forum for exercising hostilities and tensions among the powers, chiefly (but not exclusively) between America and the Soviet Union.

The Russians, frustrated and resentful, were ardent, persistent, vocal critics of the Occupation, clearly eager to foment trouble for the Americans in any way they could. The formidably grim walled compound of the old Tsarist embassy in Tokyo housed a Soviet mission of more than five hundred people. Ostensibly they were there to serve as staff for the burly General Kuzma Dereveyanko, able Soviet representative to the Allied Council. In fact, most were engaged in propaganda and military intelligence activities.

The mission was a self-contained group, the Russians even bringing over their own cooks, chauffeurs, and cleaning women, people with such extraordinary talents as to cause one American official to remark that "it had never been clear to him why the preparation of borscht required training in electronics, or why driving a car demanded an advanced degree in physics or in naval engineering."

The Far Eastern Commission and the Allied Council for Japan were both either ignored or treated with condescension, if not contempt, by MacArthur and his staff. Courtney Whitney, Military Secretary to MacArthur, would later assert: "Not one constructive idea to help with the re-orientation and reconstruction of Japan [was] offered by either the Far Eastern Commission or the Allied Council."

The Allies intended the Commission to speak its will to the American Government in Washington, which then would relay proper instruction to General MacArthur, who was both Supreme Commander in Japan for the Allied Powers (SCAP) and commander of all American forces in the Western Pacific (CINCFE). The State Department and the U.S. Army were the two parts of the American Government most concerned with the Occupation, the former being outweighed by the Pentagon. State was not eager to contest for supreme authority in Japan. And since money appropriated for the cost of the Occupation came through the Pentagon, military views tended to dominate the current of suggestions, advice, and orders flowing from Washington to Japan.

Stark, drab poverty dominated downtown Tokyo, where disorder and discomfort reigned for the Japanese. Offices were cluttered, overcrowded, dusty, poorly lit, and barely heated. Dotting the core of downtown were burned-out shells of former buildings and empty weed-grown lots, many of which remained so until long after the Occupation was over.

Opposite the sprawling grounds of the Imperial Palace, across the avenue from the ancient moat whose swans would periodically find their serenity shattered by a drunken GI toppling into the

The Dai Ichi Insurance Building, General MacArthur's Headquarters. Moat of the Imperial Palace in the foreground.

murky water, stretched in a most uncharacteristically Japanese rectilinear pattern a long line of modern buildings: the Dai Ichi Insurance Building, the Imperial Theater, the Tokyo Kaikan, the Meiji Insurance and NYK buildings. These were now taken from the Japanese. Here was the heart of authority in Occupied Japan, General Headquarters (GHQ). These offices housed four or five thousand Americans.

General MacArthur's large Tokyo establishment was commonly known as "SCAP," although strictly speaking this was his title alone. Through their own Government the Japanese provided for the occupiers top to bottom nationwide channels of command. The vital link, the interface, was provided by officials of the old Foreign Ministry, forming a body called the Central Liaison Office. Americans had only to communicate with members of this office—pol-

54

ished, aristocratic diplomats, invariably fluent in English. In this fashion the occupiers were able to minimize, even to avoid, direct contact with the Japanese civilian population, just as during demobilizing and disarming they avoided direct contact with the Japanese military. MacArthur and his headquarters, at least in theory, were the sole point of official tangency, the sole source of American policy.

Major General John H. Hilldring, director of the War Department Civil Affairs Division, spoke aptly of the advantage of utilizing the Japanese apparatus in this manner. Otherwise:

> . . . we would have to operate directly the whole complicated machine required for the administration of a country of 70 million people. These people differ from us, in language, customs, and atti-

"Occupationaire" at his desk,
GHQ, Dai Ichi Building.

Major General Whitney and his boss.

tudes. By cleaning up and using the Japanese Government machinery as a tool, we are saving our time and our manpower and our resources. In other words, we are requiring the Japanese to do their own house cleaning, but we are providing the specifications.

Around the person providing the "house cleaning specifications," the Supreme Commander, was an aura of drama and glamor. Below MacArthur, reporting directly to him, were ten or more special staff sections: Government, Economic and Scientific, Diplomatic, Natural Resources, and the like. Each was headed by a high-ranking officer, most often a general. Each section was organized along functional lines to deal with the sundry nonmilitary aspects of the Occupation.

Government Section under Major General Courtney Whitney emerged as the single most powerful body in GHQ, partly because reshaping the Japanese Government was so central to the goals of the occupiers and partly because of Whitney's closeness to MacArthur. "Whit," as MacArthur called him, had his own door to the Supreme Commander's office, through which he could enter at any time. MacArthur relied on the former Manila lawyer more than on any of his other associates.

To democratize Japan successfully required commanding, exhorting, and informing the bewildered, curious, sometimes reluctant, sometimes eager Japanese. Supervising mass vaccinations, registering important works of art, giving technical advice to a coal mining company, censoring newspapers, overseeing the rewriting of textbooks for school children are but a sampling of the enormous range of activities. They could lead to the unforeseen. After delivering a public lecture on democracy, one young American officer inquired if there were any questions. A well-dressed Japanese lady sitting in the back of the hall rose to ask: "What plans do the Occupation Forces have for the sexual satisfaction of the Japanese people?"

MacArthur was both SCAP and CINCFE. His chief of staff and certain staff sections also functioned in both capacities. The exclusively American Far Eastern Command bore responsibility for all

Lieutenant General Eichelberger with members of the House Committee on Foreign Relations and the cast of a GI production of The Mikado, *August 1946. Far left, conductor Jorge Bolet, who later became a celebrated concert pianist.* EICHELBERGER COLLECTION

military duties in the area. Japan was only part of this zone. Within the Command were two field armies, the Sixth and the Eighth, which had fought the Japanese in the jungles of the South Pacific and now shared the military duties of the Occupation, together with small detachments of the U.S. Navy stationed ashore. On January 1, 1946, the Sixth Army, General Walter Krueger commanding, was dissolved, leaving the field entirely to the Eighth Army.

During the formative months of the Occupation the Eighth Army, under Lieutenant General Robert Eichelberger (who had been with MacArthur in the South Pacific), directed all military government. Eichelberger was in Yokohama, with his I Corps in Kyoto and his IX Corps in Sendai. By radio, telephone, constant flow of paper, and frequent trips of inspection in his private train, *The Octagonian,* Eichelberger, active and restless, kept in touch with his far-flung command. Some of this he recounts in his diary, frequently fretting about the danger of Communist saboteurs blowing up the railway tunnels and paralyzing the nation. Invariably he tells us what he ate for dinner and how he liked it; whether or not his army moved on its stomach, he certainly did.

Eichelberger's chief mission was tactical, to provide troops with firepower to maintain order and enforce SCAP directives if necessary; to oversee organizations in the field, the military government teams that were scattered throughout Japan; and to supervise programs for repatriating, demobilizing, and destroying armaments. Much of what the Eighth Army was called on to do was nonmilitary, tasks for which large numbers of men were needed: transporting, storing, and distributing food for the Japanese, or supervising the building of roads and bridges. Occasionally these soldiers would help in such special missions as election surveillance.

Military government administration down to the Corps level was incorporated within the tactical command structure. Below that it roughly paralleled the organization of the Japanese Government, by region (eight regional headquarters) and by prefecture (forty-six prefectural teams). But in no way were these units of military government supposed to relate directly, officially at any rate, to the Japanese. Orders, even suggestions, were to be given only in Tokyo. "Military government" was thus a misnomer, implying greater authority and a greater measure of activity than these teams actually had. The local duties of military government were simply to observe and report. Perhaps given the highly centralized nature of the Japanese Government, with its powers concentrated in Tokyo, the situation of the local civil affairs officers did not make much difference and was a less serious flaw than might be supposed.

The prefectural teams were the lowest level of Occupation activity in Japan, closest to the "rice roots" of Japanese society. They

59

were perhaps the strongest point of contact for Americans with the Japanese people, if only because the Americans there were so few, so isolated, and so conspicuous. That they were not responsible for reform made it easier for the Japanese to bear their presence.

The occupiers were spread thin. In the city of Himeji, for example, where the great White Heron Castle soars above the plain adjacent to the Inland Sea, one or two American officers, twice that number of enlisted men, and a few Japanese interpreters ran an office nominally overseeing a prefecture with a population of more than two million. For all Japan, from the Government Section of the Eighth Army on down, there were only about 2500 officers, enlisted men, and civilians in military government.

Actually these local civil affairs teams (as they came to be called) often did far more than simply observe and report. Although officially they had no power, informally they did govern, whether or not they always were aware of doing so. As local representatives of the conqueror they bore immense prestige. The temptation for individual Americans to exploit the situation was great, the possibility of being corrupted by the opportunity not small. To the Japanese, particularly in the early phases of the Occupation, every American action, every American word, however casually uttered, was freighted with significance. Advice easily became command, with stultifying effect on Japanese initiative and inflating impact on American ego.

The Eighth Army was the cumbersome instrument whereby Americans in the field learned what SCAP had instructed the Japanese to do. But usually they did not find out about it until after the Japanese had been told. The teams learned that the fastest way to be informed was to read the English-language daily, the *Nippon Times.* Another way was directly from the Japanese. Army channels were the slowest means.

Just as it was difficult for people in the field to keep in touch with SCAP, so it was hard for SCAP to get accurate information from the field. This was not just a matter of bureaucratic inefficiency but it was also mechanical: telephone service was deplorable, the radio and telecommunications network overloaded. Local commanders were tempted to solve problems without going to the effort of consulting their superiors. Much information, particularly that which was disagreeable, was not reported to SCAP at all. No one likes the harbinger of bad news. MacArthur's firmly optimistic view of the Occupation aggravated the problem, so that conclusions drawn in Tokyo sometimes diverged from reality. SCAP believed what SCAP wanted to believe.

SCAP sometimes found it necessary to instruct local Japanese authorities to disobey any orders given by prefectural military government officials because they were illegal. Moreover, in an extraordinary effort to use the Japanese to police Americans, the former were directed to tell SCAP if they received any such illegal orders.

The civil affairs teams were abolished at the end of November 1949, with the Eighth Army losing all civil affairs responsibilities and becoming a purely tactical unit. In part this was due to a continuing shortage of qualified people. But more important was the changing mood of the occupiers. By 1949 the Occupation was winding down. Whereas critics feared that the Japanese would now be free to slide back to their old sinful ways, symbolically the withdrawal of the teams represented increased American official confidence in the success of what they had already accomplished.

After 1949 the only occupying forces left in the provinces, aside from troops confined to bases, were the shadowy Counterintelligence people. Few knew very much about their activities. Major General Charles Willoughby was the spider at the center of that particular web, serving as Intelligence Chief and close advisor to MacArthur. Willoughby's major interest was the pursuit of Communists, both within the Occupation forces and among the Japanese. He found a few. But Robert Textor, participating official and later critic of the Occupation, author of *Failure in Japan* (1951), scoffs that the "ever alert if somewhat tone-deaf ears [of the Counterintelligence Corps (CIC)] were quick to pick up rumblings of 'subversive' intent from those Occupationaires who stood to the left

Major General Charles Willoughby.

of Alf Landon. . . ." CIC did not speak for itself, being necessarily uncommunicative about what it was doing.

Cynosure of the Occupation, from the moment his feet touched Japanese soil in August 1945 until his departure in April 1951, was the Supreme Commander. Washington may have laid down the broad lines of policy, but MacArthur was the source of information upon which the evolution of that policy was largely based. MacArthur also had the discretionary authority to interpret directions as he willed, and even greater authority to choose the specific ways and means to be used. Such was the pressure of events elsewhere in the world, so strong the eagerness of MacArthur to do without supervision, and so great his prestige among both the American public and the Japanese, that Washington was glad to leave him alone. "You will exercise your authority as you deem proper to carry out your mission," Washington ordered, and MacArthur was pleased to comply.

The General and his lady. THAMES COLLECTION

5

The Hero

LITTLE of an entirely objective nature has been written about Douglas MacArthur because the "Master of the Pacific" provoked such strong reactions from those who knew or observed him. Both his authority and the power of his personality permeated the Occupation, so much so that Americans tended to evaluate that great enterprise simply on the basis of whether they thought MacArthur was doing a good job. For good or not, has any American ever exercised so much power over so many people for such a long time? No case comes to mind.

John J. McCloy remarked that being a military governor was "a pretty heady job . . . the nearest thing to a Roman proconsulship the world afforded. You could turn to your secretary and say, 'Take a law.' The law was there and you could see its effect in two or three weeks. It was a challenging job to an ambitious man."

MacArthur was an arresting personality and an ambitious man. In supreme self-confidence and histrionic ability, in pride of nation, he was not unlike that earlier American military statesman, even better known to the Japanese than to his fellow Americans, Commodore Matthew C. Perry. Neither was a cultural relativist.

Japanese political history is scarcely replete with dominant individuals; instead of rule by the Napoleonic hero, the political pattern most congenial to the Japanese has been government by committee and by consensus. Small groups of men have traditionally made the important decisions in Japanese society. But if in the Japanese political norm dictatorial rule was unusual, in another respect Douglas MacArthur fitted comfortably into it.

Customarily, real power in Japan was exercised indirectly, with the formally designated rulers standing aloof from the actual directing of daily affairs. MacArthur's use of the Emperor and the existing Japanese Government as the means of executing his will was entirely consonant with the conventions of Japanese politics. The role of the U.S. Army in the political reshaping of Japan was therefore less offensive than might have been the case in some other culture less accustomed to an aggressive military class.

MacArthur was well aware of the challenge. He had participated in the American occupation of the Rhineland following World War I. This, like that of Japan, had been indirect. The local German Government was supervised by the American Army. But the Occupation had not been successful. In his *Reminiscences,* MacArthur cites Alexander the Great, Caesar, and Napoleon Bonaparte as great captains in war who blundered when they led occupying forces.

The General and the Emperor.

Secretary of Defense Louis Johnson with MacArthur at Haneda Airport, Tokyo, June 23, 1950.

MacArthur, in his search for historical analogy, might have looked more closely at the case of General Bonaparte. Napoleon carried out military occupations but he was also a great reformer, bearer to the rest of Europe of France's new revolution.

Everyone high and low was in awe of MacArthur. Clearly he was a leader, not simply a commander. Public impression was that the Joint Chiefs of Staff "suggested and advised" MacArthur but did not "command" him. His popularity and prestige were simply too great. One of the few people to address him by first name was Franklin D. Roosevelt. Although it was not yet a custom in American public life for a high official to use the first person plural "we," MacArthur startled visitors by referring to himself during conversation as "MacArthur." In none of his known correspondence as a grown man (including that to Jean MacArthur) did he ever sign his name simply as "Douglas." Regardless of what his wife may have called him in more intimate moments, in public he was always "the General or "my General."

MacArthur had been a public figure for a long time, a soldier of prominence since he became the Army's youngest general in World

General MacArthur leaves his office at the Dai Ichi Building for the American Embassy on his seventy-first birthday, January 26, 1951.

War I. He was the most decorated senior officer in the U.S. Army, retiring in 1937 with the rank of General. In 1945 he was sixty-five, the war was over, but he was not ready to retire again.

Enlisted men scrambled for the tobacco ashes MacArthur shook out of his pipe. Presidents treated him with great care, indeed with deference. MacArthur did not come home for consultations; he came halfway—or less. In July 1944 he traveled from the Southwest Pacific to Honolulu for consultations with FDR. Harry Truman, who heartily disliked airplanes, flew all the way to Wake Island to meet MacArthur in a conference treated as if it were an international summit meeting, with MacArthur accorded the deference due a foreign potentate. In fact, MacArthur appeared to think of himself as a sovereign, a head of state, which to all intents and purposes he was.

"The role of occupation chief in Japan gave MacArthur the chance he craved to be master in his own house," Forrest Pogue, biographer of Genéral George C. Marshall, once aptly remarked. The effect was to isolate Japan from other American global considerations. MacArthur's peers and superiors chose now, as they had for many years, to let this prickly personality alone insofar as possible. Many of them admired his ability while disliking him personally. "Slick as a shithouse rat," one senior Army member of the wartime White House staff said of MacArthur to the President's naval aide. Much later Courtney Whitney told the Mayor of Norfolk, where the MacArthur Memorial now stands, that the General was looking for a suitable place for interment. He did not want to be buried in Arlington National Cemetary because there he would be "surrounded by his enemies."

MacArthur's autocratic behavior in Japan aroused remarkably little hostility at home, partly because he was the hero of American right-wingers and his policies most open to criticism were liberal if not radical. Another reason was the widespread indifference of the American public to what happened over there. The State Department may have been unhappy, but Congress did not take it amiss. As George Kennan somewhat ruefully put it:

> Americans who would have protested violently at the first sign of paternalism or arbitrariness in the behavior of the United States government at home with relation to other Americans found it not only entirely in order but wholly admirable and inspiring—a source of pride, in fact—that an American Commander should exercise a wholly autocratic power, untrammeled by legislative controls in a foreign country; and they tended to sympathize extensively with that commander whenever corrupt, distrusted Washington attempted to interfere in any way in the exercise of his power.

MacArthur told people what many of them wanted to believe about the Occupation. He discouraged probing; visitors were often willing to accept what MacArthur said. The result provided a sharp contrast with what was thought to be going on in Germany. MacArthur did not permit doubt, bewilderment, vacillation, or confusion to surface in the public view of what was occurring in Japan. Negative impressions were buried, smothered. The Civil Censorship Detachment of SCAP insured that references to MacArthur were positive and forward looking, not critical or accusatory. Although the General did not escape criticism from abroad, he fought it bitterly. And John Bennett, a SCAP sociologist, remarked later that "the prevailing doctrine in GHQ was that the 'Chief' was unchallengeable, above the mortal realm. . . ." This was one of MacArthur's major flaws as a statesman; he never hesitated to come into the kitchen, but he disliked the heat.

A second flaw was MacArthur's readiness to transcend his area of authority—and knowledge. His self-confidence was overweening, and it sometimes got him into considerable trouble. Old Admiral Hart, MacArthur's comrade-in-arms in the Philippines before the war, remarked: "General MacArthur knows a lot but at the same time knows many things that are not so." Furthermore, his Manichean world view left little room for subtle political judgments. MacArthur was prone to put emotion over logic, ideology over professionalism.

Many admired MacArthur's great intellectual capacity and the well-furnished quality of his mind. But hard work was as important to his success as natural brilliance. In an unusually self-deprecatory remark, MacArthur once said that at West Point "there were a number of my classmates who were smarter than I." But at the end he stood first in his class. During his years in Manila as Philippine military advisor and in Japan, MacArthur worked seven days a week. He seldom went out. He entertained only at luncheon, and his sole relaxation seems to have been reading, an occasional movie, and American football, which he followed with avid, indeed aggressive interest, always ready to offer advice by mail to the coach at West Point.

MacArthur had a fine, resonant speaking voice and an impressive platform manner, although his texts manifested a certain grandiloquence not unlike those of Senator Everett McKinley Dirksen. He composed this inscription over the entrance to the gymnasium at West Point:

> Upon the fields of friendly strife are sown
> the seeds that upon other fields, in other days
> will bear the fruits of victory.

With somewhat more pith, Wellington supposedly said that the battle of Waterloo was won on the playing fields of Eton. Yet to the Japanese, MacArthur's hortatory style was appropriately platitudinous and sweepingly historical, what they expected from a leader. They liked it because it offered them hope.

To the American taste, MacArthur was probably more effective in speechmaking than in writing. And perhaps best of all was his conversation, usually carried on while pacing. "General MacArthur was magnificent as he strode up & down his huge office, his khaki shirt open at the neck, and his famous corncob pipe gripped between his teeth," recalls John Allison, Foreign Service officer and later U.S. Ambassador to Japan.

A private audience with MacArthur was like attending a public lecture. He was a monologist, and yet Japan scholar Hugh Borton remarked that he had the very "rare trait of giving you the impression that the only thing of importance at the time is the topic you are discussing." Although the discussion invariably was one-sided, MacArthur often claimed he learned a great deal from such meetings. He had an excellent memory for information and for people, but sometimes he was so bewitched by his own eloquence that he would forget what he had just said. Those responsible for the General's schedule knew to allow ample time between appointments to accommodate his loquacity.

MacArthur had great style and a splendid sense of theater. During the war General Robert Eichelberger gave MacArthur the code name "Sarah" when writing to his wife, "Sarah" standing for Sarah

Bernhardt. MacArthur's corncob pipe was as jaunty as FDR's cigarette holder, his sunglasses a distinctive trademark. He chose
unusual attire, as unconventional as possible for a career military
man, accouterments that were a physical manifestation of his in-
dividuality and ego. Earlier on he was more flamboyant than during
the Japanese years. During World War I he rarely wore the regula-
tion helmet; instead he had a crushed cap, presumably the anteced-
ent of one made famous in World War II. He often carried a riding
crop or stick and muffled his throat with a long scarf—a dashing
figure indeed.

While serving in the Philippines in the late 1930s, MacArthur
had the opportunity to design his own uniform as Field Marshal. He
embellished it with his large number of decorations, giving a blaze
of color. He was known for his invariably crisp appearance despite
the wilting tropical heat.

During the Pacific War and after, MacArthur changed. He
affected a studied simplicity that served to enhance his magnifi-
cence. The trousers may have been sharply creased and the shoes
well polished, but the cap was battered, the collar open, the chest
bare of decorations. Even though MacArthur was an inch under six
feet tall, people thought he was taller because his lofty demeanor
enhanced an already overwhelming presence.

The peculiar genius of MacArthur lay in his power to convince
others of his genius. He believed that his actions were justified by
history or by divine will. Consequently he could justify overriding
the wishes of others, even his superiors. General Frank McCoy, an
old Army friend who became chairman of the Far Eastern Commission, summed it up: "MacArthur thinks of himself as a man of
destiny. . . . And he *is* a man of destiny."

Perhaps the instability of the times was conducive to the emergence of a hero such as MacArthur. He was courageous and resolute, heroic in appearance and behavior. But most important was
his absolute moral certainty, which to many was an enormously
attractive quality. And his evident sincerity appealed greatly to the
Japanese. Humor was not a conspicuous part of the General's per-

72

sonality, but neither Americans nor Japanese prize that in their leaders.

MacArthur's optimism seemed never to falter, at least in public. One cannot imagine him being quoted as saying anything like Stilwell's famous remark after the Burma campaign, "We took a helluva beating." The defeat America suffered in 1942 in the Philippines was the greatest overseas military debacle the nation had ever experienced. But Bataan and Corregidor came to symbolize, like Dunkirk, not rout but triumph. It was something heroic, and MacArthur was the hero. His attitude had much to do with the American reaction to the event. Americans needed a victory desperately; thus they had a "victory."

Despite inadequate preparation for the outbreak of the Pacific War, for which MacArthur must bear at least part blame, he was not cashiered, he was not shunted off to the sidelines. Instead he was given another active command. One press account of his arrival in Australia reads as follows:

> To the ramp the plane taxied. Now the door opened. The slim boyish-looking leader came down. The Australian sun glittered off the gold of his uniform cap. His trim, starched khaki brightened in the light. Little twinkles came from the four silver stars on his shoulder straps. "General Douglas MacArthur!" the cheering shout rose. By radio, by cable, by word of mouth the word flashed to the anxious peoples of the civilized world.
>
> "General Douglas MacArthur has arrived in Australia to become generalissimo of the Allied Forces in the Southwest Pacific."
>
> Women laughed and cried; men cheered and clapped each other on the back. . . . The stock markets jumped. Great leaders of the embattled democracies paused to cable their thanks that he had arrived safely. It was as if the sun, after a catastrophic storm, had peeped out briefly, an omen of brighter days to come.

MacArthur first visited Japan just after the Russo-Japanese War of 1904–1905, serving as aide to his father, General Arthur MacArthur. He spent a month there in 1936 and returned for a few days in 1937. But for most of his time in Asia before World War II he was in the Philippines, a country he liked and grew to know well. There is no evidence that he knew Japan well, or cared to. Faubion Bowers, his aide and interpreter during the early months of the Occupation, estimated that while MacArthur was in Tokyo, "only 16 Japanese ever spoke with him more than twice, and none of these was under the rank, say, of Premier, Chief Justice, president of the largest university." MacArthur did not mingle.

Nor did he tour. All he saw of Tokyo was his daily automobile route, with all traffic lights invariably green, between home at the American Embassy and office at the Dai Ichi Insurance Building, with an occasional trip to the airport. Of the rest of Japan he saw nothing, save for that first trip in from Atsugi and the initial days in Yokohama. General Charles Willoughby said that MacArthur "knew his authority would be the greater if it came from a Jovian

Allied personnel look on as Emperor Hirohito reads an Imperial Rescript during the opening session of the 90th Imperial Diet, June 20, 1946.

The Emperor visits the Showa Electrical Industrial plant to inspect the conversion program from war to peacetime production.

distance." Even before MacArthur arrived in Japan, the *New York Times* commented that he had "for more than three years lived on a plane of accessibility only slightly less rarified than that of the Emperor himself." With American encouragement, the Emperor broke out of the prewar pattern; he traveled extensively throughout Japan and met people of all backgrounds. But MacArthur stayed aloof. Mrs. MacArthur did move about, in the usual routine of a General's wife: opening bazaars, attending fashion shows and teas. She was a familiar, attractive, and gracious presence in Tokyo, and she also traveled elsewhere in Japan. Perhaps some of her impressions of the outside world filtered through to the General.

MacArthur owned a very large personal library, an estimated seven to eight thousand volumes, for the most part assembled by his father. It included some books on Japan, but not many. Left behind in Manila, it was destroyed during the war. His second library, considerably smaller, collected after the war, contains such standard works on Japan as Benedict's *The Chrysanthemum and the Sword,* but they are not a conspicuous part of the collection, and there is no evidence he read them. Many of these books were gifts.

Neither in his speeches nor in his conversation did the General manifest any particular interest in Japan or its culture. He seems to have thought entirely of what he and America were doing for Japan. That is, the building of a Christian democracy. MacArthur was convinced that because of the war and the Occupation, Japan had undergone a spiritual revolution, a phenomenon that included readiness for conversion to Christianity.

Ardent Christians saw in the postwar malaise of the Japanese a splendid opportunity for mass conversion to Christianity. "Since the days of Rome was there ever such a challenge flung at the Christian Church?" exulted one prominent Episcopalian layman. A thrill of excitement ran through American clerical circles. The Reverend Bob Jones of Bob Jones University, Greenville, S.C., wrote to General MacArthur: "We have . . . eleven hundred young men . . . preparing for the ministry . . . learning how to "load the Gospel gun and how to 'shoot it.' " Missionaries were eager to come to Japan, and Bibles by the million were readied for shipment there.

John Profumo, Chief of Staff of the British military and diplomatic mission to Japan (who later would achieve a certain notoriety), asserted that "if the Japanese can be Christianized, the process of democratization can be speeded up." Others agreed that nothing would help the Occupation program more "than a genuine growth of Christianity and the spread of Christian ideals among the population." Furthermore, a Christian Japan would be all the more firm a bulwark against the surging tides of Communism.

The American missionary in Japan, some ninety years earlier, had undertaken his task with certain advantages. Vessel of American culture, chief source of information about the U.S., this evangelist was usually a professional teacher or perhaps a physician, an educated person commanding respect from the Japanese. And, unlike American missionaries in China, he kept himself apart from politics. Now at least some of the missionaries hoped to capitalize on what they perceived as Japanese susceptibility to identifying democracy with Christianity, both being the bedrock of Americanism. Could the two in fact be separated? Perhaps not, these people speculated, and in Japan's eagerness to embrace democracy it would naturally take up Christianity as well. But Christianizing the Japanese was by no means an accepted goal or even a widely discussed possibility for the Occupation. "Certainly one wasn't aware of it among Occupation workers in Tokyo. I taught in a mission school whose regular Japanese and American teachers thought the American Occupation a very distant phenomenon and that it paid little or no attention to them," one American woman recalls.

The Japanese found they could have democracy without Christianity. Whatever religious zeal they may have felt expressed itself more by the mushrooming numbers of adherents to the "new religions," sects with deep native roots, than by conversions to Christianity.

MacArthur said the occupiers had "every right to propagate Christianity," yet their failure to do so consistently or officially disappointed Japanese Christians. Christianity was not forced on the Japanese, and they did not choose it.

MacArthur had no doctrine of limited war; this was evident later in Korea. He was convinced that war and peace were antithetical. He argued that you cannot control war, you can only abolish it. Hence Article Nine of the new (1947) Japanese Constitution, the famous renunciation of war clause. MacArthur saw a pacifist Japan as a genuine possibility. And regardless of who was responsible for incorporating this idea into Japanese law, MacArthur was clearly an enthusiastic proponent. Nor was he troubled by any inconsistency between the constitution and limited rearmament. That a military professional like MacArthur should be so powerfully attracted to pacifism was an extraordinary aspect of an extraordinary individual.

MacArthur spoke to American visitors with assurance about Japanese affairs. And to those back home, he seemed knowledgeable about Japan simply because he had spent so many years in Asia. He would be there, without any return visit to the continental U.S., from 1937 until 1951. MacArthur, like Secretary of War Stimson, believed that his service in the Philippines had given him special understanding of the "Oriental mind." The loyal Willoughby agreed: "MacArthur knew his Orient thoroughly, forty years of foreign service had taught him the lessons of the Far East."

But Japan for its own sake was essentially irrelevant to MacArthur. He was the Great Captain, now Peacemaker, overseeing a spectacular revolution, the success of which would expand the bounds of democracy and Christendom and propel him into the White House. MacArthur did not admit publicly his political ambitions, but his desire for the presidency was no secret. In 1944 and 1948 he was considered a live candidate. At San Francisco in April 1951, on the occasion of his triumphal return, he announced ambiguously: "The only politics I have is contained in a single phrase known well to all of you—'God bless America.'"

MacArthur epitomized the American presence in Japan. His godlike power, his ignorance of Japanese culture, his pronounced ethnocentricity, and his enormous self-confidence as well as the success he enjoyed there were common to the whole enterprise. The Japanese identify him as an agent of change in their recent past, his name inextricably linked to an era. But in his own country MacArthur was not a hero in the sense of being an encapsulation of the spirit of his times. There could be no Age of MacArthur as there had been of Napoleon, or Pericles, or McKinley. MacArthur was an anachronism, a nineteenth-century man with a twentieth-century career. He was a Victorian, more akin to William Ewart Gladstone than to John F. Kennedy. Perhaps this is why the American people denied him the political office he so wanted.

In April 1951 General MacArthur was dismissed by President Truman for insubordination. Tens of thousands of Japanese lined the streets of Tokyo to see the hero leave, many of them with genuine sorrow. The President's action in relieving the General, and MacArthur's compliance with Truman's order, powerfully demonstrated the supremacy of civil authority over military privilege in American democracy, a precept Americans had been urging upon the Japanese. American leadership judged infraction of the

78

MacArthur returns from Korea, January 20, 1951, followed by Major General Courtney Whitney.

principle in Japan, during the 1930s, to have been an important reason for the Pacific War. Fittingly, on leaving Tokyo in this dramatic fashion, Douglas MacArthur, at the sunset of his long and brilliant career, performed his final, involuntary, and greatest act for the Japanese people.

79

During the early days of the occupation an interpreter meets the Commanding Officer of an element of the 98th Division, as the unit prepares to take over a prefecture.

A card game draws a crowd.

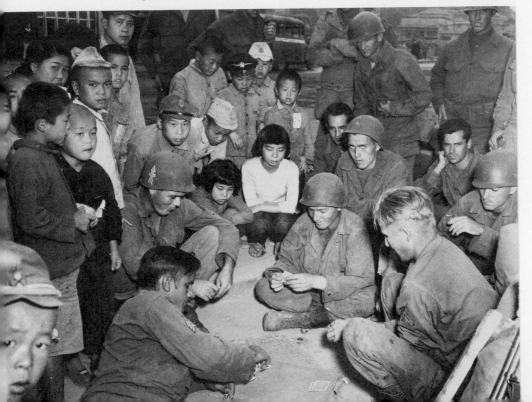

6
Disarmament and Demilitarization

AT WAR'S end nearly seven million Japanese began to lay down their arms. General MacArthur said in a radio report to the American people on October 15, 1945: "I know of no demobilization in history, either in war or in peace, by our own or by any other country, that has been accomplished so rapidly or so frictionlessly." What the General failed to mention was that the accomplishment was essentially Japanese, not American or Allied, and was well underway even before any foreign troops touched Japanese soil.

For the planning and the execution of demobilization, the Americans leaned heavily on the Japanese military, on the Imperial General Headquarters, and on the Army and Navy ministries. These Japanese were now obliged to concentrate their energies on breaking up as quickly and as thoroughly as possible the great war machine they had so painstakingly created.

To reduce the chance of clash between the occupying Army, rapidly fanning out over the Japanese islands, and the shriveling Japanese forces, the Americans tried to stay out of the way of the Japanese as much as possible. The spirit of this is illustrated by the following account.

A jeep bearing a 43rd Division Lieutenant was spinning along the road from Kazo to Kumagaya when an approaching cloud of dust resolved itself into a Japanese tank company moving to a demobilization center. As the lead tank stopped to permit passing, the jeep driver cautiously skirted it to the left on the narrow road. The soft shoulder crumbled and the American found himself tilted at a perilous angle with his vehicle mired in the soft muck of a rice paddy. Climbing out, the officer scratched his head and pointed to a cable attached to the side of one tank. Meanwhile a Japanese officer had come running up and asked in passable English if the tank driver had been at fault. Assured to the contrary, he barked orders to his men and the tank driver jockeyed his tank into position, hooked the cable on the jeep and pulled it back on the road. The Japanese captain bowed his apologies, accepted an American cigarette with thanks, ordered his tank column to continue and, waving amiably to the American, disappeared in a cloud of dust.

To which the chronicler adds, "A month earlier these men would have shot one another on sight."

Since demobilizing was a Japanese enterprise, Occupation troops were chiefly engaged with the urgent, massive, dangerous, and slow task of collecting and retaining, redistributing or destroying, Japanese war materiel. Here too Americans used Japanese to do most of the actual work.

First the ocupiers had to ferret out the instruments of war. Enor-

Japanese tanks in retirement.

Under the direction of U.S. soldiers, Japanese laborers dump bombs into a crater prior to exploding them.

mous stocks of weapons and ammunition were "dispersed amid the tangled masses of fire-blackened girders, in thousands of caches located deep in the hills, in carefully constructed tunnels, and warehouses. . . ." Very large amounts of Japan's military supplies and equipment had been successfully protected against American aerial bombardment by dispersal or by storage underground.

Under Allied supervision, thousands of aircraft were sprayed with gasoline and burned. Tanks were dynamited, poison gas carefully destroyed, ammunition detonated or burned or taken out to sea and dumped. A few remaining warships were distributed to the victors; others were broken up for scrap.

Along the shores, American patrols found hastily built bunkers, entrenchments, and forts, some with artillery pieces in place, reflecting the apprehensions of the last months of the war. Offshore the Japanese had placed underwater obstacles, and the coastline abounded with caves that were natural sites for gun emplacements or for stowing weapons and ammunition. Motorboats, for example,

Crew members of the U.S.S. Bolster, *a salvage ship, haul up silver ingots from where they were discovered in Tokyo Bay.*

were stored in seaside cavities, ready like midget submarines and human torpedoes for use in suicidal sorties against an approaching Allied armada. As one Japanese officer explained: "Japan is a poor country. . . . She couldn't always afford the type of weapon which allowed a man to keep his life. We wanted to make the best use of all our materials, and toward the end we were short on everything. All we had was men."

Americans worried most about weapons, but they wanted to find out about the entire Japanese military inventory. Goods such as shoes, socks, blankets, and medical supplies could be used by civilians and were thus turned over to the Japanese Home Ministry.

The Japanese had collected and concealed much of their treasure of gems and precious metals before the surrender. In the early weeks and months of the Occupation, newspapers carried frequent reports of sensational finds of silver and gold, platinum and industrial diamonds, secreted in remote spots.

Japanese industry was starved for raw materials. Because of this need, and as the urgency for destroying weapons seemed to wane (by October 1 no one thought there would be any shooting), more

Two lieutenants inspect some solid silver ornament, part of the war loot seized by SCAP.

and more materials were preserved from destruction and saved for alternative uses.

Coping with all the physical remnants of war was a lengthy process. Some ended as booty, spoil for GIs to send home. For one piece of equipment, American inspectors found a receipt carefully filed by a Japanese officer on which was scribbled only "John Doe, F.B.I." American patrols, relying on information given officially by the Japanese as well as rumor and gossip, crisscrossed the islands to inspect remote outposts, where post-pubescent officers had the heady experience of being deferentially received by elderly Japanese army officers. There was no outward resistance. For the most part the Japanese cooperated with sincerity, even grace.

Although most of the work was completed during the first year or so of the Allied stay, ruins of the great Japanese war machine were visible for a long time thereafter. Ten years later much of Kure, the huge Inland Sea naval base and shipyard, remained an enormous pile of rusting scrap metal; the swimmer picking his way along a rocky Misaki beach, near the mouth of Tokyo Bay, could still see empty crumbling concrete gun emplacements gaping seaward.

In contrast to American wars since, the Pacific War brought a victory that was satisfyingly thorough and utterly conclusive. Americans chose to interpret the Japanese surrender as total; the Japanese, once the Americans had landed, were in a poor position to argue the point. As MacArthur said, with some satisfaction, "Nothing could exceed the abjectness, the humiliation, and finality of this surrender. . . ."

Japan was laid bare, completely exposed to whatever penetration or manipulation the Americans wished. Access was limited only by America's inability to take full advantage of its position; its opportunity limited only by its own ignorance. Americans could talk to anyone and as long as they liked, provided they could surmount the language barrier. They could go anywhere, collect any printed information, confiscate anything they wanted.

The biggest American research enterprise for investigating

Japan, incorporating more than one thousand people, was the Strategic Bombing Survey, previously organized for work in Europe. For its analysis of the Pacific War, the Survey was able to recruit people of great ability, such as the Harvard economist John Kenneth Galbraith and Paul H. Nitze, lawyer, official, and, later, arms negotiator. Neither of these gentlemen happened to know much about Japan, but at least the ranking naval member of the Survey, Rear Admiral Ralph Ofstie, had the experience of serving before the war in the Tokyo embassy. The Survey collected voluminous information. Some Americans working in the Occupation at the time thought the Survey was intended to prove the success of U.S. bombing, and that statistics to fit that thesis were thus selected. In any case the reports went largely unused. Nuclear warfare, it was thought, made the analyses essentially irrelevant, of only historical interest. And interservice bickering over which branch had really won the war clouded a cool, rational discussion of the strategic implications of the survey.

Like demobilizing, repatriating was essentially a Japanese enterprise, not an American or Allied one. Americans watched and provided help with the logistics as more than seven million "expatriates" were returned to Japan in probably the greatest single mass movement of people by sea in history. Traveling, as one American report expresses it, "under oriental passenger standards," these people came back not only in great numbers but also over enormous distances.

Japanese soldiers and sailors had been stranded by the tides of war in places as far away from home as Bali or Burma, left to survive as best they could on a diet of sweet potatoes and snake meat. A few resorted to cannibalism. Some had been assigned to defend the coral atolls of the South Pacific; many were in Korea, China, or even farther south, garrisoning the outposts of the empire.

Four and a half million of these Japanese were civilians, colonists of the lost imperial domain. They were traders, government officials, civilian employees of the Army, engineers, schoolmasters.

Repatriates being processed at the Sasebo Reception Center load their baggage on trains which will carry thousands of Japanese from Manchuria and China back to their former homes.

A repatriated Japanese family.

DISARMAMENT AND DEMILITARIZATION

Some had spent their lives abroad and were coming to a Japan they barely knew. Korea, after all, had been under Japanese rule for thirty-five years, Taiwan for even longer. And even for those in China, their six or seven years away from Japan were during a period when Japan changed dramatically. Each person, soldier or civilian, was permitted to bring back only those possessions he could carry, plus a modest sum of money. Jobless, without homes, with little else, these people returned to add to the burden of an already staggering, emaciated homeland economy.

Removing this giant sprawl of "repatriated people" was a matter of some urgency to America's Allies, who wanted to get things back to normal. But some came to appreciate the value of the Japanese as cheap temporary labor; no one prized this asset more than the Russians.

Not until December 1946 did Japanese soldiers and civilians start to be released from Russian-held territories. Of the 900,000 Japanese troops who surrendered to Russians, only 436,000 had been returned by August 1948. Many unfortunate souls never would return. Civilians likewise. But the Soviet Government did

A repatriate at the Otake Reception Center.

not make precise statistics available, keeping relatives and friends back home in agonizing uncertainty.

An American sailor aboard an LST that ferried former Japanese soldiers from China back home remembers that his passengers were convinced they were being taken directly to the U.S.A. to be put to death. When they learned otherwise upon sailing into a Japanese port, "you've never seen anyone so happy!"

The homeward-bound came by sea, on everything from refloated Imperial Navy aircraft carriers to three-masted sailing vessels, patched up, manned, and stocked for the most part by the Japanese themselves. At the peak, in May 1946, nearly four hundred ships were being used in this service. Not one of these sank, despite the uncertain seaworthiness of many. The feat, both of seamanship and of organization, was truly remarkable.

Some people left Japan, although many more returned. Most of those getting out were Koreans, despised by the Japanese as brawling troublemakers. Living in squalid urban ghettos, they filled the least desirable and most menial jobs. Koreans were 95 percent of Japan's aliens, and their number had risen to about one and a half million by 1945.

This is still not to be likened in size or complexity to the problem of sorting out displaced persons in Central and Western Europe. Japan, an island nation, did not encourage outsiders to pass through. Despite wartime labor shortages, the Japanese did not rely on large numbers of impressed foreigners, the reason being less humanitarian than practical: transportation difficulties. The Japanese had an extremely vexatious time trying to fuse together their enormous war-created maritime empire; nor were their efforts eased by the extremely effective submarine and aerial warfare of the Americans.

Before the war economic necessity brought Koreans to Japan. After the war erupted they were "lured, even forced into Japanese mines and factories." In late 1945 life for Koreans looked better back in their newly independent homeland. After the surrender thousands of them jammed the ports of Moji, Hakata, and

90

Shimonoseki, looking for transportation across the Straits of Tsu-shima. The efflux added to the chaos of Japanese city life and the troubles of the railway system, the crowds intensifying disorder and abetting the spread of disease. More than one third of Japan's coal miners were Koreans, and the abrupt departure of many of them from the pits caused coal production to plummet.

It is estimated that more than one million people (Koreans chiefly, but also Taiwanese) left the Japanese islands in late 1945 and early 1946. But the number of those wanting to leave fell off rather sharply during the winter when the Koreans learned that conditions at home were not as good as they had anticipated; in fact, some of those who had already returned tried to get back to Japan. Today Japan has a minority of over half a million Koreans.

While the Americans may have been necessarily slow destroying Japanese weapons, the Japanese were astonishingly fast at demobilizing and disarming. Within a month, to all intents and purposes, the Imperial Japanese Army no longer existed. And everyone in Japan was out of the army by December.

The Imperial Navy was even quicker to disband as most of the ships in what had been the world's third largest fleet were already gone. By the end of November the only Japanese navy people still on duty were working as civilians, sweeping mines, doing repatriation work, or maintaining those remaining warships wanted by the Allies. A few of these last ships would go on to new careers. The *Nagato,* for example, Japan's sole surviving battleship, was taken to Bikini atoll, where she ended as a subject for nuclear testing in July 1946.

Certain major seaports could not be used at war's end because of Allied mines. Many had been dropped uncharted, and for some of them—the pressure mines—there was no known method for sweeping. Of necessity, Japanese skill and sophistication at mine removal grew; this would benefit Americans during the Korean War.

Americans were curious about Japanese military technology and eager for any lessons to be learned before it all disappeared. The Japanese scientific world had been closed to outsiders for more than a decade. The U.S. Navy, for instance, wanted to learn about the design and construction of Japanese warships, the range, power, and accuracy of guns and torpedoes, and the weight and metallurgy of armor. The Japanese had built bigger warships and bigger guns than the Americans. Were they better? If so, how? A U.S. Navy technical mission, with nearly two hundred officers and men, landed at Sasebo on September 23, 1945, and set out to learn as much as possible about such matters.

In field trips and interrogations, "NAVTECHJAP" went after documents and information: war plans, codes, training programs, scientific data on optics, meteorology, hydrography; they also collected equipment. These were highly sophisticated operations, requiring eighty language officers. Aside from weaponry, Americans wanted to know how the Japanese converted rubber into gasoline; Americans had done the reverse. Japanese tropical medicine and therapeutic drugs also aroused curiosity. By March 1946 the fruit of these labors had been sent back to Pearl Harbor, a secure and convenient place for sorting and digesting. Nearly two hundred reports were eventually printed.

The American investigators found that during the war the Japanese had conducted little organized research outside Army and Navy auspices. Consequently, Americans felt, "Japan failed, in general, to realize those tremendous and permanent scientific advances that the modern nation gains from huge wartime expenditures for research." It is certainly true that the Japanese hungered for information from Americans and other foreigners.

What did the foreigner conclude about Japanese applied science in 1945? Professor Nathaniel Peffer of Columbia University, talking with the Council on Foreign Relations in New York about reparations from Japan, reminded his audience that Americans should not regard Japanese equipment as second-rate, some being "very good indeed." Others pointed out that the Japanese did not lack originality, although this attribute was not as conspicuous as their skill at adaptation. They were, after all, late starters in modern science and industrial technology, and their material resources were slim. As it turned out, there were no great surprises awaiting the Americans in that quarter, except perhaps a new appreciation of Japanese ingenuity, of how much they had been able to accomplish with so little.

Requital, punishment, security were motives swirling about in the minds of Americans as they began working out a policy for reparations from the Japanese. War, conquest, death, disease, and injury are costs so enormous that the Japanese could not possibly recompense their erstwhile enemies. Do reparations make any sense in an age of total war? How can the loser pay for the damages of such a conflict when presumably a loser has little left with which to pay? Certainly Japan did not have much.

The deteriorated state and obsolescence of what was left in Japan made any possible reparations of dubious value. Removal might hurt the Japanese; whether the recipient could benefit was another matter. Furthermore, nations desiring sophisticated machinery as reparations from the Japanese did not necessarily know how to use it. Anyway, much of Japan's industrial plant, built to specific local circumstances, was either physically immovable or impracticable to move.

China and Korea, at least, could benefit by absorbing the substantial Japanese fixed capital investments remaining from the heyday of the Greater East Asia Co-Prosperity Sphere. And the Soviet Union compensated itself handsomely for all war costs by stripping Manchuria of industrial equipment conservatively worth two billion dollars, even though that province was part of the territory of Russia's nominal ally, China.

For the Filipinos, Indonesians, and others, there was nothing. Nothing except the angry hope—indeed the keen expectation—of exacting goods and machinery from a defeated Japan. Feelings on this issue ran so high that governments found it difficult to pursue rational policies on the matter.

93

Ambassador Edwin W. Pauley, personal representative to President Truman on reparations.

Americans, although much less passionate, recognized the importance of the issue. In Europe the U.S. was already struggling with the problem of what could be got from the Germans. In Asia, the overall American objective was to have a lean yet healthy Japan assume a place within—but not atop—a peaceful and prospering Asia. Japan was too important to be sealed off more than temporarily from international commerce. And, increasingly, America recognized that Japan could not survive without trade.

In the spring of 1945 President Truman appointed Edwin W.

Pauley, a California oil man prominent in Democratic party affairs, to develop a reparations policy for the war's aftermath. Pauley said he wanted to be stern but fair with Japan, and that the purpose of the reparations program should be to enhance American security, to perpetuate the peace. To accomplish this aim, Pauley and others believed that the victorious Americans were entitled to reform the Japanese economy drastically, and by force if necessary. The question was what controls could be imposed on the Japanese to ensure that they would not be able to revive those bad old habits of militarism and expansionism.

Pauley suggested that if Japan were to be stripped of those few key industries that had been designed and created only to support the country's military machine and imperial expansion, the Japanese would be unable to make war again. Such a loss need not prevent the nation's economy from being self-sustaining—an important consideration to the U.S.A., for Americans might otherwise be obliged to support the Japanese. This was also significant to Japan's neighbors, for they needed Japanese goods. What remained of this "artificial" industry at the end of the war was deemed surplus, available for reparations.

The Japanese people, Pauley asserted, would not suffer from the disappearance of heavy industry because they had never been permitted to enjoy its fruits. In fact, they would benefit because they would no longer be taxed to support it. But this was not a line of argument Pauley cared to push very far; he acknowledged that reparations might be painful, at least to some. Nonetheless, with an aura of the punitive lurking in the background, he insisted that there was no reason for the Japanese to enjoy a standard of living higher than their neighbors, whom they had, after all, treated rather badly. Japan would be left an industrial plant adequate for domestic needs, with enough left over to generate sufficient goods to pay for essential imports. But Pauley wanted to destroy Japan's industrial leadership in East Asia. He saw an opportunity to reorient the economy of the entire Far East.

Pauley recognized the importance of carrying out reparations swiftly so that the Japanese would know what actually was to be theirs and what was not. This uncertainty was having a devastating impact on early attempts to revive the economy. He recommended that reparations be taken in kind, but not in labor or in raw materials (Japan needed what she had for minimal economic recovery). Nor should reparations be recurring. Pauley feared that a steady stream of Japanese goods to recompense Japan's victims might revive dependency upon Japan, renewing the economic relationships of the former Greater East Asia Co-Prosperity Sphere.

The Pauley mission recommended removal of such items as tools and equipment for the aircraft industry, ball and roller bearings, most machine tools and shipyard equipment, the light metals industry, and all steel-making capacity in excess of two and a half million tons (capacity in 1945 was eleven million; in 1930, slightly under two and a half million). Pauley believed it made no economic sense for Japan to have a large steel industry without the natural resources to sustain it.

Japan's shipping was to be severely limited, with no ship over five thousand gross tons or with a speed in excess of twelve knots. Persons of a historical frame of mind would recall that the policy of Japan's own Tokugawa Government from the early seventeenth through the mid-nineteenth centuries had been much the same. The intent at that time was to keep the Japanese at home and to minimize foreign entanglements. Pauley's purpose was similar.

When Pauley and his group got down to specifics, they did not always find it easy to determine what Japan ought to forfeit. What was war industry? No one could argue about a gun factory. But chemicals? Nitrates could be made into explosives or could be made into fertilizer—which, as everyone recognized, was badly needed by Japan's farmers. How did one make such choices?

Pauley's recommendations, submitted in April 1946, were more or less scrapped. Many people criticized the Pauley report. As early as October 1947, Far Eastern expert Nathaniel Peffer told the Council on Foreign Relations that "security through reparations is a mirage." Japan, he said, could revive as a major power within a decade.

Members of the Pauley Mission. Seated at the far left is Owen Lattimore.

While machinery lay unused and rusting, or crated and waiting at dockside, two other reparations missions followed the Pauley group to Japan, in January and April 1948. These were headed by Clifford S. Strike and Percy H. Johnston respectively. Each scaled down drastically what Japan should relinquish. Strike took his argument to the pages of *American Magazine,* where he asked rhetorically: "When shall we end the drain on the American taxpayer, the preposterous situation in which parents and widows of American boys who died in the war must pay to feed and clothe those who killed them?" To Strike, it made little sense for America to make Japan pay reparations to American Allies while the U.S. was subsidizing the Japanese. In May 1949 the American Government took a final step by publicly announcing that it no longer favored any further reparations removals.

The upshot of all this was that Japan paid out little during the Occupation. Reparations remained an unsettled matter, one that finally was successfully negotiated after the Occupation ended by

97

the Japanese themselves, talking separately with most of their former Asian enemies.

Politically the reparations issue remained hot throughout the Occupation years, being one of the chief points of difference between America and its Allies. If the Chinese, chief among interested parties, had not been absorbed by their revolution, matters would have been worse. Herbert Evatt, Australian statesman and a founder of the United Nations, charged in July 1949 that whereas Australians had not changed their policy toward Japan, Americans had, and that no good would come of it. Evatt was reminded, he said, of the change in American policy toward Germany after World War I, and this had led to German rearmament.

Evatt and others were alarmed that America's image of Japan was shifting from that of a former enemy to a prospective ally; the Australians feared for their security and fretted over the threat of Japan becoming an economic rival. The alarm was quickened by Dean Acheson's speech on May 8, 1947, in which he said that America must "push ahead with the reconstruction of those two great workshops of Europe and Asia—Germany and Japan—upon which the ultimate recovery of the two continents depends." Arresting words, particularly from a man whose confirmation as Under Secretary of State in the fall of 1945 had been held up because he was thought to advocate harsh treatment for Japan.

To critics of the Occupation, chiefly Japanese progressives and a few disgruntled American newspapermen, America's failure to press the Japanese appeared to be one more piece of evidence that the goals of the Occupation had been betrayed, sacrificed to the demands of the Cold War. But most Americans at the time were satisfied.

Not only did the U.S. utterly defeat the Japanese in a physical sense, but by vanquishing them the Americans scored, they believed, a moral triumph. Most Americans did not question the righteousness of their cause. The U.S. went to war because it was attacked. America crushed the attacker; now it would punish him.

Fire bomb raids that destroyed much of Tokyo left the transportation facilities intact on this street.

That the Potsdam Declaration should promise "stern justice . . . to all war criminals" seemed entirely proper.

Nuremberg set the precedent for Tokyo, even though the German case differed from Japan's. In Japan the Allies had legal limits to their authority, whereas in Germany they did not. Japan still had a legal government.

Conventional war crimes were well defined in international law; and before World War II defendants had never been charged with anything else. But at Nuremberg something new broke forth: The Nazis were tried not only for conventional war crimes but also for crimes against peace and crimes against humanity. Americans were resolved that the Japanese should face a similar charge.

Yet the law was not defined. Justice Robert E. Jackson, American prosecutor at Nuremberg, felt that this really did not matter as long as "our test of what legally is crime gives recognition to those things which fundamentally outraged the conscience of the American people. . . . I believe that those instincts of our people were right and that they should guide us as the fundamental tests of criminality."

99

In other words, Jackson believed ethnocentric concepts of ethics could substitute for a universally accepted code of law.

Prior to the Tokyo War Crimes Trial, the Allies held no conferences among themselves to define the crimes to be tried and the procedures to be followed during the trials. Instead, a charter was drafted by Americans, principally by Chief Prosecutor Joseph Keenan. He used Nuremberg and its definition of justice as his model. Thus many principles of law and justice laid down in the Tokyo Charter had uncertain bases in established international law and were not necessarily applicable to the case of Japan and World War II.

Senator Robert A. Taft and U.S. Supreme Court Justice William O. Douglas both expressed reservations. "The trial of the vanquished by the victors," Taft said, "cannot be impartial no matter how it is hedged about with the forms of justice." Douglas remarked that the Tokyo Tribunal "took its law from its creator."

The American public was largely apathetic to all this. Nuremberg was interesting because of its novelty and because the people there were familiar. Nazism was far easier to identify, to personify—and to excoriate—than Japanese militarism. The horrors of Belsen, Buchenwald, and Dachau had become well known to Americans. At Tokyo the defendants, with the exception of Tojo, were largely unfamiliar. Tokyo was far away, the lawyers droned on for two and a half years, the trial seemed interminable.

To the Japanese the trial was vaguely embarrassing, and they were not much more engaged by it than the Americans. The shabby old men sitting in the courtroom who had led the nation into such a hopeless struggle looked more foolish than evil. And even they, stolid and impassive, seemed detached. "Day after day," one of their American lawyers remembers, "the Japanese sat in the dock, dozing or staring off into space, barely aware of their part in the courtroom drama."

Twenty-seven prominent Japanese men were accused of participating in a conspiracy to wage aggressive war. They were chosen, arbitrarily it would seem, from a list of 250 candidates. The

100

Emperor was conspicuously absent from the list, although a Gallup Poll in the summer of 1945 found that 70 percent of Americans asked favored trial or punishment without trial for him. Ironically, some of those picked, like former Foreign Minister Shigemitsu Mamoru, had been instrumental in the delicate negotiations for surrender. Apparently an important criterion for selection was American confidence the case was strong enough that there would be only a negligible chance of acquittal. In short, the twenty-seven had already been judged guilty.

Neither the Nuremberg nor the Tokyo Charters attempted a definition of aggressive war. The crime of conspiracy has no legal basis in international law, and even some of the judges in the tribunal were unfamiliar with what the charge of conspiracy implied.

Of the eleven judges, none was Japanese and none was from a country that had been neutral in the war with Japan. Several had fought in the war; one was a survivor of the Bataan Death March, perhaps the single greatest atrocity perpetrated by the Japanese. Only Justice Pal, representing India, had a background in international law. He wrote a lengthy opinion dissenting from the majority judgment, one of three justices to do so. But neither his opinion nor the other two were read by the Tribunal.

Majority rule governed all Tribunal decisions, even those involving the death penalty or life imprisonment. In American and British courts, a unanimous vote by the jury is needed to condemn a criminal to death. None of the seven men condemned to death in Tokyo was found deserving of this penalty by a margin greater than seven votes to four; a single vote was the difference in several cases. Still they were hanged.

Tojo's American defense attorney, George Blewett, published in the summer of 1950 a brief article whose title summarizes his view of the Tokyo Tribunal: "Victor's Injustice: The Tokyo War Crimes Trial." He asserted that the Americans tried the Japanese for violation of *ex post facto* law, that the Americans were much more associated with the trial and judgment than any other nation, and that

101

the long-term effects were likely to be damaging to the moral and political position of the U.S. In his view: "To a student or practitioner of international law, the Tokyo War Crimes trial can only be a source of disquiet and uneasiness. Not only were basic departures from long-accepted Western legal traditions tolerated, but a patently double standard was applied to the leaders of the victorious and defeated nations."

The American people accepted the judgment at Tokyo. For Douglas MacArthur it raised a question later to have personal implications: How far does a General follow his conscience? At Tokyo the verdict implied that he should disobey orders if they conflicted with what he believed to be in the national interest. Perhaps this was in MacArthur's mind when, after his dismissal by President Truman, he said to the Massachusetts legislature on July 25, 1951:

> I find in existence a new and heretofore unknown and dangerous concept that the members of our armed forces owe primary allegiance and loyalty to those who temporarily exercise the authority of the executive branch of government, rather than to the country and its constitution which they are to defend. No proposition could be more dangerous.

Nuremberg and Tokyo cast a long shadow, and the issues they raised are yet to be fully resolved.

In the first weeks of the Occupation many Americans heartily agreed with Admiral William F. "Bull" Halsey when he said he would have liked to deliver a kick in the face to every Japanese delegate standing at the surrender ceremonies on the deck of the *Missouri.* But such intense animosity began to erode rapidly, especially among Americans in Japan. The cheerful Japanese acceptance of the U.S. presence, as Americans perceived it, and the ready Japanese cooperation with American orders encouraged a growing spirit of magnanimity toward the former foe.

The speed and ease with which the U.S. had been able to accomplish the laying down of Japanese arms, the first part of the Occupation program, was exhilarating and immensely satisfying. Americans were buoyed at seeing, within a few months, the teeth and claws of the Japanese military establishment effectively drawn and clipped. Japan could no longer make war. And the extreme economic vulnerability of the islands meant that as long as the U.S. continued to control the approaches by sea, Japan would lie securely under American command. This was not enough, Americans judged; they sought also to wipe out Japanese militarism. But crushing the means to make war was one thing; destroying the will to do so was another. That was neither quick nor easy. Yet bolstered by initial successes, the occupiers approached their self-appointed task with high confidence and gusto.

7

Livelihood

LIVELIHOOD for the Japanese was not among the immediate American concerns upon landing in Japan. Disarming the Japanese, then democratizing them was. But the Americans soon realized they would not be able to move very far toward the latter without giving or permitting the Japanese the means to maintain themselves at a decent economic level. A starving people would have little taste for the niceties of political or social experiment.

The destruction and resulting disruption of life that urban Japan had suffered during the war, particularly in the last months, was immense. The spectacular A-bomb tended to deflect attention from what happened to cities other than Hiroshima and Nagasaki, but more than sixty of them had experienced significant damage from air attacks. At the surrender, as one reporter said, the great seaport of Yokohama was "closer to being a name than a town." Throughout the nation, two and a half million buildings were damaged or lost. Americans dropped about one bomb for every fifteen Japanese people. One quarter of the Japanese who lived in cities, about eight and a half million individuals, fled or were evacuated to the countryside.

Photographs show the devastation of the Japanese urban landscape but fail to convey the dramatic muting or disappearance of color. Everything was now monochromatic: gray, brown, or black and white. Green was virtually gone because so little vegetation was left.

There was an intensity of odors. The stench of stale urine, excre-

104

U.S. bombing raids devastated this section of Yokohama, Japan.

ment, sewer gas, rotting garbage, and, above all, the acrid smell of ashes and scorched debris pervaded the air. Winds periodically redistributed the dust that lay heavily everywhere. The ground glittered with broken glass.

"You saw people living in damp, cold, virtually windowless *kura* [storehouses] built of stone or cement," one witness recalls, and those buildings that had survived were mostly Western style, iron or steel skeletons fleshed with concrete. One could see fireproof safes here and there dotting the wide landscape. An occasional tall chimney, remnant of a public bath, punctuated the skyline, like a giant grave marker for buildings burned and pounded into ashes and dust. Little remained of the vulnerable wooden frame, tile roof dwelling lived in by most Japanese. Foreign journalists noticed that the ruins were different from those in Europe. So little was left.

105

The American Embassy, Tokyo.

Although the tonnage of bombs dropped was far smaller in Japan than in Germany, the damage was fully as great.

In the first weeks following the end of the nightmare, tentative shacks of wood or rusty corrugated metal sprouted like unsightly fungus on the landscape. The will to survive remained. Glass shards were piled neatly in vacant lots; streets were carefully cleared and neatly swept, but few people were to be seen. One could go for block after block without seeing anyone. An early foreign visitor wrote in his journal: "All of them [I saw] looked like scarecrows —they looked upon us with neither fear nor hostility nor—anything. Their eyes were blank, and if spoken to they came to and would smile in a contorted way which I have learned does not connote mirth to them."

The silence was deep, shocking to those Americans who knew the lively bustle of the prewar Japanese city. Streetcars were running, but there were very few automobiles or trucks. Many people had remained as refugees in the countryside where there was more assurance of food. The erratic supply of electricity brought dim lights; *teiden* (electric failure) was frequent. At night periodic

106

Raising the flag at the American Embassy.

West view of the Shimbashi Market in Tokyo.

plunges into total darkness seemed to illustrate the precariousness of Japan's prospect.

For Japan's man in the street in late 1945, the problems of survival, of getting from one day to the next, seemed almost insuperable. The basic order to MacArthur simply said: "You will not assume any responsibility for the economic rehabilitation of Japan or the strengthening of the Japanese economy." The General found it no hardship to be deprived of significant initiative in economic matters. No Marxist he; the revolution of which he dreamed was to be spiritual.

Because of American appreciation for the strong and effective war machine that the Japanese had been able to build, and the Americans had now to tear apart, the efficacy with which the Japanese might be able to carry out their economic recovery from the war was overestimated. The Americans judged that whatever economic problems there were—and Americans knew there were many—the Japanese themselves could handle. After all, since the Japanese started the war, they could repair the damage. Elsewhere, in the past, occupying armies had not helped rebuild the land of the former enemy. Americans saw no reason to change this practice.

Yet it was vital that the occupiers keep things going at a minimal level under what was called the "disease and unrest" formula. Sickness among the Japanese people could infect Occupation troops. Unrest among the Japanese people could make the Occupation more troublesome. What was "minimal" later became subject to discussion and dispute among the Americans. The immediate shortage of food was the chief worry for many people, Americans and Japanese.

Hunger loomed over the ruins and, to American surprise, things did not get very much better with the passing of time. How were the Japanese to survive the winter with a bad autumn harvest, an increased number of mouths to feed, and no access to former sources of supply from overseas? Precedent for feeding former enemies was established very early, one day after MacArthur's entry, when General Eisenhower said it would be necessary to bring American food into Germany to keep Germans alive during the coming winter. But no food was brought in expressly for the Japanese during the first six months of the American presence there. Brigadier General Crawford Sams, in charge of the Public Health and Welfare Section of SCAP, later said, "We were never able to verify that anyone died in Japan at any time during the Occupation from starvation." And he mused that if the situation had been demonstrably worse, more food imports might have been approved by Washington.

A few American officials after the war were prepared to watch a Malthusian correction at work in Japan: the death of enough people to bring the population in balance with the resources. Senator Theodore G. Bilbo of Mississippi even went so far as to write General MacArthur on September 14, 1945, suggesting sterilization of all Japanese.

109

Former President Herbert Hoover, chairman of the American Famine Emergency Committee, arrives at Atsugi Airfield.

Mrs. Katō Shizue, outspoken Socialist Diet member, former Baroness, and energetic proponent of planned parenthood, complained to General MacArthur, "Our daily concern with food had made us forget our traditional training not to say we're hungry in the presence of an honorable person. We are all hungry in Japan now."

The Supreme Commander was unmoved. Hunger was a worldwide phenomenon, Japan one among many suffering nations. Yet continuing Japanese pleas, a sense of charity, and fear of food riots led the occupiers to relent. They would feed the Japanese.

Herbert Hoover, serving as chairman of a special presidential advisory committee, recommended minimum imports to Japan of 870,000 tons of food to be distributed in deficient urban areas. Americans later estimated that their grain and canned goods saved eleven million Japanese.

110

In postwar Japan virtually all goods were scarce. Inflation resulted; enough to be a social leveler, destroying all wealth not founded upon real property. Taking 1934–1936 as an index of 100, wholesale prices rose to 350 in 1945, to 20,876 in 1949.

Unremitting inflation shattered incentives for producing goods or saving money; it disrupted the normal working of the economy and inhibited its real growth. Feeble government attempts to control prices and to ration goods simply stimulated a thriving black market. The new power of labor, organized into unions, forced wages up, adding to the spiral.

The Japanese seemed ready to lean heavily upon the U.S., willing to accept the Americans as masters and expecting them to assume

Japanese laborers at Shibaura warehouse, Tokyo, load trucks with Australian and American rations to go to foreign civilians and Japanese charity hospitals.

that responsibility. Slowly the Americans responded. To more than one foreign observer, the Japanese Government seemed to be doing irritatingly little to use effectively what resources it had to invigorate the economic life of the nation. The critics debated whether this was due to incompetence or unwillingness.

W. Macmahon Ball argued in the Allied Council that the Japanese intentionally made recovery slow in order to increase American aid and diminish reparations. Some Americans speculated that the Japanese wanted to make the Occupation so difficult and so expensive that the Americans would want simply to get out and quickly. Such lines of thought completely ignored both the difficulties of the Japanese Government and the wretchedness of the Japanese people. Plagued by the vagaries of Allied policy over reparations, for example, or toward big business, government officials could not plan effectively. And the Japanese people were thinking more about the absence of enough food than about the presence of the foreigners in Japan.

The near torpor of economic activity brought by defeat in war was aggravated by Japan's longstanding economic deficiencies. Japan had entered the industrial age with severe handicaps. Before the mid-nineteenth century arrival of Commodore Perry and the treaties that opened Japan to international commerce and intercourse, thirty million Japanese had lived in virtual seclusion, substantially self-sufficient. Nothing Japan really needed had to be imported. With modern times all this had changed. The population soared. In fifty years Japan industrialized and became a resource-poor nation, obliged to import heavily for economic survival. None of the major minerals required for industry was in adequate supply: iron ore, anthracite, petroleum. Nor were most of the lesser metals to be found in Japan.

Skillfully and assiduously the Japanese worked their narrow homeland and the surrounding waters, enabling them to feed 80 percent of a population which, by 1945, was approaching eighty million. They had to buy overseas what food they could not harvest and most of the raw materials necessary for their factories. Just before the war, Japan was the world's fifth largest trading nation. The Japanese exported one quarter of their manufactures; Americans exported only one tenth. The lifeblood of the Japanese nation was nourished by the inward flow of raw materials and the outward stream of processed goods.

Defeat crushed the entire delicate mechanism. Trading patterns carefully woven with other countries were sundered, and no longer were there any goods to sell. The smoke of burning cities replaced that from factory chimneys.

The Asian empire dissolved. China was now in convulsion, all but totally closed to the Japanese. Gone with the empire were the Korean and Taiwanese rice bowls that had provided large amounts of that basic foodstuff. Lush subtropical Taiwan yielded quantities of sugar and fruits; the rich black earth of Manchuria had given the Japanese most of their soybeans, humble perhaps but precious; and also there, beneath the ground, lay masses of iron ore and coking coal that Japanese capital had begun to develop and Japanese factories had just begun to exploit.

Fish, source of so much of the protein in the Japanese diet, were no longer available in adequate quantities because the fishing fleet, particularly the large vessels, had been badly decimated by the war and because the U.S.S.R. closed off access to rich fishing grounds previously exploited in the north. Most of the Japanese merchant marine, like the warships, rested at the bottom of the sea. The catch plummeted to a fraction of its prewar level.

There were also the invisible aspects of war for the Japanese to reckon with. Machinery and equipment had been heavily used and minimally maintained. Much of it was now obsolete. In the long run, rust may have been as destructive as bombs, for during the war nothing could be renewed, replaced, or even properly tended.

The textile industry, a major part of Japan's prewar economy (Japan had been one of the world's big three textile manufacturers), had been ravaged by the demand for arms and ammunition. Much of the machinery had been literally devoured, melted down, sacrificed to the desperate, insatiable hunger for metals. Per capita consumption of textiles had shrunk by 1945 to a pitiful one tenth of its mid-1930s level.

Silk textiles, the only substantial Japanese export not requiring any imported raw materials, were traditionally a principal earner of foreign exchange. Silk comprised more than half the value of pre-war Japanese exports to the U.S., for example; the American hosiery industry had consumed 90 percent. But silk became a casualty to synthetics in the postwar period. "Nylons" joined the language as a generic term. With synthetic fabric cheap, durable, and increasingly available, who needed silk?

To American advisors, men who were not manufacturers of textiles or leaders of textile unions, cotton cloth seemed a logical basis for rebuilding the Japanese economy. The machinery was outside the context of reparations, the industry was unrelated to military purposes, the Japanese had a tradition of success with it, and the world market then offered some promise. Raw materials for rayon manufacture, chiefly wood pulp, of course cost less than raw cotton. But, as one economist suggested, large American Government-held stocks of raw cotton may have weighed heavily in American advice to the Japanese. The Americans were less eager to export wood pulp.

Stockpiles of Japanese minerals were exhausted by the war. American sea and air power had choked off the Japanese home islands from the rest of the empire. Americans entered Japan on the heels of a summer that had brought forth the smallest rice crop in more than a generation. Forests were suffering from overcutting and insufficient replanting.

Coal, Japan's most important energy source, was in extremely short supply. Forty percent of the miners quit at the end of the war and headed for better opportunities. One could hardly blame them for this; the mines were in terrible condition, with perhaps the highest accident rate in the world. Mining costs remained so high that it became cheaper for the Japanese to buy American coal and ship it across the Pacific than to dig out their own. There was barely enough coal to keep the trains running, let alone fuel the factories.

114

Too many people struggling with too few resources was the bleak assessment.

At war's end the Japanese people seemed to be in utter stupor. After the exhilaration of war, defeat was psychologically prostrating. Malnourished, sickly (beriberi and tuberculosis were rife), wretchedly clothed, and exhausted, the Japanese could not do much beyond trying to meet immediate needs for food and shelter. Little preventive medicine had been practiced during the war. Now with the deterioration of sanitation, supply shortages, and a large influx of refugees from overseas, it is a miracle that except for one brief outbreak of typhus Japan was spared devastating epidemics.

For the newly arrived American it was a relief to plunge outside the ruined cities, into the fresh air of the countryside where the placid rhythm of life seemed unchanged, the beauty of the fields and mountains unscarred by war. Farmhouses with their thatched or tiled roofs still stood, timelessly at harmony with the landscape. The farmer had his house, his tools, and his land. Nitrates had been used during the war years to make explosives instead of fertilizers so the land may have lacked nutrients, but it was at least there to till. And the farmer had both the will and the skill to work it. He could eat. For the first time in modern history, the farmer became an economically privileged member of Japanese society, better off than the middle-class city dweller. The sharp pinch of hunger drove the townsman to forage the countryside; a prized antique scroll might end up in a farmer's hands, exchanged for a sack of sweet potatoes.

The material fabric of Japanese culture, its art and its architecture, suffered remarkably little from war damage despite the heavy bombing. Some treasures were spared because of their location in isolated rural places. Nara and Kyoto, sites of the greatest urban concentrations of fine arts, were not targets of American attack. Ironically, historic military architecture suffered the most. Nagoya, Osaka, Hiroshima, and Wakayama lost their two-hundred-year-old castles, ornaments to a great age in Japanese architecture. But of paintings, sculpture, and *objets d'art,* nothing of "truly unsurpassed quality" was destroyed. Natural decay, fire, typhoon, and earthquake—the old and constant threats to the preservation of Japan's artistic heritage—were far more destructive than was the war.

Officials of the Occupation tried to preserve and protect cultural property. During the invasion of China, some Japanese army officers cultivated a connoisseurship in Chinese art by seizing fine examples. But, unlike the Nazis, the Japanese Government had not sponsored a program of looting captured objects, so there were no major accumulations to be sorted out and returned to their owners.

Instead, the difficulty for American officials proved one of self-restraint: preventing erosion of the Japanese artistic heritage through the vigorous collecting activities of the American occupiers. Despite great opportunities, no significant accumulations emerged directly from this era, nothing comparable, say, to those of the Meiji Period when Ernest Fenollosa and Dr. Sturgis Bigelow laid the foundations for the superb collection of the Boston Museum of Fine Arts. During the Occupation, American museums were passive, relying on their customary dealer networks, not exploiting the new opportunities afforded by the desperate poverty of the Japanese. What appealed most to Americans discovering the richness of the arts of Japan were folk crafts, especially pottery, woodblock prints, and antique furniture. Except for amassing *samurai* swords (many Americans were avid collectors), Japan was not plundered by its conquerors.

It was easy to exaggerate the plight of Japan, and many did. Because of the extent of deterioration and destruction, few foreign observers realized the immensity of the productive capacity that remained. Japan emerged from the war with its position as the leading industrial power of Asia unchanged. Other nations had also suffered severely. And Japan's human resource, the most important resource of all, was still there, a large pool of trained and educated people. The social structure with its emphasis on obedience and cooperation was undisturbed. Institutionally Japan was intact; the government still functioned on all levels. Only the army and the navy faded away.

Aerial bombardment aside, the Japanese had not experienced war firsthand as had the Germans and Italians. There was no fighting on the soil of the Japanese home islands. Cities were bombarded from the air or, in a few cases, from the sea, but not fought over in the streets. The economy may have been severely emaciated, but it was still alive. Much of the damage, in Owen Lattimore's words, was "Dempsey damage, that is to say, it put the Japanese out of the fight but did not cripple them for life."

The electric power system remained, not working well but functioning; the lines still stretched across the countryside. The hydroelectric plants, located outside cities, had survived. Even devastated Yokohama still had its piers and warehouses.

Coastal shipping had not been completely knocked out. Railways were largely intact; trains were running through Hiroshima forty-eight hours after the bomb fell. The excellent Japanese railway network was of particular value because most roads were passable only by especially rugged vehicles, and then only in good weather. Rail transport was essential for the rapid mass movement of people and goods; the Japanese relied heavily upon it, and the occupying forces soon found they could as well. The state of the rolling stock may have been deplorable but the trains ran, with white-gloved, baton-carrying stationmasters fulfilling their duties with stiff military punctilio.

Japanese willingness to work hard immediately attracted the attention of Americans. "Never have I seen debris from bombing so quickly and cleanly cleared away," wrote Frank Kluckhohn of the *New York Times.* One soldier compared the Japanese to the Filipinos on this score. The wrong people lost the war, he grumbled; Manila was still a mess. When General MacArthur returned to celebrate Philippine Independence in July 1946, he was profoundly

117

depressed by what he saw. The Filipinos seemed primarily interested in what they could extract from the Americans, whereas the Japanese were simply trying to get things going again.

Despite Japanese efforts, the maddening slowness of genuine recovery dragged the occupiers more and more deeply into Japan's economic problems. By 1948, Japan was turning out goods at only 40 percent of the mid-1930 amount and less than one fifth of the 1940 level, despite increasing American encouragement.

Scarcity of food was a persisting malaise. The average number of calories consumed by the Japanese edged up with painful slowness. The national daily average per capita food intake in 1946 was estimated at 1898 calories, considerably higher than the minimum for survival but scarcely generous. By 1949 it had reached 2097; mineral and vitamin deficiencies were widespread. As late as 1950, when Americans had already been in Japan for five years, more than 20 percent of the Japanese suffered from malnutrition, according to one American study. The food shortage came to be linked with the population growth. More people to feed kept the amount of food available for each person below prewar levels.

In the early days of the Occupation the Americans thought that if population were to be a problem for Japan, declining not rising numbers would be that trouble. This was before they realized that well over 200,000 repatriates would be arriving every month until the end of 1946, with some to return even after that. Despite the wretchedness of life, the death rate fell from 17.6 per thousand in 1946 (a level comparable to the 1930s) to 12.0 in 1948. It continued to slide in a trend relative to the rest of the world's industrially advanced nations. By 1948 there were eight million more Japanese than there had been at the end of the war.

Americans knew three acceptable solutions to the problem of population pressure: emigrating, industrializing, practicing birth control.

For Japan's population to be held constant by emigration, two or three ocean liners, each as large as the S.S. *Queen Mary,* would have to sail from Japan every day at full capacity, carrying passengers who would never return.

Planned emigration on such a scale would smack of fascist compulsion, of prewar ultranationalism. The idea was uncomfortable, implausible. Would Japanese be willing to leave in such numbers? MacArthur believed the Japanese too fond of their homes to embark freely upon emigration to any significant degree. Furthermore, even if persuaded, where other than to, say, Brazil perhaps, where a large number had already settled, could they go? Who would want them? Making room for them at home by expanding the economy seemed a more reasonable prospect.

Increasing the agricultural yield was unlikely in view of the already intensive nature of Japanese farming. Industry was what should be encouraged, both for immediate and for long-term relief. More factories would mean more jobs for more people and, ultimately, the growth of cities. Urban life would encourage smaller families. To many demographers, such a broad economic and social trend provided the best, and perhaps the only, means of bringing population into correct balance with resources. General MacArthur clung to this mode of solving the problem.

December 1948 estimates were that Japan's population would soar to one hundred million in twenty years, necessitating both doubling domestic production and increasing foreign trade to one and a half times its prewar level in order for these people to have a decent life. Here was strong impetus for the occupiers to help speed Japan's rapid economic recovery. But could the economy grow large enough and fast enough to support such a huge number of people?

Japanese activists in the birth control field such as Mrs. Katō Shizue, suppressed during and immediately before the war, were now free to speak, to write, to organize. They did so, with the acquiescence if not approval of SCAP. SCAP could exercise benevolent neutrality, at least publicly, letting the Japanese seize the

119

initiative and knowing that they would do so.

"Sister, you just go right ahead and beat the drums all you want," is Crawford Sams's memory of the message he tried to convey to Mrs. Katō and the birth control proponents. Sams was SCAP's chief of public health. During the early years of the Occupation, SCAP made no effort to dampen Japanese interest in birth control, and made sure there would be an ample supply of what was chastely listed in economic reports as "rubber sanitary goods."

Birth control was a hot political issue, and not simply because of strong objections from the Roman Catholic Church. The American public was aware of Nazi abuses of birth control. General Sams himself used the unfortunate simile of occupied Japan being a "gigantic concentration camp," a world sealed off from others, firmly controlled by its American "guards." SCAP advocacy of birth control might well lay these Americans open to the charge of "genocide" of their helpless "prisoners." The Russians, for example, were constantly alert to the opportunity of embarrassing SCAP.

Early in 1948 the Supreme Commander received a preliminary study of Japan's natural resources prepared by Edward Ackerman, a University of Chicago geographer. Shortly thereafter the report was submitted to the House Foreign Affairs Committee of the United States Congress. Among many other suggestions, Ackerman recommended that Japan stabilize its population, and that the best way of doing so was by birth control. General MacArthur accepted the report without demur.

About the same time, probably because he had come to believe it the only practical way to handle the population problem, General Sams began to take a discreetly active role encouraging birth control. "Without Sams we could never have gotten the bill through," said the sponsor of a bill in the Diet that brought contraception under medical supervision (enabling use of the IUD) and legalized abortion. Abortion had been (and still is) widely practiced by the Japanese. The birth rate began to ease off immediately, a decline rapidly accelerating into a sharper fall than any other recorded in world history.

120

Warren Thompson, a well-known demographer, visited Japan for three months at the beginning of 1949 as an expert consultant to SCAP. He spoke warmly for birth control. Expanding the economy, he argued, would simply encourage more babies. Both the Japanese and the English-language press took up the question, and Japanese women's magazines carried explicit, graphic descriptions of birth control devices and techniques.

All this provoked angry letters to MacArthur from the American Catholic Women's Clubs of Tokyo and Yokohama, protesting SCAP policy. MacArthur replied smoothly that birth control was a Japanese affair, not SCAP policy, and that visiting consultants spoke only for themselves.

At the end of the year, when a final, expanded version of Ackerman's report was published, the Roman Catholic women again protested. The report was then recalled and expurgated; Professor Ackerman was told that he was now *persona non grata* in Tokyo. More demographers did not, as earlier scheduled, follow Warren Thompson to Japan to consult; in February 1950 SCAP denied Margaret Sanger a visa to visit Japan. A storm broke. MacArthur received much protest mail, including a letter from Eleanor Roosevelt.

To his critics the General pointed out, at some length, that the Japanese were more sophisticated in matters of birth control than Americans, and that Mrs. Sanger's views were already well known and appreciated in Japan. In other words, there was no need for her to come. Probably, although he did not venture to say so, it would have been more helpful to the international cause of planned parenthood for the indefatigable Mrs. Katō Shizue to tour the U.S. rather than Margaret Sanger come to Japan. Neither one made the trip. Possibly the Roman Catholic vote in America was on MacArthur's mind: A successful presidential campaign for him would depend heavily upon rallying a large bloc of conservatively inclined voters.

On the issue a liberal could say that, based upon what SCAP had done or had allowed to be done rather than what SCAP had said,

121

Occupation policy was clearly ahead of American public opinion. But a long-term declining birth rate had actually begun in the 1920s, and birth control was not just a postwar development.

Collecting reparations and crushing *zaibatsu* might satisfy both the American sense of justice and the American desire to proselytize democracy. But it would not help the faltering Japanese economy to recover, and without recovery of at least moderate prosperity, would democracy be possible? Furthermore, until the economy regained its health, the American taxpayer would be obliged to assume the burden of support. Relief costs alone were running about $400 million a year. As early as the fall of 1945, Colonel R. C. Kramer of MacArthur's staff, a former New York silk merchant, told reporters: "The big problem is not to keep 'em down, but to start 'em up again."

More and more, American policy toward Japan seemed to be shaped by two considerations. The first was money, the cost of subsidizing the Japanese; whether or not the Occupation was expensive, many Americans, including Secretary of State General George C. Marshall, believed it to be. The second consideration was security, Japan's strategic value in world politics to America and specifically in the rivalry between the U.S. and the U.S.S.R. Reform yielded primacy to recovery.

But "reverse course," as Japanese progressives have put it, is too facile an explanation for what happened; the phrase implies a firmness of direction, a sureness of purpose the Americans did not exercise. Perhaps a sailboat is an apt metaphor for the policy of the occupiers: Progress was made by tacking and trimming, due attention paid to currents and tide, the course plotted and the journey taken with a weather eye out for black clouds on the horizon.

Advancement of peace and democracy, those first principles of the occupiers, were sufficiently broad to be easily endorsed by a wide stripe of people. Yet when it came down to working out specific issues, deep fissures of opinion within the structure of Occupation authority were laid bare. Practical policy had to suture at

122

least some of these gaping differences; decisions had to be granulated and fused by a constant process of negotiation and compromise—very much the Japanese way.

Defeat and occupation by the Americans threw the Japanese into a new economic embrace. Since earlier sources for raw materials, such as China and the colonies, were no longer available to them, and because they were not immediately free to cultivate new trading networks, foodstuffs and minerals now had to come from the U.S. That the American market would be able to absorb enough paper fans, tea sets, or embroidered tablecloths to pay for these vital imports was unlikely. Most of the highly processed goods the Japanese could produce would not find a market in America, predicted a 1947 State Department study. One well-informed economist and Japan specialist flatly declared the future prospects of Japan's iron and steel industry to be "not very promising." And for machinery such as electrical equipment, or heavier items like vehicles, the Japanese would be obliged to find markets in the underdeveloped nations. Sale in America was unthinkable, for the quality was too poor.

Among American businessmen there was no unanimity as to what the postwar economic policy toward Japan should be. American memory of Japanese competition in the 1930s was both vivid and unpleasant. Unethical trading methods and the ruthless exploitation of labor were seen as characteristic of Japanese economic life then. Those who had suffered from such competition wanted no revival of Japanese trading vigor. And so American shipping firms, for example, were not eager to have Japan resume its highly successful oceanic traffic. Textile manufacturers, makers of cutlery and dishes, and producers of other consumer goods were wary of uncontrolled Japanese economic expansion.

For the American South, the cotton textile industry was then of major importance. Japan was both customer and competitor. Southern raw cotton found an excellent market in Japan, but Japanese cotton textiles could and did undersell American, and Southern attitudes toward Japan were correspondingly ambiguous. MacArthur invited a group of American cotton textile manufacturers to visit Tokyo and talk over the problem with him. Not surprisingly they recommended that the Japanese be strongly encouraged to direct their exports to Asian markets.

Amid the continuing upheaval in Asia, Japan was an island of stability. Americans hoped the Japanese would soon contribute to the economic recovery of the continent. Consistently Americans thought of Japan as an Asian nation, the leader among Asian nations in terms of industrial muscle, with interests confined largely to Asia, drawing its resources from Asia and selling its goods to Asia; with natural ties, in other words, to the undeveloped world. Since mainland East Asia was closed, Japan's partner would have to be Southeast Asia. Americans had no view of Japan ever becoming a global economic power.

As China faded from the American sphere, interest in Japan blossomed. "Military government is rapidly becoming a training ground for Americans who plan to go into business in Japan!" the *Wall Street Journal* suggested. "The number of paunchy, sacksuited, panama-hatted executive types in their middle fifties . . ." in the streets of downtown Tokyo gave "the illusion that the local branch of the United States Chamber of Commerce was in session."

In retrospect we can remark how little Americans did to exploit their advantages over Japan. At the time there was even some feeling that it would be morally wrong to do so. American capital did not take over Japanese industry. Carpetbagging was minimal. In fact, one could argue that the Japanese benefited more than the Americans from the peculiar relationship. Some of the seeds of future economic difficulty between the two countries were sown by Americans allowing the Japanese remarkably free entry to the American market while encouraging them to protect themselves from foreign competition.

Hollywood, Northwest Orient Airlines, and *The Reader's Digest* were among the fortunate early American arrivals to the Japanese market. Others were impatient to come in also. Those who had made money before in trade with Japan, or anticipated future op-

124

portunities for profit there—manufacturers of heavy machinery, Detroit, the big banks—wanted to reopen the Japanese market. They saw tremendous sales potential for textile machinery, for example, and trucks, buses, locomotives, railway cars. The Japanese needed everything.

Investment opportunities were tantalizing as well, made especially attractive by the security of the occupying forces, with the likelihood that Japan, after the Americans withdrew, would continue in the American political orbit. Because Japan had been largely deprived of foreign technical information for so long, beginning in the early 1930s, American business could savor the prospect of slaking the Japanese thirst for such information with lucrative sales of American patents and processes.

On behalf of the British, Sir George Sansom worried that postwar revival of the United Kingdom might be handicapped by "a too liberally assisted development of the Japanese textile industry and merchant shipping." America's Allies wondered whether the American political monopoly in Japan would squeeze them out of nurturing their economic interests there.

The ambitious American businessman could loftily dream of highly profitable joint enterprises, linking cheap Japanese labor with American capital and managerial skills. Through the Japanese the U.S.A. would be able to exploit the enormous Asian market as never before. Colonel Kramer argued the merits of cooperating with the Japanese instead of restricting them, although he pointed out almost presciently that without colonies or armies to support, the Japanese economy might come to possess a competitive ability much tougher for American business to cope with.

Shifting tides of American opinion and greater warmth toward Japan angered Japan's neighbors. "Seldom can a defeated nation have had such an important role allotted to it so soon after its defeat," W. Macmahon Ball wryly commented. Australians and Filipinos were much slower than Americans to shed the cold bitterness of war. The *Manila Times* felt (with all sympathy to the American taxpayer) that it was intolerable to contemplate Japan prospering while the Philippines, still an economic colony for the Japanese, provided them with the raw materials of industry "in exchange for the modern equivalent of glass beads, brass rings, and hand mirrors."

Many Americans, too, were apprehensive and annoyed at the notion of a restored, revivified Japan. Even so conservative a man as State Department advisor Herbert Feis was alarmed lest the old controlling groups in Japan be able to swing back into power because American attention was diverted from overseeing the Japanese build democracy.

Questions of security also muddied the waters. General Robert Eichelberger said in August 1948 that the Allied forces "should

A float used in the Thanksgiving celebration held by the Japanese in Tokyo to express gratitude for the recent emergency food shipments from the United States.

General MacArthur greets William H. Draper, Under Secretary of the Department of the Army, on his arrival in Tokyo to discuss economic conditions throughout the Far East, March 20, 1948.

stay in Japan until the country is able to defend herself against enemies from inside and outside." No longer, it seems, was there anything for the U.S. to fear from the Japanese militarily. Rather, Americans had to defend them! Indeed there was even one suggestion in the spring of 1949 that the Japanese be encouraged to resume manufacturing arms. Not only would this stimulate their economy by giving them something to sell, it might also help America's own rearmament effort. "Strategically, having some of our war production capacity located just off Siberia is worth much thought," one writer suggested.

William H. Draper, formerly of Wall Street, Under Secretary of the Army, vehement in his opposition to reparations or to the

127

breakup of the *zaibatsu,* remarked privately to the Council on Foreign Relations that, in view of an apparent early Communist victory in China, "it must be realized that Japan is the logical stopping place of Russian aggression. Therefore, aside from other considerations, it is definitely in America's national interest to rebuild the Japanese economy." During a discussion held at the State Department in October 1949, Philip Taylor, political scientist and former Occupation official, said flatly, "We have got to get Japan back into, I am afraid, the old co-prosperity sphere. . . ."

The danger of restoring iron and steel manufacture, shipping, and the making of machine tools—all of which seemed desirable, even necessary, if Japan were to recover its prewar standard of living—could be controlled providing Japan had no military power. Since Japan no longer enjoyed free and independent access to the raw materials necessary to feed these heavy industries, the U.S. could exercise leverage over such manufacturing if the sea lanes remained open. In American hands rested the power to stop the flow at any time.

It is fortunate for the sake of the historical record that the American time in Japan spilled over into the period of the Korean War (1950–1953). Had the U.S. pulled out earlier, Japan's economy would have been far weaker and more unsteady. After 1950 the Japanese began rebuilding their merchant marine and reconstituting an external banking, commercial, and insurance network, which now rose from a firm fiscal foundation because of the suggestions of Joseph M. Dodge, Detroit banker, appointed by President Truman to head an advisory group.

The Dodge Mission was the most influential to visit Japan during the Occupation. Dodge's arrival, in March 1949, was the opening salvo of General MacArthur's campaign to control inflation. The mission urged creating and maintaining a balanced budget. With solid Republican certitude, sounding much like Senator Robert A. Taft, Dodge and his associates demanded that the Japanese eliminate "excessive expenditures, wastefulness, subsidies . . . and the general dependence on Government instead of individual or group accomplishments." Because Dodge's recommendations received

Joseph M. Dodge of Detroit, far left, *arrives to advise on fiscal matters, October 31, 1949.*

the whole-hearted support of the Supreme Commander, force was implicit within his words, and those people hurt by the new fiscal austerity had to swallow it. Occupation autocracy rolled heavily over Japanese democracy. In the long run, however, the Dodge Plan was probably for the best because the economy did begin to pick up, with the "sunshine of solvency" glimmering just ahead.

From the Korean War the Japanese derived great benefit and suffered no loss. It was fully as profitable as the two wars they had themselves fought and won on that peninsula earlier in the modern era. But this time they were not participants, simply purveyors; hence the profits. Skilled Japanese hands patched American battle-damaged planes, rebore the pistons of American tank engines, milled lumber to build American barracks, and entertained American troops on leave. Rest and recuperation in Japan brought American soldiers from the Korean front to Japanese mountain and sea-side resorts by the thousands; Japan was probably the favorite

129

"R & R" spot. American dollars fattened Japanese pockets, and that nation's foreign exchange reserves began to swell. In August 1950, for the first time since the Pacific War, the Japanese sold more abroad than they imported or received in American aid. During the six years of the Occupation, the excess of imports over exports totaled $2 billion—and this was when a billion dollars was a large sum. Recovery for Japan was far slower than for Europe.

The Japanese people did not attain their prewar standard of living, modest though it was, until after the Occupation ended. And probably no one at that time would have disagreed with the heavy American pronouncement that "the Japanese people will have to work hard and long, with comparatively little recompense for many years to come, in order to survive and support their growing population." In the words of State Department economist Edwin Martin, "We thought the Japanese economy was a complete mess."

If things were so bad during the Occupation years, how did the later economic miracle happen? It was not founded upon cheap labor, imitation, or unfair trade practices. The U.S. helped the Japanese by providing technology and, what was even more important, by continuing to regard Japan as a dependent state, allowing the Japanese easy access to American markets while permitting the Japanese to protect their own.

Hard work, frugality, and commitment to study and learning are characteristic of the Japanese people. They were perhaps mindful of the words of His Imperial Majesty in his broadcast to the nation August 15, 1945:

> . . . Unite your total strength to be devoted to construction for the future. Cultivate the ways of rectitude, . . . and keep pace with the progress of the world.

With no colonies to soak up investment and no soldiers to arm, pay, and provision, the Japanese could focus their resources on the industrial development of their own land. All the energy and ability that had previously sought expression in building military muscle and empire could now go into economic growth.

8

The Great
Laboratory

MILITARY government has conventionally upheld civil order
while pacifying and punishing the vanquished former foe. In occupying Japan, the U.S. assumed not only these customary responsibilities but also another, creative one. What Americans sought to
do was smash the tight control a small number of Japanese had
exercised over the majority of their countrymen, and make that
majority assume both the will and the power for self-rule.

For the American purpose the shape of Japanese Government
had to be recast, with new institutions firmly rooting the sources of
authority in the people. The people should choose the Diet, a
parliament to which cabinet and prime minister would be responsible, with a place made in political life for those hitherto either
politically inert or lacking the vote: labor, women, and youth. The
old leadership, blamed for bringing about the war as well as for
inhibiting popular government, had to be excised and cast aside.

To smooth the way for democracy, and to sustain its progress,
American reformers strove to make changes in Japanese legal
codes, local government, and police as well as in landholding patterns and the organization of big business. Yet a working democracy can neither be established on command nor willed into life.
Passing new laws, changing the organs of government, and redistributing property was not enough; the very fountainhead of politi-

cal thought had to be gotten at. For such an effort, a massive educational endeavor was necessary. Herein, as Edwin O. Reischauer has pointed out, lay the essence of the entire American Occupation plan. With self-confidence and gusto the American reformers attacked the specific ways, as they interpreted them, by which the Japanese educational system had inhibited the growth of democracy.

Perhaps the idea that democracy could be taught was naïve. But the Japanese, because of their Confucian heritage, shared the American notion that moral improvement, the implanting of virtue, could be accomplished through formal training. Unfortunately, Americans were largely ignorant of Confucianism, knowing little of the Japanese intellectual experience. And in the American concern for the sword-brandishing side of Japanese life, they tended to overlook the rest. Even Shinto myth, which Americans saw only as a source of the irrational and the inhumane in Japanese behavior, had its positive aspect, helping make Japan a vigorous and purposeful nation. Americans therefore missed the opportunity of exploiting similarities between whatever they now brought to the Japanese and the latter's own Sino-Japanese intellectual heritage.

Nor were Americans as aware as the Japanese of the close cultural relationship that grew and flourished between the two countries in the latter part of the nineteenth century. Japan had been deeply affected by it; America had not. The flow of people and ideas to a rapidly changing and modernizing Japan had been largely one way. Americans, especially teachers and missionaries, crossed the Pacific in some number. Western ideas were in great vogue among the Japanese, while Japanese ideas were largely unknown to Americans. Undoubtedly the experience enhanced Japanese receptivity to American ideas after 1945, particularly in education, where American influence had been strong. Murray and Hepburn, for instance, teacher and medical missionary, were names still known in 1945 to many Japanese. And even today, virtually everyone in Japan remembers Professor William S. Clark's terse advice to his young students in Hokkaido: "Boys, be ambitious!"

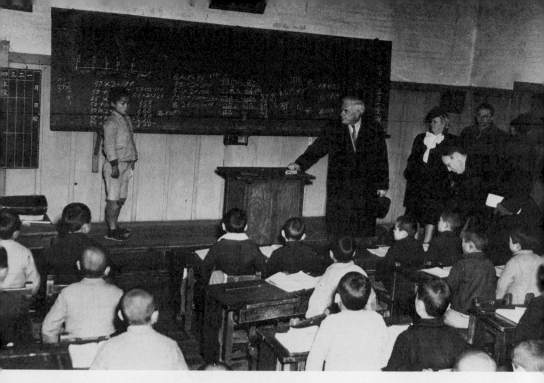

The American Educational Mission, under the direction of its chairman, Dr. A. J. Stoddard, visit an elementary school class in Tokyo.

During the Occupation, Americans believed war had come because the Japanese had been indoctrinated in militarism and extreme nationalism, acquired largely in the schools. Without basic change in this environment, Americans feared that when they left all the other reforms of the Occupation would wither away.

What ought to be done? George Stoddard, president-elect of the University of Illinois, was invited to head a delegation of two dozen prominent American educationists to travel to Japan, consult, and advise. To accomplish their mission, Stoddard and his colleagues spent three weeks during March 1946 studying and producing the single most important document of the Occupation pertaining to educational reform.

The visiting experts proposed change. Army officers plus a few American civilians in Japan were given the task of seeing it through, "to stamp out the bad and stamp in the good" as one brigadier general put it, with muddy imagery perhaps but a pithy and decisive tone.

133

The modest preparation the visitors had for their awesome task provoked little comment, at least at the time. Among the delegations of visiting experts they were certainly not unique in this respect. But one man did venture to remark that "few, if any" of the Stoddard Committee "knew a thing about the Japanese." The innocence of the members may at least have brought them to their task with open minds.

Stoddard and his group selected five broad areas where they wanted to make changes in Japanese education: teachers, content, methods, administrative ways, and scope. Two dozen Americans at GHQ would ultimately supervise fundamental changes for eighteen million students and one million teachers, studying and working in fifty thousand schools. And this does not include all those Japanese who would be indirectly affected by what the Americans proposed. Both the size of the project and the subtlety of understanding required for its success were breathtaking.

Americans decreed; Japanese executed. To the accompaniment of the scratching of thousands of pens wielded by Japanese clerks and bureaucrats, 950,000 teachers and educational officials were screened for suitability as instructors in democracy. Although only three thousand were dismissed as ideologically unacceptable, nearly one quarter (22 percent) of the nation's teachers abandoned the profession. Some did so for economic reasons, but many left for fear of being forced out if they did not withdraw voluntarily. The result may have been a more sympathetic approach to democracy in Japan's schools. Yet as a practical liability, fewer teachers were now obliged to cope with more students.

The content of Japanese education disturbed American reformers, specifically in the areas of geography, Japanese history, and compulsory ethics. Here was the source of evil—as Americans saw it. Texts and teachers both had to be purified if militarism, ultranationalism, and antidemocratic values were to be successfully eradicated from Japanese life. Daily obeisance to the imperial portrait, performed in all the schools, symbolized that which Americans

134

sought to eliminate. Religion was now to be a private matter, removed from school life.

The Japanese themselves abolished military training and drill. Americans urged substitution of competitive sports such as basketball and volley ball for the forbidden martial arts. *Kendo,* karate, and judo disappeared from public schools, but caught the admiring eye of many Americans as they went.

Americans sought to have the Japanese aspire to academic freedom. They urged the Japanese to get away from rote learning and reliance on a formal Germanic, stereotyped lecture method of teaching, to be replaced with emphasis on student initiative, critical analysis, and classroom discussion.

Perhaps the most interesting of Stoddard's recommendations was language reform, which occupiers saw as a bold, dramatic, and swift way to achieve increasing literacy and political sophistication. What Ataturk had done for Turkey was an exciting model. "Can any modern nation afford the luxury of such a difficult and time-consuming medium of expression and communication?" the language reformers now asked. To outsiders it made sense to write Japanese in a romanized script instead of Chinese characters *(kanji)* and native syllabaries. A roman script also would considerably ease foreign access to the body of Japanese culture, literature, religious thought, and even art.

American reformers urged a more democratic spoken language, so that the Japanese would converse without all the levels of politeness that so tightly specified the relative status of those speaking. The spoken language did happen to evolve in such a direction, but not particularly because the Americans so wished. Modern life inexorably carried the spoken language toward greater simplicity.

As for the written language, the Japanese established a study committee to determine what, if anything, should be done. The results were influential: simplifying many characters, writing them with fewer strokes, and an effort to cut down the number of characters commonly used. But the use of roman letters did not extend

135

beyond teaching them in the schools, much to the disgust of Commander Robert King Hall, a vocal Occupation official. He was obsessed with a conviction that the Japanese should romanize their writing system entirely; he attributed their failure to do so to differences of opinion among the occupiers. The Japanese, he argued, would have made the change if it had been strongly urged by the Occupation authorities.

Although the Americans were certainly not of one mind about the merits of romanizing the language, neither were the Japanese prepared to yield such a major part of their cultural heritage as their writing system. Some were even proud of its difficulty. The value of *kanji* is "training the eye, the hand, and the memory," and this appeared not inconsiderable; nor did the aesthetic of the pictograph escape appreciation even by the foreigner.

Mastering *kanji* takes a lot of time. But, despite American speculating, the Japanese were not afflicted by widespread illiteracy because of this. Anyone traveling in Japan on train or trolley, for example, would question George Stoddard's assertion that the Japanese "have trouble reading . . . daily newspapers and popular magazines." Japanese pursue the written word with an avidity that compares favorably with any other people. And even then Japan probably had a higher literacy rate than America.

Along with scrutinizing the teachers, the texts, and the methods, Stoddard believed the most significant feature of his report was its recommendation for decentralizing the schools. Americans judged community-managed schools more democratic than centrally-run ones. They were eager to break the power vested in the bureaucrats of the Ministry of Education who, from Tokyo, directed the education of the entire nation. The Americans had the Japanese establish local, popularly-elected school boards, to which they tried to shift power over teachers and curriculum. The Americans encouraged the Parent-Teachers Association to become something more than a fund-raising group.

Finally the Americans wanted Japanese education to embrace more people. Hence compulsory time in school was lengthened from six to nine years. The schools were reorganized to follow the American pattern of six years in elementary school, three in junior high, and three in high school, although this entailed building new schools and moving around teachers.

The Americans pushed coeducation, again on the American model. They urged adult and vocational education, to provide learning for all who could assimilate it. And, at American behest, the number of universities was considerably expanded to provide higher education for a much larger segment of the population. More pay for professors, bigger libraries, and better equipped laboratories were other goals.

Were such wrenching and costly changes appropriate, or even feasible? The American educationists responsible for the recommendations did not address financial questions. Yet lack of money was a major problem for the Japanese. Good schools really depended upon the health of the economy. Demands for government funds were enormous, the amount of governmental revenue uncertain. Virulent inflation was steadily eroding purchasing power, and such natural disasters as typhoons, floods, and earthquakes compounded the difficulty of cleaning up the mess left by the war.

The typical Japanese school, a shabby, unpainted wooden frame building, was now dilapidated, overcrowded, and unheated. Chapped faces and chilblains were legion. Construction materials were in short supply, the need for repairs acute. Before the winter of 1947–1948, the Government allotted each school 130 square feet of sheet glass to replace broken windows. That not being enough, priority was given to repairs on the northern exposure and for classrooms used by younger children. There was insufficient paper for textbooks, and libraries were grossly inadequate. The Americans estimated that half the total book resources of the Japanese nation had been lost in the war. Exhausted, underpaid teachers struggled to help malnourished, ill-clad pupils.

Not everyone was convinced that an American model would be best for Japan's schools, yet it was always that one rather than a European or native precedent which the reformers held up to ac-

claim. On close examination, much of Japanese education seemed
to have worked rather well, at least on the lower levels. Sir George
Sansom, for instance, noted approvingly that 99 percent of Japanese
school-age children attended primary school before the war, and he
was wary of "those modern educators who sedulously guard the
young against drudgery and are in a fair way to producing a generation which cannot read, write, spell or think. . . ." Sir George
presumably had little enthusiasm for the recommendation of the
Stoddard Committee that education should emphasize "child
needs" over subject matter. Those Americans who paid any attention to the Japanese noticed that in contrast to their reaction to
other Occupation reforms, the Japanese were apathetic, if not dis-
trustful, about much of the American educational program.

Some Americans, too, were skeptics. Even Robert King Hall,
ardent though he may have been for radical change of the Japanese
writing system, found fault with experts such as Stoddard who
trumpeted the virtues of the democratic process. Such lip service to
our own values, Hall said, was no substitute for the hard scrutiny
we must make of our educational philosophy. How applicable is it
to another culture? Is it something we can put in words? Another
critic pungently remarked, "We have in America . . . an educational
system that is so weak and inefficient that this nation is recognized
everywhere in the world as the most lawless—and the most wasteful."

Until the Occupation, Japan had an extremely efficient educational system with a mass base but a very small elite. The Japanese
did not object to increasing the years of compulsory schooling, but
they did fear that attempts to broaden the elite by creating a large
number of universities and junior colleges would dilute the quality
of higher education. Curricular changes, coeducation, Parent-
Teachers Associations, and 6-3-3 are Occupation reforms that have
become part of the Japanese pattern. As it turned out, demand for
schooling spiraled, both stimulated and supported by Japan's huge
economic success after the Occupation. Today almost all Japanese
go to school for twelve years. Quality, of a sort, is maintained by

Voters receive ballots as Japan takes her first wobbly step toward establishment of a democracy. On April 10, 1946, an estimated twenty-four million voters went to the polls to select representatives for a new national legislature.

the examination system and a hierarchy of universities. So the American reformers did quite well, but the degree of success their reforms have enjoyed was an accident they could not have foreseen.

Japan's leadership was a matter to which the occupiers gave high priority, for it was the final step in disarmament. Destroying weapons was not enough; SCAP felt it must rid Japan of leaders who might want to make and use them again. Americans called this change of leaders "the purge," an unfortunate term with its terrifying totalitarian overtones of midnight arrests and sunrise firing squads.

To be "purged" in Occupied Japan meant simply to lose one's job. The intent was preventive, the impression punitive. Among Americans the program was one of the most controversial Occupation policies. Some thought it went too far, others not far enough. And many did not like the way it was carried out.

Here was a clear case where Americans in Japan were influenced by what was happening in Germany, specifically by the policy of denazification. But the Japanese case was more complicated. There was no simple test to identify those responsible for Japanese militarism. In a society as homogeneous and well ordered as Japan's, it was, as W. Macmahon Ball complained, "difficult to separate the sheep from the goats."

Since war had largely destroyed the German Government, the occupiers, even had they so wished, could not have made use of it. In Japan, however, the Americans were employing all the members of the Japanese Government, from the emperor on down, with the exception of the notorious secret police. To make this legitimate, the occupiers had to cleanse the leadership. They therefore carried out what John Montgomery called "one of the largest wholesale changes in 'elite personnel' ever deliberately undertaken."

The change was accomplished through administrative process rather than judicial proceedings. That is, the Americans purged by position rather than by performance. Despite the Anglo-Saxon legal tradition that a man is innocent until proven guilty, Americans used the office to determine guilt.

The process was efficient; it was ruthlessly fast and uncomplicated; it was done almost entirely by the Japanese themselves. Americans decided the policy and the Japanese carried it out. As with the educational reform program, the number of Americans participating was very small. In the purge program only twenty or so Americans, including clerks and interpreters, were involved in the whole effort. Many Japanese were kept busy with the enormous flow of paper, screening 2.3 million individual cases and purging 210,287 of them.

Perhaps the most serious criticism at the time was the way in which this change of command was carried out. Certainly the procedure was no model for the working of democratic principles, and there were other bitter criticisms as well. "I think," Eugene Dooman maintained, "it is quite clear that there was a regular pattern designed to eliminate all those elements that could be counted upon to resist Communism and to bring up and open the way for a rise of the classes that were down at the bottom of the heap." Although Dooman was not alone in his unhappiness with the social change, others voiced their worry about the embitterment and estrangement of those who had been on top. Joseph Ballantine, Dooman's State Department colleague, now also retired, thought Americans were undermining the "traditional pro-American business group in Japan."

Kenneth Colegrove, political scientist and college professor, feared the purge policy was eliminating "the best brains" in Japanese political and economic life. Could Japan spare these highly skilled people? *Newsweek* in April 1949 quoted an American businessman as saying: "Most of the top men were honest, earnest, and hardworking. They did what they were told. Most of them weren't interested in politics. These purged men should be given the right to work to help take Japan off the neck of the American taxpayer."

For those men in their late forties and early fifties occupying senior positions the purge was catastrophic. By the time they were reinstated, they were too old to resume their careers. New faces were given a chance. Ninety-five percent of the candidates for the Diet in the first postwar elections had never been in politics before. Younger bureaucrats had great opportunities; some of the vitality of the postwar era, beginning in the late 1940s, may stem from this fresh leadership. But the impact of the purge was modified by the age-old tradition in Japanese life that those who hold nominal power are often guided, even manipulated, by those out of office. To be purged meant one could not hold office; it did not necessarily destroy one's power. Nor was purging permanent. Of those purged, like Hatoyama Ichirō, some ultimately did reappear in positions of leadership. He became prime minister.

* * *

Thomas Blakemore, an American lawyer practicing in Japan, believed that many changes would have been made in Japanese law even if there had been no Occupation. Japan was, after all, a rapidly evolving society. But from the first, Americans regarded the law as something that could be altered to allow the Japanese to practice democracy. Although laws would have to be drafted and passed before public opinion had developed to support them, Americans presumed that public opinion would eventually catch up. In the long run they knew it was vital to have law be consonant with public opinion. The Japanese had to make all of the changes their own, otherwise inevitably they would slide back to old ways after the Americans left.

For a long time Westerners had noted that the Japanese prefer negotiating to litigating. The old Confucian idea lingered that a just man does not find himself engaged in a lawsuit; as a result, Japan is not a nation of lawyers. Custom is extremely important in Japan, and not something to be changed by fiat.

Even within the realm of law, the position of the American reformers was delicate. The Anglo-Saxon legal tradition was not necessarily appropriate for the Japanese. Foreign influence on Japanese law had come, in modern times, largely from the French and the German traditions. Yet drawing primarily from their own experience, American reformers believed that judges should be appointed rather than be civil servants. In a working democracy, Americans knew that the judiciary had to be independent of the rest of government, unbeholden to a bureaucracy, particularly one as haughty and tenacious as that of the Japanese.

Along with an independent judiciary, Americans were anxious for the protection of fundamental human rights, a concern embodied in the new Constitution that the Occupation "sponsored." Whereas the Meiji Constitution (1889), which was being supplanted, had emphasized the obligation of the citizen, the new one emphasized the individual before the collective good.

The Meiji Constitution had not prevented the practice of democracy in Japan. For more than fifty years Japan had political parties,

142

parliaments, and elections. The apparatus of democracy was all there. But the system had certainly not encouraged the practice of democracy, at least as most Americans define it.

In origins, spirit, and practice, the Meiji Constitution was undemocratic. It was the gift of the emperor; it did not derive from the will of the people. It had permitted the accretion of groups that deflected power from the people, such as the Elder Statesmen, Privy Council, and Imperial Household Ministry. The full exercise of civil liberties—freedom of speech or the right to political dissent—was severely inhibited. And most important of all, considering the march toward the war, under the old order the Army and the Navy had enjoyed direct access to the Emperor with the power to circumvent all civil authority and to force the resignation of the Cabinet if they did not agree with its policies.

The new Constitution, promulgated in 1947, included a number of significant changes. The Emperor was reduced to being nothing more than a symbol of the people. The House of Peers was transformed into a weak, elected House of Councillors. A Supreme Court was established and civil liberties guaranteed. And, completely without international precedent, under Article Nine Japan renounced war and the right to maintain an army, navy, or air force. Historians still cannot determine whether this idea came from MacArthur or the Japanese. Regardless of the source, MacArthur was enthusiastic about the idea, and without his support it would not have flowered.

"The Switzerland of Asia" was how the new antimilitarist Japan was described, people seeing Switzerland as a nation that had successfully kept out of war for centuries while ignoring Switzerland's strongly armed citizen army based on universal military training. Of vast importance to Japan was the destruction of the military class, a powerful elite group in Japanese political society. This was brought about by disarmament and perpetuated by the new Constitution.

Article Thirteen in the new Constitution, prohibits discrimination in political, economic, and social relations because of race,

143

creed, sex, social status, or family origin. This is one of the most explicitly progressive statements on human rights anywhere in law.

The emergence of the new Constitution was "not entirely voluntary," as Colonel Charles Kades of SCAP Government Section dryly remarked. A Japanese joke at the time ran: Two men are talking together. One asks: "Have you seen our new Constitution yet?" The other answers: "No, I didn't know it had been translated into Japanese."

Twenty-one Americans, including four women, wrote the document. One was the charming, highly intelligent twenty-two-year-old Beate Sirota, Viennese-born, who had lived in Japan for ten years and knew its language and culture well, hence her assignment to an unusually responsible job for one so young. Combing the libraries of Tokyo in her research, Sirota drafted the clauses on civil rights. Her work was reviewed and approved by her superiors, ultimately by the Supreme Commander. The General was reportedly "convinced that the place of women in Japan must be brought to a level consistent with that of women in the Western democracies," a confidence that did not extend to entrusting any woman with a high post in the Occupation. More by accident than conviction does Douglas MacArthur emerge as a radical feminist.

How did Article Nineteen emerge unscathed? American women assigned to the lower echelons of SCAP seized the initiative, worked closely with leaders of Japanese women's groups, and overcame the opposition of men—American and Japanese. Much of this is due to the persuasive powers of Beate Sirota. But the process may also illustrate the principle that social change often comes not from the top but from the middle ranks of leadership: those who have access to the top, who can mobilize support, and who are ardent pushers for specific issues. In the case of Article Nineteen, drafters took advantage of the fact that so much else was going on at the time.

So the Japanese got their equal rights amendment long before a concerted effort was made to obtain one in America. American women are still waiting for what Douglas MacArthur delivered up to their Japanese sisters.

New law, of course, could not entirely expunge old habit; legal emancipation did not necessarily mean liberation of women. Discrimination lingers in Japan, but the law stands. If only a declaration of intent, this is important. In the whole Occupation program, probably only land reform had a similar revolutionary impact, bearing a superficial but curious resemblance to the revolution in China, cresting at the same time under radically different circumstances.

The Occupation reformers saw local self-government for Japan not only as desirable but essential: strong local government would stimulate democracy at the very roots of Japanese society. One of them, G. A. Warp, said "We made that assumption even though some of our democratic allies had highly centralized systems and even though the tendency in the United States has been in the direction of greater centralization . . ." particularly during the New Deal era.

The new Constitution with its Diet, Cabinet, and prime minister is more on the British or European model than cut to any American pattern. "We probably went further in the direction of establishing American forms of government in the local sphere than in any other aspect of Japanese life."

Local government in Japan, in modern times at least, had been weak; Tokyo made the decisions. Was this irrational? Was it necessarily dangerous? Japan was a small, compact nation, and in contrast, say, to most European countries, culturally homogeneous. Regionalism was not strong. Whether establishing local autonomy to the degree found in the U.S. was practical or desirable for Japan was a question American reformers seem largely to have overlooked. Paradoxically, however, some of them found that for programs they wanted to carry out nationwide, such as mass inoculations for public health or the development of natural resources, central authority was much more effective than local direction. Moreover, although Americans pushed for local autonomy, they

145

tended to think in terms of a uniform national pattern for all of Japan.

There was a dichotomy between the Occupation force that began as a highly centralized governing body and remained so, and the increasingly decentralized Japanese Government. The Imperial Government in Tokyo was the instrument of American power over the Japanese; the occupiers had chosen to deal exclusively with that body. Consequently, the more that power was diffused from Tokyo, the less the occupiers could do directly, at least by command. But even in the old centralized prewar Japan, Tokyo directed and persuaded; it did not enforce. The American assumption that control of the emperor and the national ministries was all they needed to enable them to exercise their will over the nation was therefore fallacious, even from the start. The Americans overlooked the need for persuasion.

Increasingly the occupiers stumbled in that direction, finding more subtle and effective means of getting the Japanese to do what they wanted. The Americans had reserved the right to intervene directly in public affairs, despite their adherence to the principle of indirect rule. The occupiers did have combat troops, albeit few of them, in the event of Japanese noncompliance, although to have used them in such a case would have been crude and distasteful.

The best and most widely used technique was hortatory: advising and counseling by Occupation officials and visiting experts invited to Japan by the Supreme Commander. This was usually informal and relaxed, allowing give-and-take and the shaping of consensus —very similar to the Japanese way of doing things. Probably more genuine change resulted from this technique than could have come from any other means.

Both sides contributed to the evolving amalgam of ideas and policies. The Americans depended on the Japanese to execute the decisions: The Japanese enacted, the Japanese promulgated, the Japanese enforced the necessary laws. Yet when they wished to resist the American will, they would drag their feet and act only on explicit order from the Supreme Commander. Such abdication was an embarrassment to the Americans, who wanted the Japanese to act as a responsible government and not as a creature of the American Army. Fiat violates the principle of democratic action. To whatever extent the Japanese threatened, tacitly, to indulge in uncooperative behavior, they had power over their nominal master. A fine line existed beyond which the Americans could not push them.

Japan's repressive atmosphere in the 1930s and early 1940s had no more obvious symbol than the policeman. Ubiquitous, officious, and arrogant, he kept the citizen in place. SCAP, aware of the crippling inhibition police power could bring to democratic life, sought to break it in two ways: through reorganizing the police and through limiting police authority in Japanese life. Lewis J. Valentine, former Police Commissioner of New York City, was brought to Japan in the winter of 1946 to give advice. He said his chief aim would be to create a Japanese police force based on "kindness, gentleness, and sympathy . . . along the lines of the New York force."

Lewis J. Valentine, former New York City police commissioner, outlines to the press his plans for reorganizing the Japanese police system.

One critic, a military government specialist, tartly pointed out that for advice on police reform SCAP should have called on a civil liberties lawyer rather than a police administrator. Where the Japanese police could really use direction and assistance was not in the area of efficiency, he remarked. "The police of the average Japanese city have more thorough control over the population of that city than Mr. Valentine ever had over the population of New York City." Where the Japanese police needed help was in arriving at a greater understanding of civil liberties. Cosmetic changes like new uniforms, with sleeve stripes replacing shoulder boards, were not the achievement of democracy.

Valentine himself recognized the problem, recounting to a reporter for the *Pacific Stars and Stripes:*

> The other day I watched an old man of about 65 crossing a street. He was crossing against the signal. The Japanese policeman first whistled at him, then shouted. The old man paid no attention. Maybe he couldn't hear. Anyhow, the policeman ran over and knocked the old man down. The old fellow got up, tipped his hat to the policeman, and walked away. We've got to democratize those police.

Pursuing this ambitious goal, SCAP first had the notorious military police, *kempeitai,* abolished, a decision easy enough to carry out. Any police agencies primarily engaged in enforcing restrictions on civil liberties clearly had to go, and few Japanese were unhappy. Purging eliminated nearly all experienced police officials of high rank, resulting in opportunities throughout the system for fresh blood to flow into vital positions. Subsequently, although the Japanese were slow to move, the Diet passed a Police Law effecting those structural changes recommended by the Americans.

Swept away was the tightly woven framework that allowed the Home Ministry in Tokyo to manage the police from the center of a nationwide web of authority. The police were now decentralized. All towns of five thousand or more were to be responsible for their own police force. And whereas a small independent National Rural

Police was formed, there was no command channel between it and the local urban police forces, except in times of emergency.

All police functions were clearly defined and rigidly limited to maintaining peace and order. No more could the police system be exploited to stifle dissent. No longer could the police harass political meetings or interfere in elections. No longer could a policeman arbitrarily arrest and imprison a potential disturber of the peace.

The functional changes seemed good. But even Americans soon questioned whether the organizational changes were the right ones. The breakup of central authority brought new problems of coordination and financing. Where would small towns, who were simultaneously assuming a new burden of support for schools, find the money to pay their police? Could necessary improvements and regular additions be made to their equipment? And what about training? With urban life suffering from extreme inflation, a large black market, and a general disruption of society, crime burgeoned —although temporarily. Many Japanese believed public order was threatened by the restive Korean minority and the noisy, recently emergent extreme left. The hitherto repressed were now free to speak out and to agitate, which they did.

The police were responsible for maintaining order; there was no other native armed force. And since the Allied forces were merely skeletal, the Occupation authorities depended on the Japanese police more than they would have wanted to admit.

What Americans had sought was a reduction of police power over the individual and a fragmentation of the system so that it would be more like the American. When the occupiers left, it was not at all clear whether these reforms would adhere, but it was certainly apparent the police would play a diminished role in Japanese life. The police chose as their new motto "Respect human rights, keep alert, always be kind and popular." In the new Japan, the policeman had become a public servant.

Politics was the most important reform of the Occupation. Even before the war was over, American planners recognized that Japanese democracy would need sound economic underpinnings: political democracy required economic democracy. Many American officials looked to the Japanese working class as a potentially strong and friendly force in the new Japan they hoped to fashion. An articulate, spirited labor movement could offset the power of big business in Japanese life, which had done so much to stultify democracy. Sustained and encouraged by the great American labor federations, the occupiers brought with them some of the zest and momentum of more than a decade of New Deal labor legislation back home.

Tiny, tough, scrappy Theodore Cohen, appointed chief of SCAP's Labor Division of GHQ, spoke in January 1946 of a "double goal" for American labor policy in Japan: encouraging the growth of democratic unions while keeping them free from the

An estimated three hundred thousand people representing labor organizations from all over Japan assemble outside the Imperial Palace on May 1, 1946, in the first May Day celebration in ten years.

predatory talons of the Communists. To that menace, American unions were keenly sensitive; they had been battling Communist attempts at infiltration since the 1920s.

Japanese workers had much to be unhappy about. They had suffered bitterly from long hours, severe health hazards, and miserable wages. Their struggle to better their lot had been ruthlessly fought by employers, backed by a repressive government. That Japanese labor unions grew phenomenally during the heady new freedom—and the appalling economic conditions—of the first few months of the Occupation is therefore not surprising. The labor movement benefited directly from the release of all political prisoners in October 1945, many of whom had been union leaders before the war. By the end of 1946, four and a half million Japanese had joined unions. Unions seemed to offer the promise of a better life, and their healthy growth defused grievances that might otherwise have exploded into violence.

Yet organized Japanese labor emerged in this new era with an intensely political, militantly leftist character, not anticipated by the Americans. After all, the American labor movement had consistently sought economic rather than political goals; few members advocated change by violent means as the mainstream remained moderate. Trade unions and collective bargaining, coupled with laws to assure workers decent standards of pay, safe working conditions, and economic security, had been the American pattern, one the occupiers anticipated for Japan. But Japanese unions, enterprise-based rather than craft-based, were aggressively political, their behavior intensified by the hostile actions of the conservative Japanese Government, whose Prime Minister Yoshida did not trouble to conceal his contempt for the labor movement.

The climax of radical action for Japanese labor during the Occupation years was the threat of a general strike, which was to take place on February 1, 1947. No transport, no electricity, and no food would be the consequences, obviously intolerable to SCAP. The danger pointed up an essential quandary of the occupiers: on the one hand America wanted Japan to pursue democracy freely, but America could not permit Japan to dissolve into revolutionary chaos.

Late in January MacArthur warned union leadership that he would not countenance a nationwide strike. After several tense days, and only two and a half hours before the scheduled start, the strike leaders yielded to MacArthur's will. Thereafter the political appeal of radical labor action appeared to wane, the Communist party suffered at the polls, and Japan did not undergo revolution.

Japanese labor became increasingly estranged from the Occupation authorities. To the Japanese, the occupiers soon seemed more interested in repressing than encouraging labor unions. Yet Theodore Cohen and others at GHQ prided themselves on cultivating friendships with labor leaders. Cohen remembers:

> The high point, to me at least, was the time a delegation from the new geisha union arrived officially to inform Gen. MacArthur, that is, me his surrogate, of their new organization. Perched on six-inch-high *geta,* with towering hairdos festooned with trinkets and little bells, their faces elaborately painted white with red-bordered eyes, and clad in the most colorful and ornate kimonos, in sharp contrast to the drab attire of the ordinary Japanese in the street outside, they paraded in stately fashion through the hall towards our building elevators and up to my office. All work in the Economic and Scientific Section stopped, offices were emptied into the halls to watch the spectacle. The three ladies accomplished in five minutes what all the Japanese [labor] . . . attacks had failed to do, put a good part of MacArthur's headquarters out of action.

The union movement continued to grow, to the ultimate benefit of the worker. Unremitting pressure on employers brought swelling wages, which meant the steady expansion of Japan' domestic consumer market. This market was a major reason for Japan's subsequent economic boom.

Inflation and an inefficient tax-collecting system gave the occupiers powerful incentive to take up tax reform in their program. Without a rational tax system, recovery of the Japanese economy seemed unlikely. Hence the telephone rang in the Columbia University office of Professor Carl Shoup on an October afternoon in 1948. The caller was Harold Moss, formerly of the Bureau of Internal Revenue (IRS), now of SCAP, Tokyo, visiting Washington in order to recruit a group of tax experts to examine the Japanese case, to diagnose it, and to prescribe for it.

Carl Shoup agreed to head what would be the last mission of visiting experts to Japan during the Occupation, stipulating that he be allowed to choose his colleagues and, with an eye on academic schedules, that they need not come until late in the spring. MacArthur had wanted them immediately but accepted the terms. He got a mission of extremely high caliber; Shoup had an eye for quality. Shoup also exacted from the Supreme Commander the significant promise that his report would be published both in English and Japanese—anyone in Japan who was interested could therefore read it. Furthermore, it would prove extremely helpful later to other American technical missions overseas, as a guide to running a consultative mission as well as for its own specific information on tax systems.

"In a pressure cooker environment," Shoup fondly recalls, "the seven of us worked, ate, and slept Japan and its tax problems for some five months or so; we were billeted in the old Imperial Hotel, and no wives being allowed to come along, we simply lived taxation at meal times and all through the day." Not that the visitors remained in their hotel rooms or even in Tokyo. They chose to get out of the capital and see things for themselves. At their disposal were chauffered automobiles and even a private train.

Stopping the car by the roadside to chat with a farmer tilling his rice, or, like Eleanor Roosevelt, going down into the bowels of a coal mine to talk with miners, the investigators gleaned impressions and gathered information they otherwise might have missed. Shoup talked to a wide variety of taxpayers and also conferred with professional tax people. The Japanese were fascinated; they liked Shoup, and his activities received wide press coverage.

MacArthur opened the country to the mission, giving them a free

153

hand. The Japanese, in economic chaos, were eagerly receptive to fresh wisdom. The Ministry of Finance supplied excellent interpreters, translators, and sources of information—young men of high technical competence, whose English was good and whose minds were first-rate. Special interests could not lobby the visitors, to try to shape or influence their deliberations. In short, conditions for the mission were ideal.

What the mission recommended was a tax system not unlike the British or Canadian. Of course the mission could not draw heavily on the Japanese experience because its members, with the exception of Jerome B. Cohen, had no special knowledge of Japan. All they knew had come from a few books, such as *The Chrysanthemum and the Sword,* or from what they were soaking up in the course of their assignment.

Although Carl Shoup believed that certain universals were applicable to Japan, he was struck by similarities between Americans and Japanese. What worked in America should work in Japan, he thought. Since diligence and civic pride could be tapped in both cases, the citizen could be trusted to compute and pay his own income tax.

Like other experts at the time, Shoup was pessimistic about Japan's economic future: the problem of what to export and how to sustain a rapidly growing population. "Yet whatever we did," he modestly says now, "it wasn't bad enough to block the subsequent success of the Japanese economy." Among tax people Shoup was on the liberal side, and he gave the Japanese an equitable system, providing few loopholes. As someone said at the time, America would benefit if Shoup had headed a mission to the U.S.

When the mission got back home in the fall of 1949, their report having been written and submitted before the members left Japan, they were somewhat taken aback to learn that their recommendations had been accepted virtually entirely. "Did we do a good job?" they asked themselves, "everything we ought to have done?"

Shoup went on to advise others; Venezuelans and Liberians would both benefit from his Japan experience. But Japan remained

154

a high point in his professional career. And he is remembered by the Japanese with respect and admiration. The tax system in any nation is likely to change in thirty years, and Japan is no exception. Yet "the spirit or essence" of the Shoup recommendations remains as a tremendous testimony to his acumen.

Nothing was more hotly discussed and less successfully resolved among Occupation reform policymakers than the matter of breaking up big business in Japan. At best, many Americans saw the combines, or *zaibatsu* ("money cliques"), as an impediment to democracy; at worst they saw them as a partner of the military in bringing about the war. Before the war, three or four of these combines had achieved a concentration of economic power in private hands probably without equal in any other major nation of the world.

Economist Eleanor Hadley, vigorous and scholarly "combine crusher" for SCAP, points out that the 1944 share in the Japanese economy of only one of these cartels, the Mitsubishi, was comparable to an American conglomerate of "U.S. Steel, GM, Standard Oil of New Jersey, Alcoa, Douglas Aircraft, duPont, Sun Shipbuilding, Allis-Chalmers, Westinghouse, A.T.&T., RCA, IBM, U.S. Rubber, Sea Island Sugar, Dole Pineapple, U.S. Lines, Grace Lines, National City Bank, Metropolitan Life Insurance, Woolworth Stores, and the Statler Hotels." To complete the parallel, the putative conglomerate would be owned by the Mellons or the Rockefellers.

Orchestrating these many diverse instruments of commerce and industry required administrative competence of the highest order. Japan's struggle to survive in the world market, and the fierce competition among the *zaibatsu* themselves, kept Japanese business leadership at concert pitch. But Americans, understandably perhaps, were quicker to condemn than to appreciate the qualities of their recent foe, in this sphere as in others.

Most Americans regarded the *zaibatsu* as both a social and an economic evil, an obstacle to everything they wanted to achieve in Japan. Ideally, they said, competitive markets should exist everywhere, not only for their economic efficiency but also for their social value. Critics noted the ferocious exploitation of labor upon which the *zaibatsu* rested; they saw immense wealth lying in few hands. One need not be a Marxist to be made uneasy by such enormous aggregations of economic power.

Eugene Dooman, on the other hand, argued that such large concentrations of capital were vital to the successful functioning of Japan's economy, and that Americans should leave them alone. A *Fortune* magazine article, implicitly agreeing with Dooman, blandly explained that the *zaibatsu* were not at all sinister; they were simply "professionally managed investment trust funds."

American attitudes toward big business in Japan, and what should be done about it, primarily reflected judgments on what the relationship between business and government ought to be. Some people were aware that even in America big business was not fully tamed, despite the Sherman and the Clayton acts. Ardent New Dealers were particularly hostile to the Japanese *zaibatsu,* seeing in them a worse version of what they had been combating at home; and although the New Deal had slackened in America, perhaps its spirit could be rekindled abroad. In such fashion Japan could enjoy an economy more democratic than America's!

How one interpreted recent Japanese history also shaped attitudes toward the *zaibatsu.* Had big business willingly cooperated with the military clique, or had it simply been dragged into the war along with the rest of the Japanese? In the drive for expansion overseas during the 1930s, *Fortune* asserted that the great combines "were the only important and active opponents of the Japanese military." Others pointed out the difficulty of showing that big business did not benefit from the swelling armaments industry, which had so much to gain from an aggressive foreign policy.

Americans proclaimed that the purpose of their antitrust program was to stimulate democracy, not to punish anyone. In fact, although many were purged, not one business leader was brought to trial as a war criminal. Yet there were some, among them MacArthur's political advisor, William Sebald, who interpreted the antitrust policy evolved by the Occupation as punitive. "Vindictive, destructive, and futile," were his words.

The issue raised some interesting ethical questions: Should businessmen and industrialists be held responsible for the moral consequences of their actions? And could a "business is business" attitude be justified by those who may have wanted war profits, if not the war that came along with the money?

Specific goals of the Occupation program were to break up the holding companies and interlocking directorates that allowed a few men to control vast resources; to eliminate the influence and wealth of the great *zaibatsu* families by forcing them to sell their stock to the public; and to enact antitrust laws to prevent reemergence of the old system. In short, the American reformers sought to establish and encourage free enterprise in the Japanese economy because they believed economic democracy was integral to political democracy.

Regulating Japanese business was an enormously intricate matter, one Americans could not handle without Japanese help. But the Japanese leadership was little interested in changing things. The *zaibatsu,* working closely with the Government, had done well in competitive international trade. Nor did public opinion seem to favor economic deconcentration as it had other Occupation reforms. The clientele was lacking. Who, for example, had money to buy shares divested by the *zaibatsu* families? Other issues interested the Japanese more.

As the economic reform program faltered, criticism of it flourished. Back home, in Congress and business circles, voices rose suggesting that the Occupation's antitrust policy was jeopardizing the recovery of the Japanese economy, and had perhaps even worse implications. If both the theory and the practice of deconcentration were successfully developed and employed by the Occupation reformers in Japan, was there not a real danger of these ideas and techniques creeping back to American shores? This did not happen. In truth the great age for the American conglomerate was yet to come.

James Lee Kauffman, a lawyer who had taught law at Tokyo Imperial University from 1911 to 1916 and thereafter practiced in Japan for many years, published a brief article in *Newsweek* in December 1947, blasting American economic policy in Japan. Later at the Council on Foreign Relations in New York City, Kauffman charged that American economic policy in Japan was

> . . . based on the distribution of private property to certain specified classes of the public with little or no compensation to owners . . . this policy does not conform with our ideas of the rights of property, or with the organization of the American economy. It will lead to socialism in Japan, despite the fact that General MacArthur feels it will save Japan from socialism by promoting free competitive enterprise . . . it goes beyond trust-busting. It amounts to the uncontrolled breaking up of the Japanese economy, a policy the American voter has already repudiated for this country . . . the U.S.A. has adopted this economic policy for Japan in order to appease Russia.

Kauffman continued, criticizing not General MacArthur but the State Department for

> failing to consult with businessmen, missionaries, and teachers who had been in Japan. Economic policy for Japan is still being kept a secret from the American people, despite the fact that Japan is costing the American taxpayer unnecessary millions. The policy is also suspect due to the type of men who have been attracted to Japan to operate it. They are bureaucrats and economic theorists, who are incapable of handling their jobs satisfactorily due to their lack of knowledge about business.
>
> The effect of this policy in Japan is to make the country economically impotent, which increases popular dissatisfaction with the occupation. As a result, a crisis is approaching which, if not averted, will destroy all the achievements of the occupation.

Those Americans favoring trust-busting in Japan were disappointed by the overall failure of the Occupation to do much to change the domination of the Japanese economy by big business.

Yet compared with the slowness and difficulty of reform in America, where the trusts were not as strong as they were in Japan, the results were hardly surprising. Not looking to the Japanese, critics tended to blame American business for exercising its influence to inhibit or prevent reform. Cold War politics also muscled in as a reason for the slowdown of reform.

Kauffman supplied bullets for the guns of these critics by asserting that the policy of business deconcentration would cause production to drop, at least for a time, and was "leading Japan to Communism. It will prevent the U.S. from using Japan as a buffer against the Soviet Union." Eleanor Hadley asked why Kauffman and others of his stripe should denounce the attempts of the Occupation reformers to strengthen freely competitive capitalism in Japan. To use Kauffman's words, there was certainly nothing "un-American" about the changes, Hadley suggests. If anything, she argues, the proposed reforms were "too American," inappropriate for small and impoverished Japan, which needed careful economic planning.

After many months of hard work developing a reform program, much of it remained on paper—evidence of General MacArthur's initial excitement but weakening resolve. By late 1949 only twenty-eight out of eighty-two holding companies had been dissolved, only 27 percent of securities held by corporations had been sold.

The leadership had been purged, with fifty-six top executives forced out, but close personal ties in Japanese business were practically impossible to control. As in political life, former leaders could still exercise their influence; it was the man, not the office, that was important. And anyway, the new men had essentially the same viewpoints. Thus in the long run all this did not matter very much.

But the upheaval of defeat, severe inflation, and a tax on capital did cause major redistribution of wealth in Japan. Nothing like the old *zaibatsu* families remain today. New companies such as Sony, Matsushita, and Honda, capitalizing on the extraordinarily rapid growth of the Japanese economy, have risen and prospered, resulting in an industrial organization extremely different from the old *zaibatsu* system. And that which has emerged is one of the most powerful economies in the world. This has not impeded the functioning of what the Japanese have evolved as their pattern of democracy.

Japan had an agrarian problem, which was important if for no other reason than because so many Japanese were farmers. The Japanese were aware of the problem, as were the Americans. It was both economic and social. The tenant farmer in particular had been poor and oppressed, a major reason for his wretched condition being the landlord system. "Farmers should neither live nor die," the old saying went; or "the farmer is like the sesame seed, the more you squeeze the more you get."

And the tenant farmer's lot had not improved. Nearly half of all employed Japanese worked as farmers, getting a high return for the area of land they worked but a low one for the amount of time they put in. The prosperous peasant was the exception. Almost 70 percent of Japan's farmers rented part of the land they cultivated; about 50 percent rented more than half of what they worked. This tenancy rate had grown rapidly since the last part of the nineteenth century, along with sprouting factories and other dramatic changes in Japanese life.

The tenant farmer had no written contract and little security. Customarily he paid more than half his yield as rent in kind. After paying for fertilizer and tools, he usually had only about 30 percent left, a marginal livelihood.

Among Americans in the Occupation, there was a widespread belief that agrarian discontent had nurtured militarism, that "the social and economic condition of the Japanese countryside was a powerful causal factor in bringing about Japan's aggressive policies in Asia." Paternalism, authoritarianism, and rigid conformity, all antidemocratic traits, had flourished in the confining atmosphere of village life. Americans used the words "feudal" and "medieval" to describe it. How could democracy be successfully planted in such soil without first uprooting these patterns of rural society? Giving the land to the tenant cultivator was a way to encourage change.

160

Robert A. Fearey, a State Department official who had once served in Japan as private secretary to Ambassador Grew, toward the end of the war wrote a memorandum, with Wolf I. Ladejinsky of the Department of Agriculture, on the desirability of Japanese land reform. If Fearey had not been transferred to the staff of George Atcheson, Jr., first State Department advisor in Tokyo to General MacArthur, and if Fearey had not brought his memorandum along and given it to Atcheson who sent it to MacArthur, the paper might simply have gone in the files, forever buried.

But it caught the eye and imagination of the Supreme Commander, whose sense of historic drama was moved by the possibilities land reform presented. Those Americans who came to be directly involved in the program felt that General MacArthur was particularly interested in what they were doing. Later the General was to remark, in one of those grand historical comparisons he so liked to make, that the Japanese land reform was comparable to that of the Gracchi in the Roman era.

The comparison is perhaps too modest. More than one third of the cultivated land in Japan changed ownership, and 30 percent of the Japanese people were directly affected. Thirty million plots of land were bought, thirty million were sold—and it was all done in two years.

Washington had its reservations about anything as drastic and sweeping as that outlined by Fearey and Ladejinsky. Eugene Dooman, again, and Joseph Ballantine, his fellow conservative senior official in the State Department during the war years, were appalled. Dooman felt that redistributing land would penalize the frugal middle class who had amassed these holdings. Ballantine argued, "There's no way in which you can shuffle land ownership about so that 6 million agricultural families can make a decent living out of 16 million acres of agricultural land," putting his finger on the basic Japanese agrarian problem. Land ownership could not solve that. But SCAP in Tokyo boldly took the initiative for reform.

From the Fearey document in late November 1945, two young men in the Civil Education and Information Section of GHQ quarried the necessary data for a paper ordering the Japanese Government to take prompt action to effect land ownership changes. What the two young Americans, a newspaperman and a radio scriptwriter, "knew about the technical problem of land reform in Japan could have been balanced on the end of a chopstick." But their ignorance was of no consequence. American initiative is what mattered.

The Japanese worked out the details and the Diet passed legislation under which the Government ultimately bought 4.5 million acres. With regional variations, nonresidents had to sell all their farmland, noncultivating residents all but 2.5 acres, and owner-cultivators all but 7.5 acres. Forest land was unaffected. The prosperous kept their woodlands, thus softening the impact of the reform.

Sale amounted to virtual confiscation because of the impact of galloping inflation on the value of the bonds given as payment to the landlords. Since the Government was unable to buy and pay for all the land at one time, the process was stretched out, yet the price remained the same. Land prices represented preinflationary values, a fraction of current worth. One estimate was that whereas in 1939 a *tan* of land (approximately a quarter of an acre) would buy over three thousand packages of cigarettes, nine years later the 1939 price of that land would buy only thirteen packages.

Opposition smoldered and emotions ran high; landowners tried desperately to play on traditional peasant subservience to authority and fear of responsibility. But without one life lost and with little violence, the reform in Japan was carried out—a reform that was probably as radical a change in the landholding pattern as in any of the Communist states. Of course the Japanese emphasis was on private, individual ownership; land was not taken for the state or for collective use. The Japanese Communist party bitterly opposed the change because it was not in the Marxist pattern and because they were excluded from leading it.

The reform did not entail destruction of a rich rural landholding aristocracy. Japan did not have such a class. For the most part tenants simply became owners of land they were already cultivating, and many landlords remained farmers. The end of tenancy was what the people clearly wanted. Thanks to the new freedom to speak out, they could say so, and no one was prepared to fight the express will of both the public and the Occupation forces.

It was feared that splitting up land holdings might cause lower production. Land reform in Japan had to avoid any such decrease, as had so often followed land reform in the Soviet Union, for example, and in the nations of Eastern Europe. The Occupation could not risk a delay in reconstruction or the political instability that a decrease in food production might cause. But in Japan smaller holdings did not result in smaller crops; production grew substantially.

Japan still had a shortage of land, at least for existing agricultural technology, and most farmers had to work hard for a decent living. Nonetheless, the Japanese were close to being able to produce at home all the food they needed; close enough that Edwin Pauley, when proposing reparations, optimistically thought self-sufficiency in food should be a Japanese objective.

Land reform not only corrected a social injustice, but the Occupation authorities had also scored a propaganda coup that could be exploited in America's growing ideological rivalry with the Soviet Union. Land reform certainly diminished the appeal of Communism to the Japanese; the new "landed proletariat" had no interest in it.

Americans could now speculate about the applicability elsewhere of what was being done in Japan. China, for example. Wolf Ladejinsky suggested that American money being spent fighting Communism there would be better used for land reform, as "the land reform of Japan is the seed from which can sprout a new agrarian order in the Orient." And Laurence Hewes, a land reform expert among the occupiers, argued that the centrality of land reform in the Occupation program "gave a stature and renown to American policy that reached beyond the confines of Japan because of its profound significance to all of Asia." A more accurate assessment, however, would probably be that each Asian nation had unique problems to which the case of Japan was not necessarily applicable.

For almost all Americans, it would seem, land reform was an attractive issue carrying no dangerous ideological overtones, no tinge of menace to any established order in the U.S. Rather, it appealed strongly to nostalgia, to the romantic Jeffersonian image of the stoutly independent citizen-farmer, bedrock of the democratic state. In Japan's case, since by terms of the settlement the wealthy were in effect punished if they happened to be rural landlords, an element of class conflict was injected into the matter. This pleased the more radical among the occupiers, yet was not sufficiently conspicuous to exercise the feelings of more conservative types, such as the General himself.

Unlike so many Occupation reforms, redistributing land was concrete, not abstract, and was positive instead of negative. There was nothing theoretical about it, and it was rapidly carried through to completion. Many people benefited; Japan became a nation of owner-farmers. Unlike much of the rest of the Occupation program, there was very little criticism of land reform either from Japanese or others once it had been completed. Even those who had lost out, the landlords, seemed rapidly to shed any bitterness. And the Occupation immediately gained not only a large constituency, for the new owners had a vested interest in preserving the change, but also a psychological momentum for other changes they wanted to initiate.

Looking back a decade later, the British sociologist R. P. Dore, could write that there had been, in his judgment, "a considerable increase in the sum of human happiness in Japanese villages" as a result of these reforms. Although Americans could be well pleased about this, they thought themselves more innovative than they really were. The Japanese had a history of Diet legislation to reduce tenancy, and wartime laws had lowered tenant rents. The Japanese had paved the way for change.

MacArthur declared that Japan had become "the world's great

Two GIs ride a Japanese trolley in Sendai, Japan.

laboratory for an experiment in the liberation of a people from totalitarian military rule and for the liberalization of government from within." What Americans were doing there not only had implications for people and policy elsewhere, but the Supreme Commander himself could use the laboratory for experimenting with national political leadership.

Old Japan hand James Kauffman thought it "impossible to expect that any foreign nation can walk into a country and completely reform it." That he was reasonably satisfied with Japan as it was may have had some bearing on his opinion. Scholar Harold Quigley was no revolutionary either, but for a different reason. He cautioned: "Neither we nor other peoples may elect to impose ourselves as mentors upon the highly cultured Oriental peoples. In that view we exhibit the same sense of superiority that is implicit in our hurtful immigration laws. Only as invited advisors, freely sought and sincerely wanted, can we function effectively." Kauffman and Quigley both remained in the minority.

165

Using its "godlike power" to change Japan was the goal of the Occupation; bringing the Japanese into "complete consonance with American policy and practice," is how one occupier defined his aim. But U.S. ignorance and ethnocentrism led Americans to exaggerate both the reach of the changes and their influence in bringing them about. Only a few Americans perceived Japanese reform as growing in a natural organic way, albeit accelerated by defeat and the prodding of the Occupation—that is, developing and progressing from what was already present. For all of the major and successful changes wrought during the Occupation, one can find sources in Japan's own recent experience.

To these Americans the prospects for Japanese doing much for themselves were unpromising. No group was harder hit by the war than the urban middle class, from which one might expect the leadership for reform to come. Food, shelter, and a job were their concerns.

There had been no politically significant defections in Japan (unlike Germany or Italy), even during the last terrible months of the war. The masses were stoic and overcome by apathy. Those people who perhaps could have come to power did not choose to make the effort. After the war, outside the ranks of the Japanese Communist party (which was a small minority), there was no thirst for dramatic, revolutionary change, no passion to be released by the trauma of defeat.

To the Americans, few Japanese appeared angry at "The System." Not a promising situation, one might say, for forging a new democratic state and society. The American theory that democracies are less apt to make war than other forms of government had occasioned little speculation. Sir George Sansom raised the question. So did American diplomat Edwin Martin, author of a 1948 report, "The Allied Occupation of Japan." Martin said that Americans know little about what causes a nation to be peaceful, yet "we cannot help but be strongly impressed by the fact that the United States, the nation about whose peaceful intentions we are most confident, is a great democracy."

166

Occupation reformers identified American democracy with such characteristics as free enterprise and commitment to international peace without asking whether these were truly parts of the American tradition. Americans were in pursuit of an ideal, not a reality. Such thinking caused historian Perry Miller to observe shrewdly, after a summer's visit to Japan in 1952, that "the policy of our Occupation was an effort to make of Japan a new Middle West—not, of course, the Middle West as it is, or in fact ever was, but as it perpetually dreams of being."

9

"Do You Have Any Kimonos?"

THE OCCUPATION involved far more Americans directly with East Asia than ever before in the American national experience. We cannot know exactly how many people went to Japan, but perhaps close to two million. In the first tense weeks after the Atsugi landing, the greatest number of American troops to be in Japan at any one time arrived to take up garrison duties. Thereafter the number fell off until the Korean War, when Japan became both a staging ground for the United Nations forces and a haven, a favorite spot for battle-weary troops on leave for rest and recreation. Throughout the eighty months of the Occupation period, the Army maintained an average of slightly more than one hundred thousand troops on duty in Japan. They were there for anywhere from a few weeks to years. The Navy, Air Force, and civilians swelled these numbers of sojourning Americans. And large numbers of women and children were there as dependents.

Each American had his or her own Japan, reflecting the infinite variety of tastes and knowledge among the occupiers. The worlds of the GI, of the high-ranking SCAP official, and of the diplomat's wife teaching in a Japanese girls' school were vastly different. Moreover nothing was static; the biggest change probably occurred around 1948 when the Japanese were no longer so desperately impoverished and when many Americans had their families with

168

GIs on a Tokyo street bargain with a former Japanese soldier selling knickknacks.

them, transforming the Occupation from what had been a predominantly male warrior society into a more normal, if still transient community.

Americans came to Japan from all parts of the U.S., bearing a wide range of background, learning, and viewpoints. Even within headquarters itself, the heterogeneity was rich; Wall Street lawyer, YMCA worker, New Deal bureaucrat, career Army officer, and Iowa agronomist all rubbed elbows. Some of the sojourners and their wives had never traveled before, others were cosmopolitan; most had never been out of the U.S. before. Few indeed knew what it was like to spend time in a society differing in race, culture, and religion from mainstream America.

Americans may still have thought of their country as a melting pot from whence emerged an alloyed but firmly Anglo-Saxon Christian society; America's leaders referred to their people in this manner, and those who were not Anglo-Saxon or Christian went along with it. But actually the nation was more heterogeneous than the melting pot image would suggest, and the Occupation reflected this diversity. The Americans in Occupied Japan were not a cohesive colonial elite like, say, the British in India. Nor were they an aristocratic presence. Glitter and starch were notably scarce; MacArthur's tarnished cap and tieless open collar said it all.

One such diversity was ethnic. Coincidentally a number of German-born Americans—Judge Alfred Oppler, Generals Walter Krueger and Charles Willoughby (né von Teppsche-Weidenbach) —held important positions in the hierarchy of the occupiers, furnishing a certain sophistication to American policies. Another diversity was religious; Oppler and Theodore Cohen, for example, were Jews. In a different way, the American presence in Japan was enhanced by blacks, from whom the Japanese received a glimpse of American racial prejudice at work.

Blacks in the Army were primarily restricted to serving as support troops, not infantry or artillery; they were segregated, suffering the same sorts of discrimination they endured in the U.S. Separate but unequal was the pattern of their life. Few whites seemed at all perturbed. John Embree, the anthropologist, was horrified to hear an instructor at one of the Army schools remark that "he saw no harm in a Civil Affairs officer being subject to racial prejudice."

To black Americans in Japan, racial issues were more important than any other problem. The general unhappiness of blacks with Army life usually focused on specific grievances such as lack of proper recreational facilities, accurately attributed to racial discrimination. They felt the large number of southern officers in the Army made discrimination worse. White troops generally were well looked after, with their snack bars, swimming pools, barber shops, and clubs. Black troops often lacked these amenities, and pent-up tensions would periodically explode into violence. Off base, fueled with Saturday night booze, white and black would go after each other before crowds of interested Japanese bystanders.

Most Japanese learned only indirectly of the racial problem in American life. Americans, whites anyway, did not talk much about it. Films distributed by SCAP, even those aimed at showing the Japanese how Americans lived, depicted only whites.

In the early days of the Occupation, one black GI wrote home that "the Japanese . . . show no signs of having been bitten by the virus of racial prejudice. . . ." He was too optimistic. The next month a black weekly, the *Pittsburgh Courier,* felt moved to say: "The Japanese [are] looking down on the colored soldiers as inferior because they see them discriminated against by their fellow Americans. . . . Here is the first lesson in 'democracy' and we may be sure that the Japanese, apt as usual, are learning it."

This may have been partially correct, but the Japanese did not need to be taught anything on this score by white Americans. They had long had their own prejudices, including an aversion to "black" skin, prizing light complexion for feminine beauty. And other physical characteristics attributed to blacks were traditionally viewed with disfavor by the Japanese. Little opportunity for showing the depth of these feelings occurred until the advent of mixed-blood children, offspring of the Occupation, of whom three to four thousand were born of black American fathers and Japanese moth-

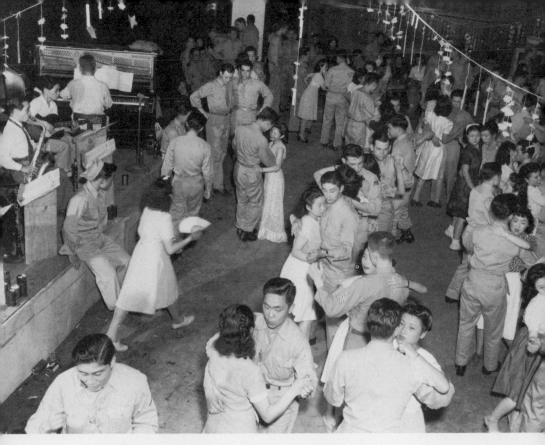

Civilians and soldiers, attached to the Allied Translator and Interpreter section, attend weekly dance for members of their unit—a popular activity in Tokyo planned for the nisei.

ers. More than their half-white counterparts, who numbered more than twenty thousand, they suffered from neglect, discrimination, and poverty. A social problem, an embarrassing reminder of something most people would like to ignore or forget, the black Japanese are shunned by almost all other Japanese, except on the stage where some have found acceptance as performing artists, their exoticism attracting the plaudits of the general public.

Most conspicuous among those who cared to help either group of interracial children was Miki Sawada, wealthy wife of a prominent Japanese diplomat. Over the years she took in hundreds of these abandoned unfortunates, housing and rearing them in her Oiso villa, "The Elizabeth Saunders Home."

Another racial group among Americans in Japan was the *nisei,*

172

second-generation Americans of Japanese descent. Without their language skills the occupiers would have been severely handicapped, as few other Americans had any facility in Japanese. *Nisei* usually spoke Japanese because they had been taught it in order to communicate with their elders; grandparents seldom knew any English at all. Often the young did not read Japanese. Yet their ability to speak it, so unusual among Americans and so useful in Japan, catapulted *nisei* into the role of "experts" on Japanese culture.

Until after the war, most Japanese-Americans were poor and few were highly educated. Among the *nisei* there was little interest in Japanese history or civilization. Like other immigrant children in America, they had discarded their parents' culture. Despite white prejudice and the wartime detention centers, most of them were "200 percent Americans."

On both sides, American and Japanese, the level of expectation for *nisei* was extremely high, indeed impossible to achieve. Japanese

Nisei *Japanese interpreters of the linguist section attend class on Japanese characters.*

expected *nisei* to be sensitive to the nuances of their ancestral culture. Because they looked Japanese, at least when they were not in motion (their walk was invariably American), they were expected to behave accordingly. Naturally they did not, and they were resented for it. That the *nisei* were privileged to be among the victors seemed especially galling to the Japanese.

Augmenting the diversity of Americans in Japan was the shifting character of the garrison troops. The first were combat veterans with a certain maturity. They were under no self-imposed obligation to prove their virility. Pragmatists for the most part, they got along well with the Japanese, and the switch from fighting to occupying seemed amazingly easy for them. It was as if having fought the Japanese hard, they subsequently felt a bond with them. Mutual respect led to camaraderie. In the hyperbole of the Supreme Commander, "The American combat soldier came, with his fine sense of self-respect, self-confidence and self-control. [The Japanese] . . . felt his spiritual quality—a spiritual quality which truly reflected the highest training of the American home. . . ."

Americans back home liked the tales of GIs befriending undernourished Japanese urchins with gifts of chocolate bars, or coercing Japanese men to give seats to Japanese women on crowded trolleys. The stories reinforced the American belief in their own moral goodness, the assumption that they had as a nation a greater impulse for kindness, generosity, and affection than other people.

But there was a darker side as well to American behavior in Japan: the soldier driving his jeep rapidly down a street crowded with people on foot, deriving evident pleasure watching them scurry out of his way; senior Army officers running the red lights on the Ginza on their way home for lunch, a common and frightening sight. Or the young corporal standing on a street corner, deliberately throwing away a half-smoked cigarette in order to see several Japanese men older than he indecorously scramble for it.

By the end of 1946 most of the combat veterans had departed. For the GI, relations with the Japanese became more formal and regulated. Gone were the insouciant days when an American Army

Two soldiers from New York greet each other on a street corner in Tokyo that they have made familiar to themselves.

major, soon to become a college professor, could choose to ride a crowded train from Tokyo up to Gotemba perched on the cowcatcher of the locomotive, carrying food to give to Japanese friends there. Japanese girls no longer lived in Army billets. GIs could no longer legally give away American food and other goods. On the trains, special first-class cars appeared, with accommodations restricted to Allied Occupation personnel. The troops rode in spacious comfort, sometimes only two or three to an entire car, in the best equipment the Japanese railways could offer. The Japanese were jammed into dilapidated, often windowless, unheated coaches.

The "high-school commandos" among the later American GI arrivals in Japan "had to show they were tough," recalls one witness. "They would deliberately do things that I hope they're ashamed of now." But much of this was sporadic and unpremeditated. These were ordinary people put in extraordinary circumstance. They were often very young and immature, far from home, without the usual constraints, surrounded by an alien culture, and in an unaccustomed position of authority and affluence. That their record was mixed should not be surprising.

Language loomed as a formidable barrier between Americans and Japanese during the Occupation period. Americans had neglected language training in the schools and colleges, even European languages. Few Americans, unless they were immigrants or scholars, spoke a foreign tongue with any fluency. America's geographical isolation, its wealth and power, had enabled Americans to maintain a "complacent indifference" to foreign languages and cultures. Even when traveling abroad, Americans rarely tried to communicate in a foreign language. The war had done something to break down this parochialism, but even those Americans in Occupied Japan who acknowledged the desirability of learning Japanese were discouraged because of what they heard about its difficulty. Also, intensive language study demanded a lot of time.

The language of the Occupation was English. The American expectation was that the Japanese would rise to the challenge of

Tokyo streets were assigned names, usually letters or numbers, to help Americans find their way around. The Japanese paid no attention to them; they did not need them.

communicating in English, despite the fact that Americans were the ones who felt they had something to say. They had won the war, and the Japanese acceded to their wishes. Anyway, the Japanese tended to think that no foreigner could really learn their language even if he tried, and so they were prepared to indulge Americans as fully as they could. They were much more determined to learn English than Americans were to learn Japanese, and the Americans accepted that determination.

Australian W. Macmahon Ball said he "had a good enough sense of my own limitations not to attempt to learn the Japanese language." And even people of European background, accustomed to mastering other tongues, despaired of Japanese. General Charles Willoughby was an exception; he picked up a working knowledge of the language. But Judge Oppler, who was fluent in at least two languages, declared he was too old to learn Japanese. Did his characterization of Japan as a "less advanced and oriental civiliza-

177

tion" have anything to do with this reluctance?

Of course many of the occupiers conscientiously studied Japanese, some even becoming quite proficient. GIs with Japanese girlfriends picked up a lot of the language. Those Americans who knew or learned Japanese found they had many opportunities to meet and mingle with Japanese people. But for most Americans in Japan the barrier remained, effectively cutting off the heavy majority from the Japanese world. For them, entry to that world was only on Japanese terms.

In the Occupation years a crude mixture of basic English was sometimes used interlarded with Japanese words and phrases, often in corrupted pronunciation. "Japlish," as it was contemptuously called, was employed more by the Japanese, particularly women, than anyone else. To both Japanese and American, the user was branded uneducated. Yet we can only applaud the initiative, good humor, and determination stimulating these people to reach out as best they could to another culture.

GI corruptions of Japanese phrases became popular with some Japanese, who took them up with gusto. In turn, Americans naïvely thought they were using Japanese idiom because they heard Japanese using it, when in fact they were merely repeating corruptions of their own making.

The nonsense ditty "Moshi, Moshi, Ano Ne," nothing more than common Japanese vocal pauses sung to the tune of "London Bridge Is Falling Down," which had been around since the 1920s, soared to new popularity. For a while this anthem was performed regularly by a Japanese female trio over the radio on the "Tokyo Mose" show of the Far East Network. Another song of authentic Japanese origin, popular with Americans as well, was "China Night," although Americans did not know it by that name. When "Shina no Yoru" (the Japanese title) became "She Ain't Got No Yoyo," bar girls began singing the American words.

Few Japanese spoke English well, but they were masters at pretending to understand the language even when remote from doing so. This provided the Americans with many a laugh. Everyone had a favorite story, such as signs. One in a Tokyo curio shop specializing in goods brought from the hinterland boasted, "Here is Curious Objects from the Backside of Japan." Or the tailor who informed his customers, "We make fur coats out of your skin."

The Victorian-era texts and grammars labored over by earnest Japanese students of English conversation sometimes led them quaintly astray. An American woman at a dinner party was startled when a distinguished Japanese gentleman sitting beside her amiably and innocently remarked, "I have always wanted to have intercourse with a nice Western lady." No one in the American community seems ever to have reflected on the howlers Americans perpetrated when they attempted to speak Japanese. Yet when trying out their few Japanese phrases, some did have the disheartening experience of being misinterpreted as speaking English.

Tradition reinforced the isolation of the foreigner. History had created certain expectations on both sides as to how Westerners should behave in Japan, and the occupiers were the heirs of this

American soldiers and Japanese geisha watch a show.

tradition. The "treaty port" had been the white man's world in East Asia, first springing up in China as a mutually agreeable manner of segregating foreigner from Chinese. Both sides wanted controlled contact rather than free association.

From the East Asian viewpoint, the alarmingly uncouth foreigner was inevitably an outsider—*waijen* to the Chinese, *gaijin* to the Japanese, written with the same characters. No one expected the cultural barriers to be penetrated, or wanted them to be, except perhaps the missionaries, whose zealous persistence periodically embarrassed even alarmed other Westerners, and irritated the East Asians. The treaty port tradition, although much weaker in Japan than in China—Japan had preserved its sovereignty—nonetheless remained during the Occupation as a subtle influence from the past, an historical justification for keeping the two cultures apart.

The language barrier and the way Westerners in Japan had lived in the past simply deepened what was a profound culture gap between America and Japan. The war helped bridge it; after the war a few more Americans knew something about Japan. The Army

A mixed crowd at Meiji Stadium, Tokyo, to see a rodeo.

and Navy Language Schools had a profound influence by training the people (like Donald Keene, Robert Brower, and Robert Ward) who laid the foundation for postwar Japanese studies in America. But war does not nourish tolerance. War is, one might say, the worst preparation for peace, for it goads and aggravates ethnocentrism and chauvinistic nationalism. The winner is especially vulnerable to these powerful emotions. Yet the period immediately after a war provides unusual opportunity for the flowering of relationships between peoples because of the intimacy which, brief and unnatural though it may be, exists between victor and vanquished. The outstretched hand raises hopes of long-term friendship. But since genuine attachment seldom happens easily, the fruit of this encounter can be misunderstanding, enhancement of mutual prejudice, frustration, and even anger. That intercultural relations necessarily produce goodwill is a myth.

The Americans and Japanese were pleasantly surprised at what they first learned directly about each other. But American impressions of the Japanese were certainly mixed. Americans often found Japanese behavior perplexing and annoying, the ready laugh or giggle being a particularly disconcerting trait.

This anecdote was related in the April 1946 *Atlantic Monthly:* "After a few tributes to our . . . B-29s, they asked me if their balloon bombs had done any damage in the States. I replied that as far as I knew, they had done no damage and were not worth a damn. Everybody around us laughed heartily; evidently I had said something very funny."

A young naval officer in Japan during the first weeks of the Occupation wrote home: "If only they were proud and hostile and looked upon us with hate—possibly then I could sympathize with them. But when they titter and scrape the ground in front of you and say 'welcome' or 'alo' in that oriental way of theirs. . . ." About the same time *Life* magazine commented: "The slavishness and obsequiousness . . . [of the Japanese people] is offensive. It comes because we are stronger, because we beat them, not because they feel that they or their country have done wrong."

181

There were those Americans for whom Pearl Harbor died hard. A Marine general remarked that he had "dedicated too many Marine cemeteries to be really friendly with the Japanese people." A letter to *Pacific Stars and Stripes* in late November 1945 said: "We're not here to beat up Japs, starve women and children, or punish any except war criminals. However we still have a duty—to let the Japanese people know that we won this war, that they have been defeated, that they were terribly wrong in starting the war and that we do not feel that all is 'forgotten and forgiven.' Selling smokes and elaborate handshaking is no way to perform that duty." A senior naval officer at Yokosuka posted a large photograph with the caption:

> Remember. This is a photograph of an American sailor who was a prisoner of the Japs. The Japs did this to him. They did the same and worse to thousands of other Americans. They'll do it again if they ever get a chance. Remember this if you ever catch yourself getting soft and being nice to a Jap.

Although Japanese ways drew unfavorable American comment, this was nothing new. In the nineteenth century, when Westerners first began coming to Japan, Japanese customs concerning nudity were invariably ciriticized. Every visiting writer felt obliged to express his horrified disapproval of the Japanese practice of mixed bathing, if possible including an illustration of it in his article or book. The Japanese, on their part, were somewhat appalled by the low-cut dresses popular with Western ladies and the public display of nude paintings and statuary.

The twentieth century would label such reactions "culture shock," to which no one is altogether immune. Intellectually one may prepare for it; emotionally one cannot. Reading and thinking about it are not the same as confronting it. One American woman thought herself well prepared for living in occupied Japan. She was quite familiar with Japanese customs and knew, for example, that Japanese men sometimes urinate publicly; she accepted that fact. One day, walking down a Tokyo street, she encountered at rather close range a gentleman she knew slightly relieving himself against a fence. Too late to retreat, she determined to ignore the man as she hurriedly endeavored to pass. But courtesy compelled the man to acknowledge the lady's presence. So with a gesture of exquisite gentility, he tipped his hat and bowed, the stream continuing without interruption. To her, this was culture shock!

Smells seem to have an important role in the way one culture reacts to another. To East Asian nostrils, the Western diet, rich in animal fats, imbues Westerners with a distinctive and unpleasant odor. Intensifying the problem for the Japanese was that Westerners did not always bathe with regularity. In Japanese the phrase *bata kusai*, "stinks of butter," was for some time a common pejorative for things Western.

Most Westerners believed the Japanese practice of saving night-soil to use for fertilizer was noisome, unhealthy, and generally unattractive. To the Japanese the practice—and the smell—was so common as to go unnoticed. When circling over Haneda Airport in the late 1940s, a descending plane would suck in fresh air for its passengers from the currents rising off the farmers' fields below. The odor of nightsoil delicately wafting to the noses of the arriving foreign passengers would cause some of them to stir uneasily. Whereas those who grew to like Japan tended to accept such things, those who disliked Japan often seized on the smells as one of their prime reasons, equating the use of nightsoil not with frugality but with filth.

In the preface to his novel *The Stainless Steel Kimono* (1947), Elliot Chaze writes: "I believe the reaction of most occupation troops in Japan is that of a person suddenly handed a brimming bedpan and told to guard its contents carefully. It comes as a shock to the average American to find himself custodian of such a smelly and strange country." The chief medical officer of Admiral Halsey's Third Fleet broadcast over the radio in October 1945: "Japan is a land of fish, fleas, vermin and rodents . . . all the factors which promote disease. She has been and is a stench in the nostrils of the world."

Sprawling outside the gates of every American military base in Japan was a tawdry strip of shops catering to GIs: tailors crowded against souvenir vendors, bars intermingling with bathhouses and brothels. In this milieu, a wasteland between cultures, real intercultural penetration occurred with Japanese women acting as go-betweens.

For a time the Army attempted half-heartedly to forbid fraternizing with the Japanese, frustrating those who wanted to break out of the American world, to see more of Japan than "the strip." One irate soldier complained early in 1946: "If we are supposed to represent American culture in the Orient, why in hell are we barred from partaking of the best that remains in Japanese civilization, and allowed only the vice and drunkenness for which we are rapidly becoming famous?" There were no such restrictions in Europe, he pointed out; nothing was off limits there. Why should there be restrictions in Japan? He wanted to go to the *No* theater, concerts, print shows—but only bars were open to him. Such would not be the case after the early months of the Occupation, but he was out of luck. Actually, in Tokyo MPs would drive GIs out of nightspots and the movies but rarely went near the *No* or *kabuki* theaters because there were few GIs there.

"Fraternization" in a congenial sense was not of course what most GIs wanted; they wanted Japanese women. Signs in English directing GIs to Army prophylaxis stations and advertisements for VD clinics were all over the cities, even near the shrines in Kamakura. American newspaper cartoons in Japan began depicting Japanese women with voluptuously Western figures, a GI's dream of feminine pulchritude—not at all the Japanese reality, or even ideal. Appreciation of the latter would come later, and then only to some. Just as the ideal of feminine beauty in modern Japan changed under the influence of the West, a change which accelerated after the Pacific War, so did American appreciation of Japanese beauty grow along with a greater understanding and tentative acceptance of Japanese aesthetics: the houses, the gardens, prints and pottery.

184

The traditional behavior of Japanese women was immediately appealing to the foreigner. American men found their demure deference captivating. Many friendships bloomed out of the Occupation.

James Michener's popular novel *Sayonara,* a variation on the Madame Butterfly story, uses miscegenation as its central theme. His protagonist says:

> No man could comprehend women until he had known the women of Japan. As I could never have known even the outlines of love had I not lived in a little house where I sometimes drew back the covers of my bed upon the floor to see there the slim golden body of the perpetual woman.

Half a century earlier, Lafcadio Hearn set the pattern for this romantic image when he described the Japanese woman as "the fairest artistic product of 2,000 years of Japanese culture."

Military red tape discouraged marriage. But from the end of the war until the present, fifty to sixty thousand Japanese women have married Americans and come to the U.S. Many of these marriages occurred during the Occupation. Many were *nisei*-Japanese unions. Others crossed racial lines, white or black meeting yellow, in what is probably the largest number of legally sanctioned interracial marriages in such a brief space of time in American history.

During the period of the Occupation, the law of many states in America still prohibited miscegenation. Applicants in Japan were obliged to fill out a lengthy questionnaire, obtain permission from their commanding officer, be interviewed by the chaplain, and so forth, in what could be a discouragingly time-consuming and disagreeable experience, the intent being to eliminate women who were prostitutes, criminals, or chronically diseased.

The would-be bride needed a sheaf of documents including a physician's certificate, police clearance, and a copy of the entry for her in the temple register *(koseki)* which all Japanese used as proof of identity. Once, in Yokohama, a 6'6" black sergeant with a diminutive Japanese girl was quizzed by the Consul General himself, who was helping his overworked staff. Looking through the girl's papers, the Consul General saw that one document was missing. "Have you seen her *koseki?*" he demanded of the sergeant. "Oh no, I ain't seen nuthin yet," was the earnest reply.

Not all Americans liked Japanese women. Letters in *Pacific Stars and Stripes* expressed puzzlement over those who did, especially those wanting to marry Japanese. "I guess they didn't associate much with American women while in the States, or they wouldn't talk so foolish." "Are these men trying to compare them with American women? Surely they must be out of their heads or are 'Gook Lovers.'" "The flat-chested, button-nosed, splay-footed average Japanese woman is about as attractive to most Americans as a 100-year-old stone idol. In fact, less so. They like to take pictures of the idols."

The *Saturday Evening Post* commented tartly on the ignorance of many Japanese women of American life and customs, summing up by saying they wanted girdles but did not know how to use them. Few of the GI brides were highly educated, even in their own culture; their English, learned from GIs, was often limited, crude, and coarse. They did not always make a good impression, even on those prepared to be objective.

In an attempt to help, the Red Cross ran "brides' schools" to teach cooking, child care, etiquette, and something about American dress. Otherwise the Japanese bride might know American ways only through movies and mail-order catalogs, through visits to the commissary and the PX. The American was particularly eager to have his wife able to prepare food he liked. Frying a hamburger was easy enough; baking a cake was something else, for ovens were not normally a part of the Japanese kitchen, and this sort of cookery was alien to the Japanese tradition.

The burden of adaptation in all these matters was thrust entirely on the Japanese bride, the presumption being that the couple would ultimately go to America to establish a permanent home. For every marriage there were many informal liaisons, from the one-night stand to the "shack up." Many a man had his "moose."* Although agreeable to the American male, these temporary arrangements were less so to the Japanese female, who was more likely to experience trauma at the end of the relationship. Like Madame Butterfly, she stayed and he left.

Occupation society, particularly in the early period, was essentially masculine. Drinking, whoring, and souvenir hunting were among the most popular activities. Even in the first tense days after the initial landing, when among the pile of rubble there was very little to buy, GI shoppers were on the prowl. Someone remarked that the two most frequent American questions in the early days were "Do you Japanese hate us?" and "Do you have any kimonos?"

At that time kimonos and swords were the most prized acquisitions. Battle flags, rifles, bayonets, sabers, pistols, and binoculars were also sought after, with some opportunity to obtain such trophies free through Army sources—the Army had confiscated large stocks of Japanese weapons.

At first the Japanese, not knowing what to expect, hid many of their valuables. But as the avid GI shopper rapidly depleted the market and inflation kited the prices, the Japanese entrepreneurial skill surfaced quickly to turn out souvenirs in quantity for the eager Americans. Lacquer ware, fans, cloisonné, woodblock prints, and ceramics—some moderately tasteful, most not—were produced in increasing amounts. The line of goods was very much the same as that with which the Japanese had flooded the U.S. before the war. In other words, it was what Americans expected from Japan.

Cheap pottery souvenirs stamped "Occupied Japan" became widely available: children's tea sets, tiny figurines of mildly indecent subjects, cup and saucer sets, cream pitchers, bookends, etc. Or if one wished, a decorative plate inscribed "Souvenir of Oklahoma City, Oklahoma."

---

*"Moose" was a corruption of the Japanese word *musume,* "young girl."

Opening day at the new Tokyo Post Exchange proved a busy one, November 2, 1945.

Haggling over prices at street corners provided amusement and served to ease the tension during the early days of the American presence. "An old man selling a *haori* (short coat worn over a kimono) protests an offered price by pointing to his wife, making gestures imitating sewing and then drawing fingers down his face indicating tears and exhaustion from such labor. This provides laughter all around."

Post exchanges were soon established so that the soldier, in theory at least, could get good value for his money. They grew in size and number and they prospered, some becoming virtual department stores. Japanese manufacturers, supplying the PXs and serving them on concession, had a cross-section of the American buying public—from the general's wife to the lowest ranking GI. Japanese manufacturers learned American ways of quality control and packaging, and they learned what the American mass market wanted. The more discriminating among the occupiers learned their way directly to Japanese shops.

Many GIs did not know why they were in Japan, which made them restless and unhappy. For the new arrivals, orientation programs were often weak, typically a lecture or two delivered to a bored audience by a junior officer who might or might not be a good speaker and who did not necessarily know anything about Japan. The Army's principal interest seemed directed toward controlling venereal disease.

A chaplain complained that instead of telling the soldier specifically what his country was trying to do in Japan, the soldier was threatened with another war in twenty-five years if he did not remain in Japan. There must be, the chaplain argued, a positive ideology for the Occupation. "The best we have yet taught is a negative idealism," he said. "The result is the GI's present negative attitude."

The press and radio, chiefly the *Pacific Stars and Stripes* and the Far East Network, provided a limited informational diet of sports, comics, U.S. and foreign news, and trivia, as well as large amounts

Members of the Tachikawa Motorcycle Club pose in front of Kamakura's Great Buddha.

of popular music. Although the English-language Japanese press, notably the *Nippon Times,* steadily improved and began to inform its readers of art, music, and theater in Tokyo, information generally available about Japanese politics and activities was scanty. Japanese life remained vague and shadowy to most Americans.

Books in English on Japan were neither numerous nor easy to get except in libraries; secondhand volumes could sometimes be found in Tokyo bookshops. But the only new books on Japan in English had to be obtained through the PX, where the supply was short and the demand was great. Frederick Melcher of *Publishers Weekly,* visiting Tokyo in the spring of 1947, pointed out how impoverishing it was that the occupiers, making important policy decisions for an entire nation, did not have ready access to new books, those he called "opinion-making books," and thus were cut off from new ideas. Gradually libraries grew; the Ernie Pyle, across from the Imperial Hotel, had a good reading collection by early 1948, and more books became available in the stores. Charles Tuttle, ex-Occupationaire of Rutland, Vermont, established a still-thriving bookselling business catering to Americans.

In the early months of the Occupation most officers in the garrison forces wanted to go home rather than have their families join them. As a *Stars and Stripes* reader asked: "Does he [MacArthur] really think that the boys over here want to bring their families to this hole? . . . I wouldn't bring my dog here to live." After a year or so, with the maturing of the Occupation, these attitudes changed.

An adversary relationship did not develop despite the rich opportunity for it. The Japanese people were prepared to be unusually objective about themselves, to take a new look at their old culture; defeat led them to question at least some of their traditional values. In no way were they ready to challenge the Americans. Within a few weeks of the American arrival it was apparent that no physical trouble would develop. General Robert Eichelberger reported to a Cincinnati audience in November 1947 that Japan was "one of the few places in this world where an American soldier can walk

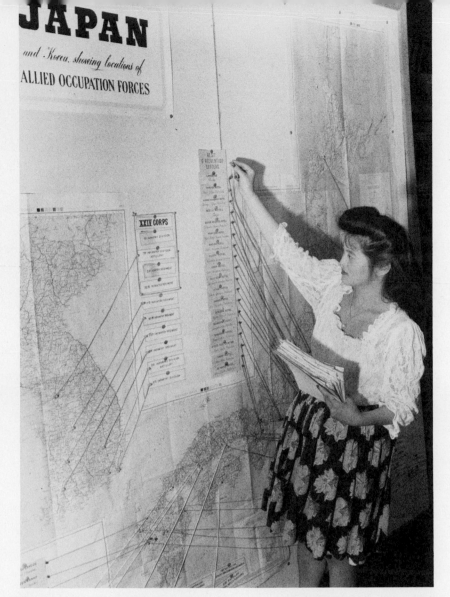

Yukie Kozai, nisei *clerk, pinpoints a GI rest area. Miss Kozai arrived in Tokyo from New York City in 1940 and was forced to remain in Japan until the end of the war.*

in a foreign land among the civilian population on the darkest of nights, unarmed and unafraid.''

For most Americans, Japan became an extremely attractive assignment; for some, the experience of a lifetime.

Two Americans brace for the camera on the balcony of the Gamagori Hotel, overlooking beautiful Gamagori Bay, at the Takeshima Rest Center, March 20, 1947.

In May 1946 American dependents began to arrive. Most were quite content to enjoy "Stateside" comfort at one of the bases outside Tokyo or at Pershing, Grant, or Washington Heights, large self-contained military housing developments in Tokyo. Playing the slot machines, drinking at the Club, watching a movie, they felt little need to venture outside. One woman who would be returning to the U.S. the next week with her husband and children, excitedly confided to friends that she was going "off base" that night for the first time since she had arrived in Japan two years earlier. "Off base" in her case meant an Army Officers Club in downtown Tokyo.

Not all were so timid. With servants readily available, many wives had abundant leisure time, more than their husbands; and they were free to explore Japanese culture, joining Japanese-American clubs, enrolling in language classes, collecting folk arts and crafts, or studying a traditional Japanese art form such as flower arranging *(ikebana)*. Ellen Allen, a general's wife, was a notable

192

example. Instrumental in founding Ikebana International, an organization that now has branches all over the world, Mrs. Allen was subsequently decorated by the Japanese Government for her accomplishment. "Fearing they had upset the sexual balance," a friend later commented, "the Japanese belatedly decorated General Allen even though he hadn't really contributed much to Japan-American relations, unless it was Ellen."

Some women busied themselves in typically American volunteer work, for instance raising money for scholarships to enable Japanese students to attend American colleges and universities, and providing them with clothing and pocket money as well. The College Women's Club in Tokyo, with both Japanese and American members, began to sponsor an annual sale of new woodblock prints. Not only was this an excellent way to raise money for worthwhile purposes but also it became a cultural event, stimulating the art form by attracting interested collectors.

Life for the occupiers could be very rich indeed, particularly

Lieutenant Donald C. Mills in No *costume.*

when contrasted against the gray Japanese world. General Eichelberger wrote to *Time* magazine: "We have more to offer a soldier and his dependents than I have ever before seen in over forty-four years service."

Housing may not always have been of the quality Americans expected. Modern plumbing and central heating were amenities not readily available in Japan, even to the rich; Japanese had not prized these aspects of life as fully as Americans did. GIs were usually housed in barracks, often newly built, similar to those on an American Army base anywhere. More difficult was finding suitable quarters for military and civilian personnel working in Tokyo or scattered about the countryside on civil affairs teams.

Typically the upper-ranking occupier in Tokyo would be given a "U.S. House" commandeered by the Army from its Japanese owner, perhaps an imposing Victorian gingerbread structure of the Late Meiji or Taishō eras (circa 1890–1920) favored at the time by some of the rich. Such a house would have large public rooms, several bedrooms, and a comfortable Japanese-style wing. These houses were ideal for entertaining on the grand scale, a custom

Army jeeps in front of Tokyo's Imperial Hotel.

The Dai Ichi Hotel served as quarters for occupiers of officer rank.

many Americans now found easily affordable and altogether pleasant. Labor was abundant and cheap (in the early part of the Occupation servants were supplied free to SCAP officials).

Majors and captains, Department of the Army civilians (DACs) and diplomats (DIPSECS, those in the Diplomatic Section of SCAP) also had houses. Not all were big or grand, but most were in the Western style. "Those of us who had houses, serious business with Japanese officials, and a wonderful standard of living spent lots of time entertaining Japanese officials and their wives. By mid-Occupation they were busy reciprocating. The Americans were able to make friends with every kind of important Japanese besides the officials—*kabuki* actors, artists, musicians, old aristocratic fami-

195

U.S. House No. 594 for dependents, Tokyo.

lies and imperial household people, even members of the imperial family. Many of us took advantage of the opportunity," recalled one diplomat's wife.

Even a lowly PFC living off base could afford a maid. For some families with children their maid might be the only Japanese person they really knew, and this relationship could be very close. "Our Japanese servants—and *everyone* had servants—were important links to the Japanese world. It may sound condescending but it was true. They loved to explain Japanese customs, they taught our children their songs, recommended food and suggested excursions. They were often not low-class uneducated people; many of them had simply fallen upon hard times. We Americans indulged and enjoyed our servants, and of course they lived with us in our houses. The ties often still persist."

196

The servants may not always have been skillful, but most Americans found them good-natured and eager to please. An Admiral's wife noticed "their ornate, huge, Western-style house growing very cold around noon on Christmas Day. She called her Number One Boy and asked him the reason. He replied: 'Madame, today is your happy day. Tomorrow I will tell you that yesterday we ran out of coal.' "

With cigarettes available to Occupiers at ten cents a pack and gasoline at sixteen cents a gallon, it was hard to get too exercised over forgetful servants. Food also was cheap. A family of two adults who entertained frequently could maintain three maids and live on fifteen dollars a week.

Virtually all the food eaten by Americans in Japan was imported. Initially, because the practice seemed nonexploitative, this had a most favorable impact on the Japanese. Yet when Japanese food production increased and supplies were entirely adequate, the occupiers continued to import their food. Eating locally-produced food ("indigenous" as the Army Commissary labeled it) was somewhat discouraged by American authorities. Raw vegetables grown in uncomposted nightsoil could harbor intestinal parasites, and one's salad could be dangerous if the ingredients had not been carefully washed. The Army set up a large hydroponic farm outside Tokyo to grow lettuce and other vegetables that would be safe for the American table.

But American squeamishness was excessive; the Army imported frozen beef even though Japanese beef tasted better, was then no more expensive, and offered no threat to good health. Those living on bases tended to rely almost exclusively upon military sources of food supplies, whereas those who lived in "U.S. houses" often sent out their servants to buy fresh fish, vegetables, and fruit in their own neighborhood. These Americans were exposed to the Japanese cuisine.

Train travel for the occupiers was free until August 1946; thereafter it cost one cent a mile. In such desirable resorts as Nikko and Hakone, oases of Americana catered to American comfort at

197

Dinner party given in honor of a distinguished guest by Major General Paul J. Mueller, Chief of Staff to General MacArthur, at his home in Tokyo.

very low cost. Chinese and Western-style restaurants in Tokyo became popular with SCAP people although they were more expensive than military clubs. The manager of the Army-run Imperial Hotel remembers that a Colonel's wife was giving a dinner for twenty guests and wanted it to be memorable. " 'I want it to be a marvelous party,' she told me, 'so don't hold back on anything. You can go as high as a dollar a person if you have to.' "

"Yes, those were good years," Jean MacArthur would later recall. Many would echo the sentiment.

Largely by their own choice, or at least by that of the ruling elite, the Japanese had been virtually isolated from the Western world during the 1930s. The Pacific War intensified that isolation. Japan's relations with Italy and Germany, the Axis partners, were never intimate and in no way compensated for the loss of ties with the U.S. and Great Britain.

Medicine, for example, showed the crippling impact of Japan's severance from the West. An American doctor visiting Kyushu in

198

late 1945 remarked that he had found no foreign medical literature there dated beyond 1935, and that Japanese medical people were "pitifully ignorant" of recent science.

The Japanese were aware of their cultural impoverishment and in 1945 hungered for a renewal of direct intellectual ties with the Western world. Yet Japan was not permitted by the Occupying authorities to send many of its people abroad or to maintain diplomatic relations overseas. Even getting books and journals from abroad was difficult. Slowly this improved.

The Occupation remained the funnel through which had to pass all information from overseas, filtered by the Americans. Americans thought little about this. Nor did most of them appreciate the importance of the Occupation community as an intellectual authority to the Japanese. The occupiers represented a culture of which the Japanese were now prepared to think the best. As the losers in a disastrous war, the Japanese were more aware of their failures as a nation than of their successes.

Americans were less disposed to learn from the Japanese. Yet for Americans the Occupation era was vastly important as a time of cultural exposure; much would later come of it.

10

The Homecoming

DOWN the crowded street staggered a tousled young American soldier, lurching wildly from side to side, hardly able to maintain balance or momentum. Circling the soldier protectively, remaining beyond his reach yet ready to prevent his escape, moving wherever he did, were five Japanese policemen, immaculate, impassive. Back and forth the street they moved, as if in an elaborate dance, the GI altogether unconscious of his human shield, or indeed of any part of the environment beyond his path. Passers-by, all Japanese, scrupulously averted their eyes and carefully chose their steps so as to avoid physical or emotional involvement in what was going on.

Suddenly a siren shrilled and an Army jeep drove up. The circle of Japanese police immediately parted; a few American MPs abruptly thrust the soldier into the jeep and rushed him away. At the second-floor window of a coffee shop, two American missionaries watched. They had been talking over the whole Occupation experience and, being fond of parables, one of them speculated whether what had just happened was not a parable for the Occupation.

The film *Rashomon* (1951), acclaimed by foreign critics as a masterpiece, created a sensation among Americans who go to foreign movies. Seen by more Americans than any other object of Japanese art until then, few in the audience recognized the allegory within the film. Japanese critics noted that the bandit protagonist, a loud, uncouth barbarian who did not even look Japanese, could be taken as symbol for the foreign occupier. Terrifying, unpredictable, ridic-

200

ulous, the bandit could also have been that drunken GI.

The *Rashomon* image is of course grotesque, a caricature. So also is the drunken GI, a figure hardly representative of the nobler part of the American enterprise in Japan. There were, after all, the two MPs as well. True, without the buffer of an existing Japanese Government both sides would have found getting along far more difficult than they did. The occupiers were often ignorant, insensitive, and blind to much of what was going on in the Japanese world around them.

But the Japanese emerged from the Occupation with no thirst for vengeance and no appetite for overturning the changes wrought by the occupiers. The Japanese admit that a military occupation by them would not have been as agreeable an experience for the loser; their record in Korea and China bears this out. It would appear that the Japanese are better losers than winners, whereas Americans are better winners than losers.

By military standards the American presence had been benign. Political evangelism rather than exercise of brute force was the American tactic. To induce the Japanese to cooperate, Americans relied heavily upon persuasion. Instruments of force were there, and everyone knew it. But except for ceremonial occasions they remained discreetly in the background.

With the Japanese becoming an active part of the whole effort, American choices were necessarily limited. And since American success depended on Japanese help, those parts of the Occupation program that proved most permanently successful were those Japanese authority was most enthusiastic about and around which Japanese public opinion could most easily rally.

Departing Japan, Americans by and large had good feelings. For the U.S., the Japanese experience stood out as an exception to America's generally unhappy role in Asia after World War II. Forty years of growing American hostility with the Japanese ended in 1945.

Many Americans, idealizing the Occupation effort, radiated a tremendous moral earnestness that touched the Japanese. No virtue

201

is more appreciated by the Japanese than sincerity. Above all else, Americans exhibited that trait. At their best, the occupiers were superb. The nobility of American ideals is no better expressed than by Clarence Pickett of the American Friends Service Committee, writing to President Truman on September 18, 1945: "Though Japan stands today at the bar of judgement, in a deeper sense it is America that is on trial. . . . Not only Japan . . . but all the countries of the Eastern world will watch us now to see whether we manifest in our conduct those principles of justice, humility, and respect for the individual for which we have fought and sacrificed." In most American policies and American attitudes, the propitiatory prevailed over the vindictive.

The inequality of the new American-Japanese relationship lent itself to a cloying condescension on the part of the Americans, expressed in a rhetoric that a more cynical age may find hard to read without squirming: "One can not serve in this enormous undertaking without being filled with the greatest desire to help in every way possible this struggling people, longing as they do to find a better way of life; longing to understand and be understood by other peoples; longing to leap ahead a thousand years in a single century and walk beside the other nations in fellowship and equality."

Condescension bred complacency, and "MacArthur's champions, led by a sizable force of devoted public relations officers, proclaimed the entire Occupation a success, because order had been maintained, hunger averted, and the cities dusted with prodigious quantities of DDT."

The smugness of SCAP invited and indeed provoked criticism; Washington, the actual source of the policies, somehow avoided the brunt of the attack. Angry American critics, some of them former SCAP officials, argued that Cold War exigencies—the deteriorating tie with the Soviet Union and the rising star of revolution in China, making a new American need for Japan—had compromised and corroded the basic ideals with which the Occupation had been launched.

Indeed the occupiers had not, for example, crushed the *zaibatsu*.

"The old princes of privilege are lurking behind bamboo screens, furtively throwing monkey wrenches and fattening their bank rolls at the expense of the Japanese masses," wrote one critic. Labor unions, initially encouraged, were later repressed. And with the outbreak of the Korean War, Americans showed little reserve or reluctance in spurring the Japanese to build their own defenses. Somewhat lamely, SCAP's supporters declared that the "anti-war Constitution" was never intended to bar measures for self-protection.

Of course the self-interest of the U.S., not the benefit of Japan, was the ultimate purpose for the Occupation. Americans often glided over differences between the two. That the Japanese might judge their "best interests" to be different from the way Americans chose to define them did not occur to most Americans. Among both detractors and supporters of Occupation policies, leftists or right-wingers, ethnocentrism rode high.

Americans found the new Japanese dependence both flattering and irritating. Flattering, for obvious reasons. Irritating, because the Japanese appeared to be using this special relationship to their advantage. As early as January 1946, a writer in the *Saturday Evening Post* pointed out how well off the Japanese were compared to the rest of Asia. In Japan, he noted, the presence of the American Army prevented civil disturbances. Furthermore, "Japan doesn't have to drain her resources, as we do, to keep up a strong army and navy. She is free to concentrate entirely on the development of her country and people. Come to think of it, she's better off than we [Americans] are in that respect."

At a time of growing conservatism in America and a corresponding readiness in the U.S. to find Communist conspiracy everywhere, Japan seemed to be shaping up reassuringly as a Far Eastern showcase of democracy and "Christian capitalism," a bulwark against Communism and a friend of America. What critics of the Occupation often overlooked was the inexorable intermeshing of foreign relations with domestic politics. No leader of a democratic state could overlook public opinion when shaping foreign policy.

For example, in the U.S. during the Occupation the Wagner Act (1935), sympathetic to the labor movement, gave way to the far more conservative Taft-Hartley Act (1947) as the keystone of American labor law. Is it therefore surprising that Occupation labor policies should become far less liberal than they had been initially?

The radical reform measures endorsed by SCAP in its early months might well have made the Occupation vulnerable to the same sort of hysterical probing America's China policy received had it not been for the MacArthur aura. To the American public the General personified the Occupation, and it would have seemed ludicrous to suggest that he was either sympathetic to Communism or susceptible to manipulation by Communists.

Americans went to Japan confident of their superiority over a largely unknown but thoroughly defeated country. American dominance in the postwar relationship between the two nations simply bolstered this lofty self-assurance. The consequences were serious, for Americans persisted in perceiving Japan as poor and fragile, long after Japan's new economic power burgeoned and Japan's new political and social order stabilized. This severely inhibited the receptivity of Americans to learn from the Japanese. Compton Pakenham of *Newsweek* reported in 1949 that he had heard the Japanese say, "Americans have learned nothing about Japan in four years, but we have learned much from them." The disparity still exists.

While the war was waning, geographer Edward Ackerman speculated on America exercising strategic command over Japan by simply sealing it off from the rest of the world. Employing the might of its air and sea power, America could manipulate the Japanese by remote control. Ackerman believed the Japanese could, with heavy effort, eke out an adequate if monotonous diet, and their ample forest resources, their water power, their coal and copper could take care of all other needs, albeit in a very modest way. No occupation would be necessary and the U.S. could remain aloof, entirely free of the workings of Japanese politics and society, the

Japanese being obliged to cope with their own problems. Japan could survive as a closed nation only if the number of people were controlled; that was vital, Ackerman judged. He pointed out that many other areas of comparable size were infinitely poorer in natural wealth. Japan's problem, as he saw it, was primarily of its own making: too many people for the available resources.

Putting aside the moral questions such a Draconian proposal as isolating Japan might raise, would it have worked? Certainly it would not have permitted the Japanese to participate in the economic life of the other Asian states to the extent that Americans soon came to believe those nations needed. For this essential role, Japan required revival of its manufacturing, with free access to foreign materials and markets.

Many Americans, particularly those unaware of Japan's progress, felt that Japan's future was bound to Asia, not to the West. Basic cultural and racial affinity were already there, with economic linkages more recently overlaid. Exports from Japan of rubber boots, cheap cotton cloth, flashlights and sewing machines would not find as convenient or natural a market in the U.S. as in Asia. Japan's most likely sources of raw materials also lay in Asia. Foreign observers tended to look at Japan's large agricultural population with its low standard of living, rather than at Japan's highly educated urban population with its history of economic growth. Japan's similarities to the rest of Asia were more apparent than the differences.

Despite the unprecedented opportunities for gathering and analyzing information which the occupiers possessed, none of them anticipated Japan's later economic triumph. But, for that matter, neither did the Japanese, which may say something about the art of economic forecasting. The "have-not nation" attitude, so prevalent in the 1930s and so popular among the Japanese during the war, lingered in the minds of Japanese and foreigner alike.

Japan's modern technology was essentially borrowed. Within the modern Japanese experience, foreigners saw few instances of fresh ideas or bold invention springing up to compensate for the severe handicaps posed by the nation's essential poverty. Writing at the

205

twilight of the Occupation, Professor Ackerman, by then a former SCAP official, doubted Japan's future ability to earn enough from foreign trade to reach at least the moderate living standard achieved before the war, "in view of its rising population, world shortages of basic commodities, and uncertainties in the outlook for Japanese exports." Even the goal of a radio for every home seemed ambitious.

Not for decades would middling success at best be likely, with that depending upon availability of foreign advice and assistance, Ackerman thought. In fact, simultaneous with his observations, the Japanese were trying to persuade John Foster Dulles to include in the peace treaty, which he was then drafting, a guarantee that America would provide economic support for Japan.

An impoverished, restive Japan could choose to undo the reforms of the Occupation and turn back to military adventure. And the economic collapse of Japan would damage American prestige. "It would be proof-positive that the American way, the American concept for Asia, is meaningless . . . , " wrote Edwin Reischauer. Without a modicum of prosperity, democracy could not flourish. And "if our experiment in democratic government in Japan is permitted to wither away in a few years, how can we expect the other nations of Asia to have any confidence in our leadership?" questioned David Eichler.

Should capitalism in Japan seriously falter, Communism, rising to success in China, could provide an alternative. Americans were apprehensive about Japanese vulnerability to Communism; as Albert Craig observed, Japan had at the time the makings of "the ideal Communist state."

The underlying authoritarianism of Japanese society was conducive to Communism. Weakening of the middle class, erosion of big business, and the disappearance of the army and navy left a temporary power vacuum. The trauma of defeat made the Japanese people as a whole peculiarly susceptible to sweeping change. Had Japan gone Communist, everyone would have nodded sagely, saying how predictable it had been.

The angry, unanticipated politicizing of the Japanese labor movement and the clamorous estrangement of Japanese intellectuals pointed up to Americans the fragility of Occupation democracy. And ready Japanese compliance with Occupation authority, pleasing as it may have been to Americans at the time, was nonetheless disturbing when Americans pondered the long-range prospects for Japanese democracy.

If Japanese poverty was dangerous to America, Japanese prosperity was also a menace, if somewhat less likely. Irene Taeuber, the demographer, pointed out that Japan needed an industrial development greater than that of the 1930s in order to survive. Yet in terms of potential both for military development and for ability to compete with American manufactures, this was dangerous. Owen Lattimore expressed the dilemma in 1949: "There is no way of getting a really free and independent Japan that is not also a Japan capable of bargaining against us at our expense. There is no way of having a dependent Japan that is not an embarrassing drain on us."

The Allies were not as pessimistic about Japan's prospect as the Americans. More than anything else, they feared rebirth of Japanese power. Australia saw a continuation of the same basic circumstances that provoked Japan to go to war: rising population with limited food potential. And if Japan were to be in truth "the workshop of Asia," as Dean Acheson proclaimed, where would this leave Australia and the other neighbors? Would such an event simply be the realization of what Japanese expansionists had sought in the 1930s, what the Allies had so bitterly fought?

Americans shared this anxiety. "I have heard more than one Japanese predict," Harold Strauss said, "that the American Army would win for Japan what its own army failed to win." Back in December 1943 *Fortune* had pointed out: "Japan could win the war by making it appear that she had lost it, and that well may be the basis of her present grand strategy." Indeed postwar Japan, despite abject misery, was better off in some respects than many nations on the winning side. By one swift stroke her colonies were removed, less painfully and less traumatically than the agonizingly protracted surgery undergone by the West European maritime powers.

Japan today is a very different political culture from the country of the 1930s. Like the 1868 Meiji Restoration, 1945 is a key date in the history of the nation, marking the beginning of a new era. Whether defeat in war or the Occupation itself is the responsible agent remains a question. But the Occupiers enjoyed their greatest success with reforms that had roots in previous Japanese experience, of which the war was obviously a part.

After seven years of Occupation, Japan emerged with a working democratic system and a high degree of social stability. Ultimate economic success subsequently made population pressure a dead issue. Japanese democracy continues to function in its distinctive consensus fashion under the unchanged Constitution of 1947. Military officers are not among those making the most important decisions for the nation; the Japanese military faded as the American military flowered.

Not long before former Prime Minister Yoshida Shigeru died, he boasted to a friend that Japan did better as a loser at the San Francisco Peace Conference in 1952 than as a victor at Versailles in 1919. In the long term perhaps he was right. Versailles was disappointing to the Japanese. Since San Francisco, although Japan has not recaptured the economic dominance over China and Korea that the Empire made possible, the U.S. has become a larger and richer substitute. America has replaced Manchuria as a source of raw materials, a market for manufactures, and an outlet for investment.

According to the old saw, *"influence* has been the graveyard of many historians." The historian can suggest influence but cannot prove it, and he gets into trouble when he tries. Americans undertook and carried out the Occupation of Japan unaware that teachers can be influenced by their students; the occupiers did not expect the experience of guiding Japan to affect them. Many probably would have agreed with Russell Brines, who wrote: "By and large the Japanese gave the Americans only one thing—a deeper love and respect and yearning for what they had left behind." Nonetheless, occupying Japan was an experience sufficiently vivid to be brought back home, where it worked in various subtle and even profound ways.

The war had kindled a white American perception that the U.S. had a race problem. Like other underprivileged groups, blacks benefited from participating in the war, and ultimately the American civil rights movement took on strength and fire. Blacks pushed; some whites encouraged.

In Japan many white and black Americans found they could live comfortably among people of a different color. Whites learned what it was like to be a racial minority, albeit a highly privileged one. The great number of interracial marriages also was an eye-opener; despite enormous problems, many of these American unions with Japanese proved exemplary.

The Japanese war bride, wherever she lived in the U.S. outside of Hawaii and California, was a conspicuous person. To a few she was a reminder of racial tensions and wartime rage. To many more she provided living evidence of a new and peaceful era for America and Japan, as well as proving the feasibility of harmonious interracial life.

The average American accepted the Japanese woman more readily than he did the Japanese man. The latter was often viewed with suspicion and even distaste, emotions that reverberated with white America's later reaction to the new Asian-American ethnic pride.

Quickly and quietly after the war, Japanese-Americans have arisen from the psychological debasement brought by interment and crippling economic losses, achieving new distinction in politics and in the professions. Daniel K. Inouye of Hawaii and S. I. Hayakawa of California sit in the U.S. Senate. Isamu Noguchi in sculpture and Minoru Yamazaki in architecture are well known. The hard-working Japanese-Americans have become a "success story" in the classic American immigrant pattern. Spiro Agnew provoked widespread criticism by referring to a correspondent as "that fat Jap." With some Americans, prejudice lingers.

The American media still seldom portray the Asian-American male as a forceful or admirable character. Those Californians who, during the war, were so anxious to put Japanese-Americans in detention camps, may now enthusiastically elect them to high political office. Yet in movie and television roles demanding an Asian hero, as in the "Kung Fu" series, Hollywood's tendency is to try to use a Caucasian actor. White America, it seems, clings to its stereotype for "the oriental."

The "counter culture" that sprang up so vigorously in the 1960s was led for the most part by people too young to have been among the occupiers of Japan. But parts of that culture—interest in Zen and meditation, the cult of frugality, the macrobiotic diet—are certainly akin to elements within the Japanese tradition. Earlier, the popular culture of the GI had washed hints of that back to American shores. Some of the occupiers were taken with the simplicity of the Japanese aesthetic ideal, reinforced by that nation's postwar poverty.

Many Americans returning from Japan were startled, even repulsed, by the lavish, materialistic way of life they saw in lush tropical Hawaii and *al fresco* California, those parts of the U.S. usually visited first by Americans returning from East Asia. Culture shock on returning home could be even greater than going to Japan, in part because no one anticipated it. Readjustment could take awhile. As one distraught American mother wailed, "He's been in his room, with the door closed, during the entire two weeks since he's been back, just playing those Japanese records." Some Americans who had been in Japan for a long time, living among the Japanese, found themselves unconsciously behaving like Japanese when they returned. They had learned the usefulness of go-betweens and the value of preserving face for another person. Indirect means, they had found on occasion, could be more effective than direct.

In the realm of higher culture, American practice and under-

210

standing of Zen, for example, may have only shallowly comprehended this facet of Japanese religious culture. The goal of Zen meditation, Harvey Cox pointed out, is not self-enlightenment as many Americans seemed to think, but a way of escaping ego. Yet whether "American Zen" was genuine is probably not the important point. What matters is that Americans were reaching for fresh ideas, for intellectual and emotional nourishment, outside Western civilization toward a tradition hitherto highly exotic and largely unknown. Zenist principles appeared to fit what those in the *avant garde* were trying to express in dance, poetry, music, and ceramics.

From Japanese classical dance, knowing little of the literary or philosophical roots of the form, American performers nonetheless have learned techniques, the outward forms if not always the inner meanings, using, as one example, suspended movement to convey intensity. Increasingly, choreographers such as Jerome Robbins in "Watermill" have tried to go beyond technique to reach the ideas of Japanese culture in order to transpose them to the American. Awareness by the general public of the breadth, excitement, and sophistication of the Japanese performing arts has been enhanced by the enthusiastic efforts of Beate Sirota Gordon, Constitution-drafter turned New York impressario. Today she heads the Asian Performing Arts Society.

John Cage, who studied for two years under Zen philosopher Daisetsu Suzuki, says he learned from Suzuki "of a multiplicity of centers in interpretation and nonobstruction (rather than a single goal toward which we move). Thus I was able to conceive of a music in which each sound (each at its own center) could be itself rather than subservient to a theory or a more important tone. . . . Thus my work is unthinkable (if it is thinkable at all) without Zen. . . ." The studied casualness of Zen blossoms in the poetry of Gary Snyder, serious student of Japan for many years. Nor is poetry limited to the Zenists; even American elementary school pupils try their hand at the *haiku* form.

Modern Japanese material culture, represented by the goods produced with such elegance, skill, and profusion by Japanese factories, has powerfully attracted the American consumer. Those who were in Japan during the Occupation had the opportunity to observe that most Japanese seemed to enjoy working and that what they made showed their pleasure. While American five-and-tens began turning elsewhere for their stock, buyer resistance to the "Made in Japan" label faded. Honda, Sony, and Pioneer are known primarily for their quality, secondarily for being Japanese.

In the middle and late 1950s, while Japanese popular culture was enthusiastically embracing blue jeans, fast food, and Elvis Presley, a burst of American interest in Japanese aesthetics caused the word "shibui" to have brief vogue among the cognoscenti. The decorating magazines embraced it enthusiastically, and the Museum of Modern Art in New York drew admiring crowds to its display of a fully assembled traditional Japanese house. Contemporary American architecture, landscape design, and ceramics were profoundly influenced by the Japanese. No single foreign civilization has been so aesthetically pervasive in postwar America.

John D. Rockefeller III, consultant to John Foster Dulles when the San Francisco peace treaty was being prepared and a founder of the revived Japan Society of New York, built a superb collection of Japanese and Asian art, much of it given to the Asia House gallery. Another notable New York collection was made by Mary and Jackson Burke. But the most extraordinary one to come out of Japan after the war was Harry Packard's. When the Metropolitan Museum of New York acquired it in 1975 for $5 million, the largest group of objects the museum had ever bought, New York immediately joined Boston, Cleveland, and Washington as a major center for Japanese art in the U.S.

Harry Packard had walked around with holes in his shoes amassing this great collection. "I have used every means of collection that any man without money could use," he said. Single-minded, tenacious, fiercely energetic, and knowledgeable, Packard began in China at war's end, combing the pawnshops for bargains, then abundant, in Japanese art. Trained by the U.S. Navy as a Japanese language officer, he was subsequently stationed at Nagasaki, in

212

charge of a camp for Japanese repatriates. During the years of the Occupation, first at Nagasaki and later in Tokyo, Packard concentrated on buying woodblock prints, beginning with those of the Meiji Period and working back to Hiroshige, Utamaro, and the other great masters of a century earlier. His aim was to get pieces in as fine condition as could be had. While traveling and collecting all over the country, he studied hard.

After the Occupation Packard enrolled as a graduate student in Art History at Waseda University in Tokyo, regularly going to Kyoto to attend lectures. His teacher recalls that Packard would travel down on the night train, third class, spreading newspapers on the floor of the coach where he would sleep. Princeton art historian Shimada Shūjirō remembers him as "the most devoted American student of Japanese art I ever met." The print collection was ultimately dispersed. What the Metropolitan acquired, Packard had

*Harry Packard: "I have used every means of collection that any man without money could use."—Richard Halloran/*THE NEW YORK TIMES

not begun to assemble until 1958: a choice group of sculpture, paintings, and ceramics illustrating the whole history of Japanese art, ranging from the neolithic to modern times. Appraisers put a value of $11.3 million on the collection at the time the museum acquired it.

David Potter argues in *People of Plenty* that "no other part of American activity has been so consistently and so completely a failure as our attempt to export democracy." American success, he claims, has been an unconscious message, material rather than ideological: the pursuit of abundance rather than the pursuit of democracy.

The American pattern of a society enjoying a high living standard, pouring forth an ever-increasing quantity of goods, was an implausible model for little Japan with its many people and its slender resources. Within the economic sphere it is paradoxical that Japan should have achieved such startling success. But the American-Japanese encounter is rich with paradox.

Throughout the war the Japanese fought Americans with fanatical zeal; the more desperate the odds, the harder they fought. But after the surrender they baffled Americans by putting up no outward resistance. They appeared docile, amiable, even cooperative, and their habitual deference to authority helped Americans establish the means to destroy that prewar authority.

Officially Japan was governed through "the Allied Occupation of Japan"; in fact, virtually the whole show was American. Americans scrupulously excluded their wartime allies from any policymaking. The occupying authorities exercised tight control, allowing only those few foreigners of whom it approved to enter Japan and a scant number of Japanese to travel abroad. The occupiers censored the press, theater, and books, a policy evocative both of the repressive militarists of the 1930s and, a century earlier, of the feudal, authoritarian, "closed nation" era of the Tokugawa regime—in short, exhibiting many of those characteristics of Japanese political behavior that were anathema to Americans.

214

Preaching freedom of religion, the Americans endeavored to destroy State Shinto and to encourage Christianity. Under the heavy guiding hand of the U.S. Army—like all armies an authoritarian and hierarchical body—the Americans attempted to fashion a working democracy in Japan. Under the leadership of the Army, whose business was waging war, the U.S. tried to make Japan a state legally committed to giving up war. And the American military leaders of the Occupation gave little thought to the future defense needs of Japan. Renouncing the right to make war was of particular interest to the Supreme Commander, General Douglas MacArthur, a war hero who wanted, he said, to be remembered in history for his accomplishments in peace, not war. In this democracy by fiat, the Japanese were given a Constitution providing more liberal rights than Americans enjoyed, least of all the occupiers themselves, living and working under military law.

The greatest paradox of all was that despite intense American ethnocentrism, despite profound American ignorance of Japanese culture and society, despite every reason for failure in terms of the goals Americans defined, the Occupation of Japan was extraordinarily successful, a landmark in human history.

Notes

FOREWORD

xii   waging the Pacific War. As Hubert G. Schenck put it, "What is being done in Japan to build a good society, economically, socially, and politically, may if it is successful, serve to justify the efforts and sacrifices of millions of people in fighting this part of World War II." "Natural Resources Problems in Japan," *Science,* Oct. 8, 1948, 367.

xiii   "hackneyed within a week." Albert K. Weinberg, *Manifest Destiny, a Study of Nationalist Expansionism in American History* (Baltimore, 1935), 301.

xiii   "Christian men of enterprise." Quoted in a review of Anthony F. C. Wallace, *Rockdale: The Growth of an American Village in the Early Industrial Revolution* (New York, 1979), in the *New York Times Book Review,* Jan. 21, 1979, 32.

xiii   "they made the Americans feel superior." Dallas Finn to author, August 28, 1979.

xiv   capital of goodwill. The suggestion is that of Okita Saburo, expressed in a speech at the Woodrow Wilson Center, Washington, D.C., April 16, 1979.

CHAPTER 1

1   efficiency . . . was impressive. Kato Masuo, *The Lost War, a Japanese Reporter's Inside Story* (New York, 1946), 257. On the touchdown, see also Colonel Tench's own version, "Advance Party: Mission Surrender," *Infantry Journal* 59:30–36 (August 1946); also the *New York Times* and the *Washington Post,* and *SCAP, Reports of General MacArthur* (Department of the Army,

217

Washington, D.C., 1966), Volume I, Chapters 13 and 14. Cited hereafter as *SCAP.*

3   Kades's trip is described by him in an interview, Columbia University Oral History Collection, December 12, 1961.

3   biggest airborne operation of the Pacific War. "When you realize that logistic plans for the support of army operations are frequently made as many as six months ahead of time, and when you realize that ordinarily a lapse of 120 days must be allowed between the time a theatre requests an item to be procured and the time that it actually arrives in the theatre, you can marvel at the speed of the massing and moving of the armed forces to Japan within the short space of weeks. Add to the fact that almost immediately upon arrival in Japan a huge demobilization program got underway, and you wonder more than ever that the forces were able to accomplish anything at all in those first few months." Robert Neville Ginsburgh, "Between War and Peace" (unpublished Ph.D. thesis, Harvard University, 1948), 388.

3   edge of the strip. *SCAP,* I, Supplement, 25.

4   "a lawn party." *New York Times,* Aug. 29, 1945, 6.

4   "place in history." Ben Z. Kaplan, "Tojo Doesn't Live Here Anymore," *Free World,* December 1945, 33.

6   "some mountain fastness." Council on Foreign Relations, *American Interests in the War and the Peace, Problems of the Peace Settlement with Japan* (July 1944), Major George Fielding Eliot, "Problems of Japanese Disarmament," 2.

6   "flooded rice fields." Hugh Borton, *American Presurrender Planning for Postwar Japan* (New York, 1967), 23.

6   than ever before. Bernard Seeman, "Life in Japan Today," *American Mercury,* July 1945, 15. ". . . the closer the storm of American fighting power approaches the Japanese homeland, the greater becomes the hysterical resolve of the Japanese people to go down fighting." Seeman was a consultant to the Office of War Information.

6   "not necessarily to Japan's advantage." The speech is quoted in entirety by John Toland, *The Rising Sun, the Decline and Fall of the Japanese Empire* (New York, 1970), 838.

7   "shoot them down in friendly fashion." Quoted in the *New York Times,* Aug. 15, 1945, 1.

7   "once more saved by the Divine Wind." Quoted by Eric Svens-

son, "The Military Occupation of Japan" (unpublished Ph.D. thesis, University of Denver, 1966), 137 ff.

8   "C rations, a canteen, and a carbine." M. D. Ingram, "The USN in Japan, 1945–1950," *Proceedings,* United States Naval Institute, April 1952, 379.

8   "It's too damn quiet here." Quoted in the *New York Times,* Sept. 1, 1945, 2.

8   "Three Cheers for the U.S. Navy and Army." MS Diary of Ensign John M. O'Connell USNR.

8   On the POWs, see *SCAP,* I, Supplement. A graphic firsthand account is provided by Alfred A. Weinstein, *Barbed-Wire Surgeon* (New York, 1948), especially 90–115.

10   synonymous with "destruction." Hanson W. Baldwin, *New York Times,* Aug. 7, 1945, 10.

10   "fanatical samurai." John F. Embree, "How to Treat the Japanese," *New York Times Magazine,* Sept. 9, 1945, 5.

10   "kill a goddam Jap." Professor Gregory Henderson was that Marine lieutenant. Henderson to author, Oct. 20, 1978.

11   "oriental stoicism." Walter Krueger, *From Down Under to Nippon* (Washington, 1953), 344.

11   "better than their own." Lieutenant General Robert Eichelberger, MS Diary, Duke University Library, entry for Nov. 11, 1945. Japanese resentment was largely directed against their own wartime leaders who had proven themselves so inept. Grant K. Goodman, *The American Occupation of Japan* (Kansas, 1968), 2–3.

11   "what did not happen." Theodore White, "Episode in Tokyo Bay," *The Atlantic Monthly,* Aug. 1970, 60.

11   "oriental" troops. National Archives, Record Group 319, JCS, Joint Staff Planners, May 6, 1945. "Composition of Forces to Occupy Japan Proper" (courtesy of Professor Iokibe).

12   "single British Commonwealth identity." J. M. Walsh, "British Participation in the Occupation of Japan," *Army Quarterly,* October 1948, 72.

12   "Japanese generals in Piccadilly." D. P. Capper, "Japan in Transit," *National Review* (London), April 1949, 429.

13   "world politics and commerce." *The Economist,* November 1947, 722.

13   "below the salt." Capper, *op. cit.,* 428.

14 "freely expressed will of the people." *United States Initial Post-Surrender Policy for Japan,* Part I (b), Aug. 29, 1945.

CHAPTER 2

15 On the belief in universality of American values see, for example, Roger Nash Baldwin, "New Liberties in Old Japan," *Survey Graphic,* August 1947, 425; Douglas G. Haring, *Japan's Prospect* (Cambridge, 1946), 22; Philip Wallenstein Buck and John Wesley Masland, Jr., *The Governments of Foreign Powers* (New York, 1950), 644; and D. C. S. Sissons, "SCAP's Statements on the Occupation of Japan," *Australian Outlook,* March 1950, 36.

17 "the most perfect society." J. Hector St. John Crèvecoeur, *Letters from an American Farmer* (Gloucester, 1968), 47.

17 "finish the great circle." *Ibid.,* 49.

17 Timothy Dwight, from the poem "Greenfield Hill," quoted by Henry Nash Smith, *Virgin Land* (Cambridge, 1970), 10.

17 Thomas Hart Benton, quoted by Henry Nash Smith, *Ibid.,* 26.

17 "by its light." A. A. Bennet quoted by Ralph H. Gabriel, *American Values, Continuity and Change* (Westport, Conn., 1974), 13.

18 Woodrow Wilson and the "principles of America." N. Gordon Levin, Jr., *Woodrow Wilson* (New York, 1968), 18.

18 Henry L. Stimson and "moral superiority." Henry L. Stimson, "The Decision to Use the Atomic Bomb," *Harper's,* February 1947, 103.

19 Japan as the chief enemy. William L. Neumann, *America Encounters Japan* (Baltimore, 1963), 292. For information about the economic relationships between America and Japan, *Ibid.,* 137 and *passim.*

24 scarcely a dozen. "Japanese Studies in the United States, a Report on the State of the Field, Current Resources and Future Needs," SSRC-ACLS Joint Committee on Japanese Studies, February 1970, 12.

24 Europe in order to get graduate training. Hugh Borton, Oral History, Columbia University, 4.

25 Not commented upon by the reviewers when his book was published. Kenneth Colegrove, *Book Review Digest,* 1940.

25 Lattimore on Norman. Owen Lattimore, *Solution in Asia* (Boston, 1946), 38*n.*

25 "what the Japanese were like." Ruth Benedict, *The Chrysanthemum and the Sword* (Boston, 1946), 3.

25 Harold Strauss's review. *New York Times,* Nov. 24, 1946, 4.

26 provoking one critic to remark. He was Frederick Nichols Kerlinger, who wrote "Behavior and Personality in Japan," *Social Forces,* March 1953, 251.

27 Rosinger on reforming the Japanese. Lawrence K. Rosinger, "What Future for Japan?" *Foreign Policy Reports,* Sept. 1, 1943, 148.

27 Henry R. Luce to Douglas MacArthur, June 8, 1944, MacArthur Archive, RG-10, VIP Correspondence.

27 "victory will take decades." *Fortune,* December 1943, 121.

27 "hysterical and mystical." Sydney Greenbie, *Asia Unbound, A Pattern for Freedom in the Far East* (New York, 1943), 17.

27 "or individual expression." James Young, "The Menace of Shintoism," *Proceedings,* United States Naval Institute, April 1948, 465.

27 "Japan is not our intellectual equal." Eliot Janeway, "America's Moral Crisis," *Asia and the Americas,* October 1945, 468.

27 *Know Your Enemy Japan.* War Department film, Audio-Visual Center, Dartmouth College.

28 "actions of the masses." Waldo H. Heinrichs, Jr., *American Ambassador* (Boston, 1966), 368.

28 Eliot on complete destruction. Quoted by Lawrence K. Rosinger, "What Future for Japan?" *op. cit.*

28 Ernest Hooton on treatment of the Imperial family. Julius W. Pratt, "The Future Status of the Japanese Emperor," Council on Foreign Relations, *American Interests in the War* (New York, July 1944), 12.

28 November 1944 Gallup poll. Lousie M. van Patten, "Japan, An American Problem," *Far Eastern Survey,* May 9, 1945, 117.

29 "into a liberal republic." Commander Glynn quoted by Neumann, *op. cit.,* 24.

30 Potemkin structure. Doris Schwartz, "Letters from an Army Nurse in Japan," *New York Times Magazine,* April 14, 1946, 57.

30 Americans and foreign affairs. Ernest F. May, *American Imperialism* (New York, 1968), 22.

30 the warship canard. I am indebted for this to Professor Robert G. Albion of Harvard University.

31 Einstein in Japan. Sir George B. Sansom, "Postwar Relations with

Japan," Tenth IPR Conference (Stratford-on-Avon), September 1947, 15.

31 on tariffs. Neumann, *op. cit.,* 222–223.

32 "Jap trap." personal experience of author.

33 over the racial struggle. Good discussion of these attitudes can be found in Jacques Barzun, *Race: A Study in Superstition* (New York, 1965), and Thomas F. Gossett, *Race, the History of an Idea in America* (Dallas, 1963).

34 "A Jap's a Jap." Dennis M. Ogawa, *From Japs to Japanese* (Berkeley, 1971), 11.

34 "distinction . . . between the Japanese and the German." David MacIsaac, *Strategic Bombing in World War II* (New York, 1976), 203–204.

35 "racial and nothing but racial." Pittsburgh *Courier,* Sept. 29, 1945, 7.

35 racial epithets ("bandy-legged," etc.). Part 3. Richard Tregaskis, "Road to Tokyo," *Saturday Evening Post,* Oct. 13, 1945, 108.

35 "fighting for them?" Saul K. Padover, "Japanese Race Propaganda," *Public Opinion Quarterly,* Summer 1948, 197.

35 "satanic depths." Major General Charles Willoughby and John Chamberlain, *MacArthur 1941–1951* (New York, 1954), 312.

35 "mistreatment and killing of a few thousand prisoners!" Presumably the *Courier* would emphasize the mistreatment. "Thousands," of course, were not killed. Pittsburgh *Courier, loc. cit.*

35 praising Japanese efficiency, cleanliness and courtesy. *Idem.*

36 our democratic institutions. David M. Potter, *People of Plenty* (Chicago, 1954), 112*n.,* quotes Frederick Jackson Turner, *The Frontier in American History* (New York, 1920), 244.

CHAPTER 3

37 Stimson memorandum. Secretary of War Henry L. Stimson to Secretary of State James F. Byrnes, Memorandum for President Truman, Potsdam, Germany, July 16, 1945. Stimson Papers, Yale University Library (courtesy of Professor Iokibe).

38 On the importance of the Hunt memo, see Dan Charles Allen, "Franklin D. Roosevelt and the Development of an American Occupation Policy in Europe" (unpublished Ph.D. thesis, Ohio State University, 1976), 5.

39 University of Washington program. Franz H. Michael, "Civilians

and Soldiers Study Pacific," *Far Eastern Survey*, Aug. 23, 1944, 159.

40 "nothing in the world I couldn't do!" R. P. Wheeler to author, October 30, 1979.

41 "the situation they were going to get into." Hugh Borton, Oral History, 12.

41 Meanwhile papers flowed. For all of the section following I am much indebted to Professor Makoto Iokibe, "Blueprint for Japan," unpublished paper prepared for the New England Japan Seminar, April 7, 1978, and for many conversations with him.

41 right to "reorder . . . the vanquished." Peter A. Adams, "Eugene H. Dooman" (unpublished M.A. thesis, University of Maryland, 1976), 166.

42 " 'poor dear Japan' Blakeslee," Marlene J. Mayo, "Planning Japan's Economic Future," unpublished paper prepared for Seminar on Modern East Asia: Japan, Columbia University, Dec. 8, 1978, 22.

42 "a Sunday School flavor." Svensson, *op. cit.*, 27*n.* The remark was made by Herbert Feis.

43 "successful occupation." Borton, Oral History, 16, speaks for the Japan hands.

43 For the differing views within the State Department I am indebted to the detailed and illuminating discussion by Marlene Mayo, *op. cit.*

44 origins of unconditional surrender. Iokibe, *op. cit.*, 2–3.

47 "give Japan back to the Japanese." Tregaskis, "Road to Tokyo." Part 5. Oct. 27, 1945, 114.

47 Kades not entirely clear about what he was to do. Kades to author, May 22, 1979.

CHAPTER 4

48 "if we stay too long, it won't be successful." Kades, Oral History, 58–59.

48 "more than 500,000 men." Harold J. Noble, "What It Takes to Rule Japan," *Saturday Evening Post*, Sept. 29, 1945, 108.

48 Truman hoped it would speed up getting the men out of uniform. *Pacific Stars and Stripes*, February 7, 1946, 2.

48 "toss away the fruits of victory?" *Christian Century,* October 1945, 1119.

49 problems in the Army. William Mervin Wix, "The Army's Plans for Its Postwar Role" (unpublished Ph.D. thesis, Columbia University, 1976), 4 and 13.

49 sixteen hundred American generals facing demotion. *Christian Century, loc. cit.*

51 MacArthur nonetheless resented it. R. B. Finn to author. August 28, 1979.

51 "and of course couldn't." Sansom, Oral History, 36.

52 "Russian-American relations." W. Macmahon Ball, *Japan: Enemy or Ally?* (New York, 1949), 35. MacArthur found Ball irritating. For "a people who had never really intended to fight north of the Equator," MacArthur thought the Australians later had too much to say. Frank R. Kelley and Cornelius Ryan, *Star Spangled Mikado* (New York, 1947), 239.

53 to cause one American official to remark. Rodger Swearingen, "The Soviet Presence in American Occupied Japan," paper presented at the annual meeting of the Association for Asian Studies, March 30, 1979, 5.

53 "not one constructive idea." Major General Courtney Whitney, *MacArthur* (New York, 1956), 299.

57 "providing the specifications." Merle Fainsod quoting the *Department of State Bulletin,* Oct. 8, 1945, 541, from Douglas Haring, *op. cit.,* 300.

59 "as election surveillance." For a general description of Eighth Army activities, see Henry L. Hille, Jr., "Eighth Army's Role in the Military Government of Japan," *Military Review,* February 1948, 9–18. Also on military government, John D. Montgomery, "Administration of Occupied Japan," *Human Organization,* Summer 1948, 4–16; and Ralph Braibanti, "Administration of Military Government in Japan at the Prefectural Level," *American Political Science Review,* April 1949, 250–275. Braibanti, Montgomery, and Richard Park (below) were all political scientists who served with SCAP early in their careers.

59 "rice roots." Richard L. Park, "Transition in Japan," *Far Eastern Survey,* Sept. 21, 1949, 226.

60 only about 2500 in military government. Hille, *op. cit.,* 14.

60 read the *Nippon Times.* Carl J. Friedrich, *et al., American Experiences in Military Government* (New York, 1948), 344.

60 On information flow, see Braibanti, *op. cit.,* 268–269.

61 "to the left of Alf Landon." Robert B. Textor, *Failure in Japan* (New York, 1951), 78.

63 "to carry out your mission." U.S. Department of State, *Occupation of Japan* (New York, 1969), Appendix 16, Authority of General MacArthur as Supreme Commander for the Allied Powers, 89.

CHAPTER 5

65 John J. McCloy on being a military governor. Daniel Yergin, *Shattered Peace* (Boston, 1977), 374. McCloy said much the same thing at a conference, "Americans as Proconsuls," Smithsonian Institution, May 20–21, 1977.

69 MacArthur as head of state. Ambassador William J. Sebald with Russell Brines, *With MacArthur in Japan* (New York, 1965), 119.

69 "master in his own house." Forrest Pogue, *American Historical Review,* June 1976, 689.

69 "surrounded by his enemies." Vice Admiral John L. McCrae to author, Nov. 19, 1979.

69 "exercise of his power." George F. Kennan, *Memoirs* (Boston, 1967), 371.

70 "above the mortal realm." John W. Bennett and Iwao Ishino, *Paternalism in the Japanese Economy* (Minneapolis, 1963), 14.

70 "knows many things that are not so." McCrae to author, Nov. 19, 1979.

70 "smarter than I." Gavin Long, *MacArthur as Military Commander* (London, 1969), 7.

71 MacArthur's conversation. Allison, *Ambassador from the Prairie or Allison Wonderland* (Boston, 1973), 129.

71 "the topic you are discussing." Hugh Borton, Oral History, 37.

71 accommodate his loquacity. Lieutenant General Frank Sackton in conversation with author, April 14, 1978.

72 "man of destiny." William A. Kelley, *MacArthur, Hero of Destiny* (Greenwich, Conn., 1942), 5.

73 they had a "victory." This would bear out Santayana's dictum,

quoted by Sidney Hook, *The Hero in History,* 21, that " 'for those who believe, the substance of things hoped for becomes the evidence of things not seen.' "

73 "brighter days to come." William A. Kelley, *op. cit.,* 8.

74 "largest university." Faubion Bowers, "Twenty-five Years Ago: How Japan Won the War," *New York Times Magazine,* Aug. 30, 1970, 35.

74 "Jovian distance." Major General Charles Willoughby and John Chamberlain, *op. cit.,* 306.

75 "of the Emperor himself." *New York Times,* Aug. 26, 1945, IV, 3.

76 conversion to Christianity. "General MacArthur Replies," *Fortune,* June 1949, 204. Also Luman J. Shafer, "Report on Japan," *Christian Century,* April 14, 1948, 327. And E. Stanley Jones, "Report from Japan," *Christian Century,* June 13, 1951, 711.

76 "since the days of Rome." Francis Bowes Sayre, *Glad Adventure* (New York, 1957), 338.

76 "how to 'shoot it.' " Quoted by Lawrence S. Wittner, "MacArthur and the Missionaries," *Pacific Historical Review,* February 1971, 82.

76 "democratization can be speeded up." J. D. Profumo, "Japan Under MacArthur," *Journal, Royal Central Asiatic Society,* April 1947, 183.

76 "Christian ideals among the population." Council on Foreign Relations, *Records of Groups,* Vol XII, Jan. 23, 1947, Ken R. Dyke (former head of C.I. & E., SCAP, Tokyo).

76 Could the two in fact be separated? MacArthur himself wrote: "Democracy and Christianity have much in common, as practice of the former is impossible without giving faithful service to the fundamental concepts underlying the latter." Quoted by Wittner, *op. cit.,* 82. See also Francis J. Horner, "Japan and the Ideal," *Commonweal,* April 16, 1948, 633.

77 "to propagate Christianity." Wittner, *op. cit.,* 78.

77 disappointed Japanese Christians. Ralph J. D. Braibanti, "Religious Freedom in Japan," *Christian Century,* July 9, 1947, 851–852.

78 Stimson and the "Oriental mind." Elting E. Morison, *Turmoil and Tradition* (Boston, 1960), 374.

78 "lessons of the Far East." Willoughby, *op. cit.,* 295.

78 desire for the Presidency. See Howard B. Schonberger, "The

General and the Presidency," *Wisconsin Magazine of History*, Spring 1974, 201–219.

78 " 'God bless America.' " *New York Times*, April 19, 1951, 1.

CHAPTER 6

81 nearly seven million began to lay down their arms. SCAP, *op. cit.*, states that "on the day of surrender, the Imperial Japanese Forces totalled 6,983,000 troops." Roughly half were on the home islands.

81 "so frictionlessly." *Ibid.*, I, 131.

82 "shot one another on sight." *Ibid.*, 131, 143.

83 "tangled masses." *Ibid.*

85 "All we had was men." Philip H. Gustafson, "What If We Had Invaded Japan?" *Saturday Evening Post*, Jan. 5, 1946, 93.

86 "John Doe, F.B.I." Arnold van Benschoten, "Success of a Mission," *Proceedings*, United States Naval Institute, May 1947, 534.

86 Kure and a Misaki beach. Author's personal observation.

86 "finality of this surrender." SCAP, *op. cit.*, 131.

87 On Strategic Bombing Survey and "irrelevance" of its report, see David MacIsaac, *op. cit.*, 165–166.

87 "oriental passenger standards." SCAP, *op. cit.*, 155.

89 returned by August 1948. *Ibid.*, 131.

90 "anyone so happy!" Richard Delmore to author, Dec. 14, 1979.

90 "mines and factories." Edward Wagner, *The Korean Minority in Japan* (New York, 1951), 25.

91 during the Korean War. James E. Auer, "The Postwar Rearmament of Japanese Maritime Forces" (n.p., 1973), 66 ff.

92 "huge wartime expenditures for research." Winthrop Slocum, "The Naval Technical Mission to Japan," *Proceedings*, United States Naval Institute, January 1949, 7.

92 "very good indeed." Council on Foreign Relations XIV, Oct. 27, 1947.

93 Feelings ran so high. *Ibid.*, III, 301.

96 major power within a decade. *Ibid.*, XIV, Oct. 27, 1947.

97 "those who killed them?" Clifford S. Strike, "Revenge Is Expensive," *American Magazine*, September 1947, 50.

98 no good would come of it. W. F. Petrie, "Reparations Since the Surrender," *Australian Outlook*, March 1950, 56.

98 "recovery of the two continents depends." Acheson's speech of May 8, 1947, *New York Times*, May 9, 1947, 3.

98 harsh treatment for Japan. At the time I. F. Stone said: "Who would have dreamed that within four years of Pearl Harbor a nominee for high office would be attacked in the Senate of the United States for advocating severe treatment of Japan?" "Behind the MacArthur Row," *Nation*, Sept. 29, 1945, 298–299.

99 "stern justice . . . to all war criminals." Department of State, *Occupation of Japan*, Appendix 3, 55. Not all Americans were that keen on punishing the Japanese. Admiral Raymond Spruance USN said, "I think the most we can ever expect from them is an admission that they made a bad mistake in starting the war. I never heard of a Southerner feeling that the South was in the wrong in starting the Civil War." Thomas B. Buell, *The Quiet Warrior* (Boston, 1974), 370–371.

99 For the discussion following, I am much indebted to Richard Minear's *Victor's Justice* (Princeton, 1971).

99 "fundamental tests of criminality." *Ibid.*, 16.

100 "forms of justice." *Ibid.*, 74.

100 "from its creator." *Ibid.*, 66.

100 "their part in the courtroom drama." George F. Blewett, "Victor's Injustice," *American Perspective*, Summer 1950, 287.

101 trial for the emperor. Shirley Jenkins, " 'Uninformed' Opinion on Japan," *Far Eastern Survey*, Sept. 12, 1945, 251.

102 "victorious and defeated nations." Blewett, *op. cit.*, 283.

102 Colonel L. E. Bunker wrote home that SCAP had wanted quicker handling of war criminals instead of "this cumbrous, inefficient, ostentatious show forced upon us. I hope everyone back there realizes that this is not what the General wanted but was forced upon him over his continued protests." Bunker MS, June 5, 1946.

102 "No proposition could be more dangerous." William J. Bosch, *Judgment on Nuremberg* (Chapel Hill, 1970), 183.

102 among Americans in Japan. Halsey quoted by *Christian Century*, October 1945, 1119.

CHAPTER 7

104 "closer to being a name than a town." D. P. Capper, "Japan in Transit," *op. cit.*, 425.

105 "living in *kura*." Dallas Finn to author. August 28, 1979.

106 "does not connote mirth to them." MS Diary, Ensign John M. O'Connell, September 1945.

108 "strengthening of the Japanese economy." "Basic U.S. Directive for Post-Surrender Military Government in Japan," JCS 1380/15, 3 Nov. 1945, II A, 13. (Courtesy of R. B. Finn).

109 "died . . . from starvation." Brigadier General Crawford Sams, quoted by Deborah Oakley, "Population Policy in Japan" (unpublished Ph.D. thesis, University of Michigan, 1977), 148.

109 Malthusian correction. Robert King Hall, "Education in the Development of Postwar Japan," 10. Prepared for symposium at the MacArthur Library and Archives, 1975.

109 sterilization. MacArthur Archives, RG-10, VIP file, Bilbo, Theodore. Also quoted by Oakley, *op. cit.,* 146.

110 saved eleven million Japanese. SCAP, "History of the Nonmilitary Activities of the Occupation of Japan, 1945–1951" (typescript on microfilm), Introduction, 23. Cited hereafter as "History."

111 wholesale prices. Martin Bronfenbrenner in Grant K. Goodman, *The American Occupation of Japan* (Kansas, 1968), 18. Also OSS/OIR, "Intelligence and Research Reports," #4748, Nov. 1, 1948.

112 incompetence of Japanese Government. Jerome B. Cohen, "Japan: Reform vs. Recovery," *Far Eastern Survey,* June 23, 1948, 137. Sherwood Fine, Director, Economics and Planning, Economic & Scientific Section, GHQ, SCAP, said, "The gulf between Western and Japanese economic thinking was never successfully bridged." "Japan's Post-war Industrial Recovery," *Contemporary Japan* (1952), 174.

112 diminish reparations. W. Macmahon Ball, *op. cit.* (New York, 1949), 103.

112 get out and quickly. Joseph Fromm, "Sabotage of Recovery Within Japan," *World Report,* Jan. 6, 1948, 11.

113 Americans exported only one tenth. These data represent 1936. Roswell H. Whitman, "Economic Recovery in Japan," *Military Government Journal,* January 1948, 2.

114 large American Government-held stocks of raw cotton . . . advice to the Japanese. Jerome B. Cohen, *Japan's Economy in War and Reconstruction* (Minneapolis, 1949), 484.

114 highest accident rate in the world. Robert Y. Grant, "Japanese Mining and Petroleum Industries; Programs Under the Occupation," *Science,* Nov. 17, 1950, 587.

114 than to dig out their own. Robert S. Schwantes, *Japanese and Americans* (New York, 1955), 69.

115 devastating epidemics. A vigorous U.S. Army inoculation program had much to do with this.

116 nothing of "truly unsurpassed quality" was destroyed. Charles F. Gallagher, "War Damage to Japanese Art Treasures," *Oriental Art,* Winter 1948, 117.

117 "Dempsey damage." Council on Foreign Relations, Records of Groups, Vol XI, 1945/46–1945/1947, remarks by Owen Lattimore, Feb. 8, 1946.

117 trains running through Hiroshima. David MacIsaac, *The United States Strategic Bombing Survey,* (New York, 1976), VII, 17.

117 "cleanly cleared away." Frank Kluckhohn, *New York Times,* Sept. 9, 1945, 8.

117 Manila still a mess. James Cox to author, Aug. 17, 1977.

118 MacArthur depressed. Bunker MSS, July 1946.

118 malnutrition. "History," I, 25. But Edwin Pauley had asserted in his report to the President that there was "no serious or unusual malnutrition in Japan," with at least 4 percent and perhaps as much as 8 percent of the rice crop going into the production of alcohol.
On the whole question of population policy I am much indebted to the work of Deborah Oakley, *op. cit.*

118 declining not rising numbers would be that trouble. *Ibid.,* 143.

119 passengers would never return. *Ibid.,* 160.

119 solving the problem. *Ibid.,* 167.

120 "beat the drums all you want." *Ibid.,* 173.

120 "rubber sanitary goods." *Ibid.,* 185 ff.

120 "gigantic concentration camp." *Ibid.,* 261.

120 birth control interpreted as genocide. *Ibid.,* 176.

120 "we could never have gotten the bill through." *Ibid.,* 198, 392.

121 Margaret Sanger denied visa. *Ibid.,* 260 ff. SCAP sent out a three and a half page single-spaced letter to those protesting this decision. MacArthur Archives, RG-5: SCAP, Japanese Birth Control File.

122 "start 'em up again." Quoted by Richard Tregaskis, "Road to Tokyo," *Saturday Evening Post,* Oct. 27, 1945, 115.

122 believed it to be. General Marshall said: "Japan is costing us a great deal of money; that cannot go on indefinitely. . . . What we have to be so on our guard against is that we don't weaken

ourselves economically so that the whole structure collapses."
H. Alexander Smith Papers, 1949, Princeton University Library, 393–395. For copies of these papers I thank Professor
Shindo. See also *U.S. News,* March 4, 1949, 24–25.

123 iron and steel industry "not very promising." Jerome B. Cohen,
Japan's Economy in War and Reconstruction (Minneapolis, 1949),
475.

124 "business in Japan." Harold Strauss, "Right Face in Japan," *Nation,* Nov. 30, 1946, 607, quoting the *Wall Street Journal.*

124 "Chamber of Commerce was in session." *Ibid.*

124 morally wrong to do so. Edwin M. Martin, *The Allied Occupation of Japan* (New York, 1948), 26n.

125 in the American political orbit. Gunther Stein, "American Business with East Asia," 10th IPR Conference, Stratford-on-Avon, September 1947, 33.

125 "and merchant shipping." Sir George B. Sansom, "Conflicting Purposes in Japan," *Foreign Affairs,* January 1948, 311.

125 economic interests there. Harry Roskolenko, "Letter from Japan," *Monthly Review,* July 1947, 376.

125 American business to cope with. R. C. Kramer, "Japan Must Compete," *Fortune,* June 1947, 176.

125 Ball wryly commented. Ball, *op. cit.,* 102.

126 "and hand mirrors." *Manila Times,* May 7, 1948, quoted by Jerome B. Cohen, "Japan's Economy Under Occupation," *Foreign Policy Reports,* Feb. 1, 1949, 223n.

126 the Japanese build democracy. Council on Foreign Relations, XIV, May 20, 1948.

127 "from inside and outside." Eichelberger, San Francisco News Conference, *Contemporary Japan* 17 (1948), 393.

127 one writer suggested. Buford Brandis, "The South and Japan," *Georgia Review* 3 (Spring 1949), 8.

128 "to rebuild the Japanese economy. William H. Draper, Council on Foreign Relations, XVI, Oct. 21, 1948.

128 "the old co-prosperity sphere." H. Alexander Smith Papers, 346, B-28.

128 "or group accomplishments." C. A. Bouchier, "American Help Has Transformed Japan's Economy," *Great Britain and the East,* June 1950, 41.

130 "support their growing population." Council on Foreign Relations, XVI, 2.

130 "a complete mess." Remark made by Ambassador Martin at conference, "Americans as Proconsuls, U.S. Military Government in Germany and Japan, 1944–1952," Smithsonian Institution, May 20–21, 1977.

CHAPTER 8

132 cultural relationship . . . nineteenth century. Robert S. Schwantes, *op. cit.,* 129 ff.

133 "stamp in the good." Robert King Hall, "The Battle of the Mind," *Columbia Journal of International Affairs,* Winter 1948, 63.

134 "knew a thing about the Japanese." Carroll Atkinson, "Japanese Education," *School and Society,* Aug. 17, 1946, 115.

134 abandoned the profession. "History," XI, Social, Part A, Education, 239.

135 of Stoddard's recommendations. George D. Stoddard, "MacArthur and the U.S. Education Mission to Japan," *National Parent-Teacher,* September 1946, 24.

135 "expression and communication?" William C. Bagley, "The Report of the U.S. Education Mission to Japan," *School and Society,* June 1, 1946, 389.

136 urged by the Occupation authorities. Robert King Hall, "Education in the Development of Postwar Japan," unpublished, 1975, 22.

136 "the eye, the hand, and the memory." Sir George B. Sansom, "Education in Japan," *Pacific Affairs,* December 1946, 414.

136 "daily newspapers and popular magazines." Stoddard, *op. cit.,* 24.

137 broken windows. "History," 130.

137 book resources of the Japanese nation had been lost. *Ibid.,* 306.

138 "cannot read, write, spell, or think." Sansom, *op. cit.,* 414.

138 "child needs" over subject matter. "History," 95.

138 "our educational philosophy." Hall, "The Battle of the Mind," *Columbia Journal of International Affairs,* Winter 1948, 70.

138 "most wasteful." Atkinson, *op. cit.,* 115.

140 "sheep from the goats." W. Macmahon Ball, *op. cit.,* 165.

140 "ever deliberately undertaken." John D. Montgomery, *The Purge in Occupied Japan* (Chevy Chase, Md., 1954), vii.

140 210,287 of them. Figures from *Ibid.,* 2.

141 "bottom of the heap." Eugene B. Dooman, Columbia Oral History interview, 1962, 145.

141 "pro-American business group in Japan." Joseph Ballantine, Oral History, 1961, 251.

141 eliminating "the best brains." H. Alexander Smith Papers, *op. cit.*, 324, B-24.

141 "off the neck of the American taxpayer." *Newsweek,* April 18, 1949, 45.

142 even if there had been no Occupation. Thomas L. Blakemore, "Post-war Developments in Japanese Law," *Wisconsin Law Review,* July 1947, I, 637.

144 Kades dryly remarked. L. H. Redford (ed.), *The Occupation of Japan: Impact of Legal Reform,* Symposium, MacArthur Memorial, April 1977, 163.

144 "women in the Western democracies." Stoddard, *op. cit.,* 23.
I am much indebted to the penetrating discussion of women's rights by Susan J. Pharr, "The Politics of Women's Rights Reform During the Allied Occupation of Japan," to appear in Robert E. Ward and Sakamoto Yoshikazu (eds.), *Policy and Planning During the Allied Occupation of Japan.* See also Ms. Pharr's "A Radical U.S. Experiment, Women's Rights Laws and the Occupation of Japan," in Redford, *op. cit.,* 125–134, and discussion following.

144 pushers for specific issues. Pharr, "Politics," 41.

145 "direction of greater centralization." George A. Warp, "In Our Image and Likeness," *National Municipal Review,* April 1953, 175.

145 "than in any other aspect of Japanese life." *Ibid.*

146 for all of Japan. But even the reformers soon questioned whether the organizational changes were all to the good. Osborne Hauge to author, April 18, 1979.

147 "along the lines of the New York force." *Pacific Stars and Stripes,* Feb. 9, 1946, 2. Valentine studied the metropolitan police until May 15, 1946. Oscar G. Olander, former Commissioner, Michigan State Police, headed the Rural Police Planning Commission which completed its report on June 6, 1944, after twelve months of study.

148 "over the population of New York City." Carl J. Friedrich, *et al., op. cit.,* 353.

233

148 "we've got to democratize those police." *Pacific Stars and Stripes,* April 1, 1946, 4.

149 "always be kind and popular." Kurt Steiner, *Local Government in Japan* (Stanford, 1965), 90.

152 "headquarters out of action." Theodore Cohen, "Labor Democratization in Japan: The First Years," unpublished paper presented at symposium, MacArthur Library and Archives, April 1977, 5.

153 "all through the day." letter of Carl Shoup to author, Feb. 22, 1979.

154 "success of the Japanese economy." *Ibid.*

154 mission to the U.S. Stanley Surrey to author, June 4, 1979.

154 "everything we ought to have done?" letter of Carl Shoup to author, Feb. 22, 1979.

155 "and the Statler Hotels." Eleanor Hadley, "Trust Busting in Japan," *Harvard Business Review,* July 1948, 429.

156 for their social value. Hadley points out that American attachment to democratic capitalism—and American ethnocentrism—led Americans to believe it the best pattern for Japan, despite the difference between the Japanese and American economies. Hadley, *Antitrust in Japan* (Princeton, 1970), 13.

156 "professionally managed investment trust funds." "K. B.," "SCAPitalism in Japan," *Fortune,* September 1948, 6.

156 "opponents of the Japanese military." *Ibid.*

157 "Vindictive, destructive, and futile." Ambassador William J. Sebald with Russell Brines, *With MacArthur in Japan* (New York, 1965), 89.

157 other Occupation reforms. Jerome B. Cohen said, "The whole trend is completely contrary to past custom and practice in Japanese economic life, and therefore, if enforcement or policing should lag, no real gains will have been achieved. . . ." *Foreign Policy Reports,* Feb. 1, 1949, 217.

157 perhaps even worse implications. W. I. Ladejinsky, "Trial Balance in Japan," *Foreign Affairs,* October 1948, 100. Cites speech by Secretary of the Army Kenneth Royall, January 6, 1948, at San Francisco: " 'Deconcentration must stop short of the point where it unduly interferes with the efficiency of Japanese industry.' "

158 Kauffman's criticisms. Council on Foreign Relations, XIV, January 27, 1948.

159   "too American." Hadley, "Trust Busting in Japan," *op. cit.,* 426–427.

159   fifty-six top executives were forced out. Hadley, "Japan: Competition or Private Collectivism?" *Far Eastern Survey,* Dec. 14, 1949, 293–294.

159   the same viewpoints. Hadley, "Trust Busting in Japan," *op. cit.,* 435.

160   "Farmers should neither live nor die." William M. Gilmartin and Wolf Ladejinsky, "The Promise of Agrarian Reform," *Foreign Affairs,* January 1948, 314.

160   "the more you squeeze the more you get." Darrell Berrigan and Wolf Ladejinsky, "Japan's Communists Lose a Battle," *Saturday Evening Post,* Jan. 8, 1949, 28.

160   "aggressive policies in Asia." R. P. Dore, *Land Reform in Japan* (London, 1959), 115.

161   done in two years. W. I. Ladejinsky, "Japan's Land Reform," *Foreign Agriculture,* September 1951, 188.

161   amassed these holdings. Eugene B. Dooman, Columbia Oral History interview, 1962, 144.

161   "16 million acres of agricultural land." Joseph Ballantine, "Japan: Nationalization vs. Free Enterprise?" *Far Eastern Survey,* Feb. 8, 1950, 253.

162   "balanced on the end of a chopstick." Harold Strauss, "MacArthur in the Paddy Fields," *Nation,* Nov. 9, 1946, 521.

162   only thirteen packages. Andrew J. Grad, *Land and Peasant in Japan* (New York, 1952), 219*n.*

163   self-sufficiency in food should be a Japanese objective. Edwin W. Pauley, *Report* (Washington, 1946), Appendix 8, "Agriculture," 10.

163   "a new agrarian order in the Orient." Gilmartin and Ladejinsky, *op. cit.,* 324.

163   "to all of Asia." Lawrence I. Hewes, Jr., *Japan* (Westport, Conn., 1974), 50.

164   injected into the matter. *Ibid.,* 60.

164   "happiness in Japanese villages." R. P. Dore, *op. cit.,* xvii.

164   "the world's great laboratory . . . liberalization of government from within." Douglas MacArthur, *Reminiscences* (New York, 1965), 322–323.

165   "completely reform it." James Lee Kauffman, Council on Foreign Relations, Jan. 27, 1948.

165   "can we function effectively." Harold S. Quigley, "Evaluating the Japanese Occupation," *Far Eastern Survey,* Oct. 10, 1951, 178.

166   "godlike power." The phrase is used by John D. Montgomery, *Forced to Be Free* (Chicago, 1957), 191.

166   "American policy and practice." Ball, *op. cit.,* 171.

166   Sansom raised the question in "Conflicting Purposes in Japan," *Foreign Affairs,* January 1948, *passim.*

166   Kurt Steiner argues that the Occupation's "justification for democratization was not that democracy was the best system for all of mankind, but that it might serve Japan in the second-half of the twentieth century better than the myth-based authoritarianism of the past." See Alfred C. Oppler, *Legal Reform in Occupied Japan* (Princeton, 1976), x.

167   an ideal, not a reality. Edwin O. Reischauer points out in *Japan, the Story of a Nation* (Boston, 1970), 242, that since Americans were largely not cognizant of Japan's democratic tradition, they felt much more radical and revolutionary than they actually were.

167   "dreams of being." Perry Miller, "Teacher in Japan," *The Atlantic,* August 1953, 65.

CHAPTER 9

168   from a few weeks to years. Monthly Reports, Office of the Chief of Military History, "Strength of the Army" (Washington, D.C.).

171   "officer being subject to racial prejudice." John F. Embree, "Military Occupation of Japan," *Far Eastern Survey,* Sept. 20, 1944, 173.

171   more important than any other problem. Samuel A. Stouffer, *et al., The American Soldier, Combat and Its Aftermath* (Princeton, 1949), 501.

171   made that discrimination worse. Mary Penick Motley, *The Invisible Soldier: The Experience of the Black Soldier in World War II* (Detroit, 1975), 99. Lieutenant General Robert Eichelberger, who settled in Asheville, N.C., was probably typical in his racial attitudes, expressed in his MS Diary.

171   "virus of racial prejudice." Pittsburgh *Courier,* Oct. 13, 1945, 14.

171   "the Japanese, apt as usual, are learning it." *Ibid.,* Nov. 3, 1945,

6. See also Hargis Westerfield, "Failures in GI Orientation," *Free World,* April 1946, 62–63.

171 for feminine beauty. Hiroshi Wagatsuma, "The Social Perceptions of Skin Color in Japan," in Irwin Scheiner (ed.), *Modern Japan* (New York, 1974), 51.

172 neglect, discrimination, and poverty. Hiroshi Wagatsuma, "Mixed Blood Children in Japan," *Journal of Asian Affairs,* Spring 1977. Wagatsuma provides statistical estimates.

173 "200 percent Americans." Daisuke Kitagawa, *Issei and Nisei* (New York, 1967), 36.

174 "the highest training of the American home." Ball, *op. cit.,* 11.

176 to give to Japanese friends there. John C. Pelzel to author, Feb. 12, 1979.

176 "I hope they're ashamed of now." Harold Henderson, Columbia University Oral History, 1962. See also Herrymon Maurer, "The U.S. "Does a Job," *Fortune,* March 1947, 186.

176 should not be surprising. George C. Marshall said of the occupation of the Philippines (but it might as well have been Japan) " '. . . however quiet you may be in your home district, when you get abroad on a wartime basis under conditions that are extremely difficult, you are likely to do things that you would utterly discountenance at another time . . ." Forrest Pogue, *George C. Marshall* (New York, 1963), I, 81.

176 "complacent indifference." Robert S. Schwantes, *op. cit.,* 189.

177 "not to attempt to learn the Japanese language." Ball, *op. cit.,* xi.

177 "less advanced and oriental civilization." Alfred Oppler, *op. cit.,* 291.

179 "Backside of Japan." John Morris, *The Phoenix Cup* (London, 1947), 138.

181 should necessarily produce goodwill is a myth. Harold Isaacs, *No Peace for Asia* (New York, 1947), 7.

181 "something very funny." John Ashmead, "The Japs Look at the Yanks," *Atlantic Monthly,* April 1946, 88.

181 "in that oriental way of theirs." MS O'Connell Diary, Oct. 28, 1945.

181 "they or their country have done wrong." "Life in Tokyo," *Life,* Dec. 3, 1945, 32.

182 "friendly with the Japanese people." Major General Harry

Schmidt USMC, quoted in *Pacific Stars and Stripes,* Dec. 4, 1945, 2.

183 "smelly and strange country." Elliott Chaze, *The Stainless Steel Kimono* (New York, 1947), vii.

183 "a stench in the nostrils of the world." *Pacific Stars and Stripes,* Oct. 16, 1945, 2.

184 "rapidly becoming famous." *Ibid.,* Dec. 28, 1945, 3.

185 "slim golden body of the perpetual woman." James A. Michener, *Sayonara* (New York, 1957), 128.

186 "wouldn't talk so foolish." *Pacific Stars and Stripes,* Jan. 31, 1946, 3.

186 " 'Gook Lovers.' " *Ibid.*

186 "pictures of the idols." William L. Worden, "GI Is Civilizing the Jap," *Saturday Evening Post,* Dec. 15, 1945, 104.

186 "wanted girdles but didn't know how to use them." Janet Wentworth Smith and William L. Worden, "They're Bringing Home Japanese Wives," *Saturday Evening Post,* Jan. 19, 1952, 79.

187 "Do you have any kimonos?" Ashmead, *op. cit.,* 91.

188 "This provides laughter all around." *Christian Science Monitor,* June 15, 1946, 5.

188 what the American mass market wanted. Charles Tuttle to author, May 20, 1979.

189 know anything about Japan. Westerfield, *op. cit.,* 63.

189 "the GI's present negative attitude." *Pacific Stars and Stripes,* Feb. 5, 1946, 3.

190 cut off from new ideas. Frederic G. Melcher, "Booksellers in Japan and Their Buying Public," *Publishers Weekly,* June 14, 1947, 2936.

190 "my dog here to live." *Pacific Stars and Stripes,* Feb. 21, 1946, 3.

191 "unarmed and unafraid." Quoted in *Contemporary Japan,* 16, 508.

193 Dallas Finn to author, August 28, 1979.

194 ". . . more to offer a soldier . . . in over forty-four years service." Lieutenant General Eichelberger is quoted by Helen Mears, "Our Far-Flung Correspondent," *The New Yorker,* Nov. 23, 1946, 92.

195 recalled one diplomat's wife. And "ties often persist." Dallas Finn to author, August 28, 1979.

197 ". . . yesterday we ran out of coal." Erwin D. Canham, "Can This Be Japan?" *Christian Science Monitor Magazine,* April 26, 1947, 2.

197 relying on American or other imported food. George DeVos suggests that a person thrust into a foreign culture may feel he is keeping his social identity by eating his customary diet. "Towards a Cross-Cultural Psychology of Caste Behavior," in George DeVos and Hiroshi Wagatsuma, *Japan's Invisible Race* (Berkeley, 1966), 372.

198 " 'a dollar a person if you have to.' " J. Malcolm Morris, *The Wise Bamboo* (Philadelphia, 1953), 57.

198 "good years." Remark to author, April 1978.

199 "pitifully ignorant" of recent science. Richard B. Berlin, "Impressions of Japanese Medicine at the End of World War II," *Scientific Monthly,* January 1947, 46–47.

CHAPTER 10

200 parable for the Occupation. One of the two missionaries was Robert Wood. Robert Wood to author, Feb. 17, 1978.

200 allegory within the film. John D. Montgomery, *"Rashomon,* Gateway to the New Japan," *Contemporary Japan,* 21 (1952), 252–263.

202 Pickett letter. Clarence Pickett to President Harry S Truman, Sept. 18, 1945. American Friends Service Committee Archives.

202 "fellowship and equality." Gertrude Tormey, "Nine Days in Japan in April 1950," *Education,* September 1950, 45.

202 "prodigious quantities of DDT." Mark Gayn, *Chicago Sun,* Sept. 3, 1946.

203 "expense of the Japanese masses." William Costello, "Japanese 'Plunderbund,' " *New Republic,* Jan. 5, 1948, 16.

203 did not occur to most Americans. See for example Eric H. F. Svensson, *op. cit.,* 3.

203 "better off than we are in that respect." *Pacific Stars and Stripes,* Jan. 6, 1946, 2. Also Douglas Haring, *op. cit.,* 367–368.

203 "Christian capitalism." The phrase is used by Anthony F. C. Wallace, *op. cit.,* 32.

204 ". . . but we have learned much from them." Compton Pakenham, *Newsweek,* Sept. 12, 1949, 31.

204 sealing off Japan. Edward Ackerman, in Douglas Haring, *op. cit.,* 40–41.

206 "outlook for Japanese exports." Edward Ackerman, *Japan's Natural Resources* (Chicago, 1953), 564.

206 radio for every home seemed ambitious. Douglas Haring, *op. cit.*, 280.

206 trying to persuade John Foster Dulles. John M. Allison, *Ambassador from the Prairie* (Boston, 1973), 381.

206 "the American concept for Asia is meaningless" Edwin O. Reischauer, in "Transcript of Round Table Discussion," H. Alexander Smith Papers (Princeton University), 474. Professor Reischauer also remarked: "We have to succeed in Japan immediately; the Communists don't have to succeed in China for decades," 477.

206 "any confidence in our leadership?" David K. Eichler, "The Future of the New Japan," *Yale Review,* Winter 1952, 176.

206 "the ideal Communist state." Professor Albert Craig in conversation with author. See also Talcott Parsons in Haring, *op. cit.,* 109.

207 in order to survive. Robert E. Ward and Frank J. Shulman, *The Allied Occupation of Japan* (Chicago, 1974), quoting Irene Taeuber, 636.

207 "drain on us." H. A. Smith Papers, 491.

207 expansionists had sought in the 1930s. Yale Granada, "Should We Rebuild Japan?" *Nation,* Aug. 14, 1948, 214.

207 "what its own army failed to win." Harold Strauss, "Reply," *Ibid.,* 214.

207 "present grand strategy." *Fortune,* December 1943, 129.

208 Yoshida's boast. Yoshida said this to Admiral (Ret.) Yamanashi Katsunoshin, IJN. Repeated in conversation with author, April 1962.

208 America has replaced Manchuria. The point is made, in essence, by Ezra F. Vogel, *Japan as Number One, Lessons for America* (Cambridge, 1979), 13.

209 "what they had left behind." Russell F. Brines, *MacArthur's Japan* (Philadelphia, 1948), 299.

210 prejudice lingers. The *American Historical Review,* June 1976, 690, notes that in a history by Lenore Fine and Jesse A. Remington, *The Corps of Engineers: Construction in the United States,* the authors refer to American citizens of Japanese ancestry living on the West Coast as "west coast Japanese."

210 the "Kung Fu" series and "the oriental" stereotype. Tom Kagy Nahm, "Stop Stereotyping Me," *Newsweek,* Jan. 15, 1979, 15.

211   a way of escaping ego. Harvey Cox, *Turning East, the Promise and the Peril of the New Orientalism* (New York, 1977), 77.

211   "unthinkable without Zen." letter of John Cage to author, June 7, 1979.

212   On the history of the Packard Collection, see the *New York Times,* Aug. 24, 1975, 1 and 42; and Sept. 4, 1975, 30.

214   "our attempt to export democracy." David M. Potter, *op. cit.,* 127.

Bibliography
for Sources Beyond
Those Listed in the Notes

THOSE interested in pursuing subjects raised in this book should turn first to the monumental work by Robert W. Ward and Frank Joseph Shulman, *The Allied Occupation of Japan, 1945–1952, an Annotated Bibliography of Western-Language Materials* (Chicago, 1974). Rarely has a field of study been served so well. Just by turning the pages of this book, the browser can learn a great deal about the Occupation.

I have drawn heavily upon Ward and Shulman; many of its listings appear in my footnotes. It would seem unnecessary for me to list below the hundreds of other books and articles in it that I consulted for background information. Therefore I mention below only those works not included by them or published since their book appeared.

Frank Shulman comments further in an unpublished paper presented at a symposium sponsored by the MacArthur Library and Archives (April 1977), "Bibliographical Controls for Research on the Allied Occupation of Japan, 1945–1952: Current Resources and Critical Needs." On the same occasion, James J. Hastings presented "A Survey of the Records in the National Archives of the United States Pertaining to the Occupation of Japan."

UNPUBLISHED PAPERS

Peter K. Frost, "The Failure of the *Shinteki,* The American Reform of Higher Education in Japan, 1945–1954," prepared for the American Historical Association, 1977.

Richard Minear, "Japanese National Character, the Wartime Studies," 1979.

Ray A. Moore, "Democracy and Christianity in the American Occupation of Japan," prepared for the American Historical Association, 1977.

————, "Soldier of God, MacArthur in Japan," prepared for the New England Japan Seminar, March 1976.

Howard Schonberger, "American Labor's Cold War in Occupied Japan," prepared for the American Historical Association, 1977.

Joseph Jay Tobin, "Dependence, Independence, and *Amae;* American Reactions to Living in Japan," prepared for the Association for Asian Studies, March 1979.

UNPUBLISHED PH.D. THESES

Richard Jorgensen, "The Honorable Bridge: An Historical Study of Japan's Cultural Reputation in America" (Georgetown University, 1973).

Robert Alan Kern, "The Work of Gary Snyder" (Harvard University, 1972).

Michael John Yavenditti, "American Reactions to the Use of Atomic Bombs on Japan, 1945–1947" (University of California at Berkeley, 1970).

BOOKS

Frances Baker, *Jeeper's Japan* (Tokyo, 1949).

John Morton Blum, *V Was for Victory: Politics and American Culture During World War II* (New York, 1976).

Otis Cary (ed.), *War-Wasted Asia, Letters, 1945–46* (Tokyo, 1975).

Harlan Cleveland, G. J. Mangone, and J. C. Adams, *The Overseas Americans* (New York, 1960).

Roger Daniels, *The Politics of Prejudice, The Anti-Japanese Movement in California and the Struggle for Japanese Exclusion* (Gloucester, Mass., 1966).

George A. DeVos, *Personality Problems and Problems of Adjustment in American-Japanese Intercultural Relations* (Taipei, 1973).

John K. Emmerson, *The Japanese Thread, a Life in the U.S. Foreign Service* (New York, 1978).

Gene Florence, *The Collector's Encyclopedia of Occupied Japan Collectibles* (Paducah, Ky., 1976).

Joseph C. Goulden, *The Best Years 1945–1950* (New York, 1976).

BIBLIOGRAPHY

John Higham, *Strangers in the Land: Patterns of American Nativism, 1860–1925* (New Brunswick, 1963).

John Hohenberg, *Between Two Worlds; Policy, Press, and Public Opinion in Asian-American Relations* (New York, 1967).

Akira Iriye (ed.), *Mutual Images* (Cambridge, 1975).

Sheila K. Johnson, *American Attitudes Toward Japan 1941–1975* (Washington, 1975).

Anne and William Johnstone, *What Are We Doing with Japan?* (New York, 1946).

Joyce and Gabriel Kolko, *The Limits of Power* (New York, 1972).

Alexander Leighton, *The Governing of Men* (Princeton, 1945).

David MacIsaac, *The United States Strategic Bombing Survey* (New York, 1976), volumes VI, VIII, IX, and X.

Eric L. McKitrick, *Andrew Johnson and Reconstruction* (Chicago, 1960).

Ernest R. May, *The Truman Administration and China 1945–1949* (Philadelphia, 1975).

Thomas D. Murphy, *Ambassadors in Arms* (Hawaii, 1954).

Pacific Stars and Stripes, Out of Line, a Collection of Cartoons (Tokyo, 1952).

E. B. Potter, *Nimitz* (Annapolis, 1976).

Edwin O. Reischauer, *The Japanese* (Cambridge, 1977).

Theodore Roszak, *The Making of a Counter Culture* (New York, 1969).

Bruce M. Russett, *No Clear and Present Danger, a Skeptical View of the U.S. Entry into World War II* (New York, 1972).

Paul W. Schroeder, *The Axis Alliance and Japanese-American Relations, 1941* (Ithaca, 1958).

Mark Seldon (ed.), *Remaking Asia, Essays on the American Uses of Power* (New York, 1974), especially Herbert P. Bix, "Japan: The Roots of Militarism."

Martin J. Sherwin, *A World Destroyed: The Atomic Bomb and the Grand Alliance* (New York, 1975).

T. G. P. Spear, *The Nabobs, a Study of the Social Life of the English in Eighteenth Century India* (Oxford, 1932).

Tokyo News Service, *Japan in Pictures 1945–1951* (Tokyo, 1951).

Otto Tolischus, *Tokyo Record* (New York, 1945).

Justin Williams, Sr., *Japan's Political Revolution Under MacArthur, a Participant's Account* (Athens, Ga., 1979).

Lawrence S. Wittner (ed.), *MacArthur* (Englewood Cliffs, N.J., 1971).

Earl F. Ziemke, *The U.S. Army in the Occupation of Germany 1944–1946* (Army Historical Series, Washington, D.C., 1946).

Barton J. Bernstein, "The Perils and Politics of Surrender: Ending the War with Japan and Avoiding the Third Atomic Bomb," *Pacific Historical Review,* February 1977.

John W. Dower, "Occupied Japan as History and Occupation History as Politics," *Journal of Asian Studies,* February 1975.

Douglas G. Haring, "Japanese National Character: Cultural Anthropology, Psychoanalysis, and History," *Yale Review* 42, Spring 1953.

Colonel Joseph P. Harris, "Selection and Training of Civil Affairs Officers," *Public Opinion Quarterly,* 7, #4, Winter 1943–1944.

Ikuhiko Hata, "Japan Under the Occupation," *Japan Interpreter,* Winter 1976.

Charles S. Hyneman, "Wartime Area and Language Courses," *Bulletin,* American Association of University Professors, 31, Autumn 1945.

Shirley Jenkins, " 'Uninformed' Opinion on Japan," *Far Eastern Survey,* 14, Sept. 12, 1945.

Bok-lim C. Kim, "Asian Wives of U.S. Servicemen: Women in Shadows," *Amerasia Journal,* 4:1, 1977.

John W. Masland, "American Attitudes towards Japan," *Annals of the American Academy of Political and Social Science,* 215, May 1941.

J. A. Michener, "Why I Like Japan," *Reader's Digest,* 69, August 1956.

Ray A. Moore, "Reflections on the Occupation of Japan," *The Journal of Asian Studies,* 38, #4, August 1979.

Nicholas Read-Collins, "Japan Crusades for Culture," *Asian Horizon,* 2, Spring 1949.

Robert A. Scalapino, "The American Occupation of Japan—Perspectives After Three Decades," *The Annals of the American Academy of Political and Social Science,* November 1976.

Gerald J. Schnepp and Agnes Masako Yui, "Cultural and Marital Adjustments of Japanese War Brides," *American Journal of Sociology,* 61, 1955.

Howard B. Schonberger, "The Japan Lobby in American Diplomacy 1947–1952," *Pacific Historical Review,* Autumn 1977.

—— "The Occupation of Japan Through American Eyes," *The American Studies News-Letter,* #41, May 1976.

—— "Zaibatsu Dissolution and the American Restoration of Japan," *Bulletin of Concerned Asian Scholars,* 5, #2, September 1973.

Lieutenant Robert B. Sheeks, USMC, "Civilians on Saipan," *Far Eastern Survey,* 14, May 9, 1945.

Eric W. Sheppard, "Bombers over Japan," *Spectator,* January 10, 1947.

BIBLIOGRAPHY

Marguerite Ann Stewart, "Asia in the School Curriculum," *Far Eastern Survey,* 14, Sept. 12, 1945.

S. B. Williams and H. J. Leavitt, "Predictions of Success in Learning Japanese," *Journal of Applied Psychology,* 31, April 1947.

Harold Zink, "The Contribution of Universities to Military Government," *Bulletin,* American Association of University Professors, 32, Winter 1946.

INTERVIEWS

I am deeply grateful to the following people who graciously consented to be questioned by me about their various Occupation experiences: James Cox (August 14, 1977); Richard Delmore (December 14, 1979); Osborne Hauge (April 18, 1979); Gregory Henderson (October 20, 1978); Charles L. Kades (May 22, 1979); Vice Admiral (Ret.) John L. McCrae USN (November 19, 1979); John D. Montgomery (June 9, 1977); John C. Pelzel (February 12, 1979); Carl Shoup (April 24, 1979); Stanley Surrey (June 4, 1979); Mary Tonougar (May 24, 1979); Charles Tuttle (May 20, 1979); Raymond Vernon (June 6, 1979); R. P. Wheeler (October 30, 1979); Justin and Ellawitt Williams (October 29, 1979); Robert and Mary Wood (various times, Winter 1978).

Index

Page numbers in *italics* indicate illustrations.

INDEX

INDEX

INDEX